HOW TO CREATE SMART VILLAGES

HOW TO CREATE SMART VILLAGES

Open Innovation Solutions for Emerging Markets

Solomon Darwin, Werner Fischer

& Henry Chesbrough

Peaceful Evolution Publishing
Berkeley, California

Peaceful Evolution Publishing
Suite 402J
2220 Piedmont Avenue
Berkeley, CA 94720

Links to third party websites are provided by Peaceful Evolution Publishing in good faith and for information only. Peaceful Evolution Publishing disclaims any responsibility for the materials contained in any third party website referenced in this work.

For feedback and other inquiries, please send us an email to sdarwin@berkeley.edu and werner.k.m.fischer@gmail.com.

ISBNs: 978-1-7321353-6-9 (Paperback), 978-1-7321353-5-2 (eBook)

DEDICATION

This book is dedicated to the 3.4 billion rural people currently deprived of sustainable economic development due to lack of connectivity, information, resources, training, and tools for the digital era. We hope that sharing our experience and learnings with Governments, NGOs, Philanthropists, and Corporations all around the globe fosters a future in which they can thrive.

CONTENTS

POST COVID-19 CONTEXT

FOR THE SMART VILLAGE MOVEMENT

By Solomon Darwin

During the Covid-19 crisis, we have seen millions of Indians fleeing cities in a historic reverse-migration from cities back to their home villages. Many returned on foot as transportation was not available or not affordable. My grandparents faced a similar crisis during the Japanese bombing of Burma during World War II. They migrated to the commercial and prosperous city of Rangoon, Burma in search of a better life. When food became scarce and safety and security became an issue, hundreds of thousands of migrant workers risked their lives and returned on foot along with their families leaving their belongings behind. My grandparents and their four small children were among those refugees that returned. During their three month journey, many died along the way due to starvation, sickness, snake bites, bombing, and being devoured by wild animals. We are now fighting a different war having the same effect. The vast majority of migrant workers who left their villages in search of a better life, live in slums under substandard conditions and separated from their families. In times of crisis and distress, their souls desire to return home.

Here are four reasons why this exodus has taken place based on my analysis. Villages offer four value propositions that cities cannot offer to people:

1. Community: Sense of belonging, coexistence, the comfort of extended family, and emotional security.
2. Ecosystem: Relationships that meet one another's needs – interdependence prevails vs. independence
3. Natural Resources: Access to sources of life – arable land and water sources to grow food
4. Brand Value: Identity, Legacy, Lineage, Ancestral Pride and Tacit knowledge of ancestral trades

Creating sustainable villages are those where people do not need to relocate to create value for others and capture some of the value they create for themselves in the form of income. The Covid-19 crisis brought us to this new realization. We need not leave our homes to do our jobs or add value. Much can be done sitting in our villages through digital technology that is now available and affordable to villagers today. Some 600 + million young people in India can learn anything including coding and AI on mobile devices. They can now be tested, trained, certified, and placed in jobs to do them right from their home village. Once they are connected digitally they can severe the world from wherever they are. This also contributes to the eco-friendliness of our planet as evidenced during the Covid-19 crisis. May the waters of Ganges run pure and the splendor of Taj Mahal be visible so we may behold its glory.

Villages are natural habitats and a lifeline for the big cities. Let us not get our priorities reversed. Also, rural dwellings offer natural social distancing when compared to urban dwellings to slow the spread of pandemics. For this reason, I am passionate about what I do. The Smart Village Movement was birthed and founded at the Garwood Center for Corporate Innovation following the Innovation Round Table discussion hosted by the President of the world's largest republic, the honorable Pranab Mukherji, at the Rashtrapati Bhavan in New Delhi on March 12th, 2016. During this time I was teaching courses called "Building Smart Cities" at UC Berkeley. However, I felt a compelling heartfelt need to make my proposal for the creation of Smart Villages to take India forward. I had taken my inspiration from the sentiment expressed by Mahatma Gandhi, the father of that great nation who emphatically declared: "The soul of India lives in its villages". It was at this forum that proposed the idea of the Smart Village Movement through an open innovation approach to empower the subcontinent. The idea was well received and endorsed by the President and the distinguished participants of the roundtable.

The Berkeley Open Innovation Approach to Smart Villages was first sponsored and adopted by the Honorable Chief Minister Chandra Babu Naidu of Andhra Pradesh in the summer of 2016. Chief Minister Naidu was the first to finance the pilot study in the Mori Village where a prototype was developed where many lessons were learned discussed in this book. The success of the pilots in the Mori Village and showcasing how digital technologies can improve the lives of rural people helped to establish the Smart Village Movement. The movement continues to gain traction among academics, governments, global firms, and startups. Then, Covid-19 disrupted our lives. However, it will also create opportunities for new technologies and business models to emerge around the world. We can come out of this crisis stronger if we learn from it and serve one another's interests.

The Post Covid-19 World will be a game-changer requiring a new way of thinking if the 3.4 billion underserved people on earth, living in villages, were to prosper. In this interconnected and globalized world, what effects those hidden away in rural areas affects each one of us very rapidly. Welcome to the domino effect where small changes in one place are felt and sometimes magnified around the world the bad news travels fast. We can no longer say "I am not my brother's keeper" During the Covid-19 Crisis, many supply chains from "Farm-to-Plate" are broken or disrupted and need to be fixed. We cannot do it without the inclusion of villagers and rural workforce. The movement continues to draw interest and participation governments, global businesses, startups, and academics under the dynamic operational capabilities of Dr. Anil Shah, the Executive Chairman of the Smart Village Movement.

Historical Context: Open Innovation at work in times of crisis

During this Covid-19 Crisis, we are seeing open innovation at work through a faster FDA approval process, collaborations in faster drug development, and partnerships across industries to accelerate solutions. Here is another example of how a crisis liberated people in bondage giving birth to the world's largest democracy. In 1918 Spanish Flu infected a third of the world's population and claimed over 50 million lives. Out of which a total of 18 million lives from India. This is more than total casualties in WW1. India lost 6% of its people in a matter of months. This was a heavy price for one country to pay but Indians emerged out of the crisis stronger and a people of talent contributing significantly to the global economy.

The Spanish Flu Pandemic was a wake-up call to the people of India. It was only then they collectively realized that the British neglected them and they were poorly equipped to save their own lives. This unprecedented loss helped Indians discover their blind spots and rethink and evaluate their strengths and weaknesses. It took a crisis such as this for people to open up to create something new that did not exist before. The crisis brought an urgency among the people to act as one and galvanize their efforts under

Mahatma Gandhi, whose campaigns for freedom went unnoticed and were not previously taken seriously. The crisis empowered Indians to collaborate and overcome the largest empire the world had ever known upon which the sun never set; the pandemic helped fuel the birth of the world's largest democracy and establish the largest republic on earth. India is a subcontinent, it houses over 2,000 people groups that are culturally, religiously, ethnically, linguistically, and regionally diverse. The pandemic united the most diverse groups of people on earth under one umbrella and brought down the barriers that enabled a free exchange of ideas for collaboration. The spirit of open innovation was at work. Henry Chesbrough was yet to be conceived who later taught us the principles of Open Innovation and coined the phrase.

The diverse groups of India came together bringing their individual contributions to build a new nation. The surrounding 584 princely states, ruled by various kings, that were not formally part of British India came together and united to establish freedom and independence. The freedom movement, under Mahatma Gandhi who studied the peaceful principles of Jesus Christ of non-violence and turning the other cheek, finally gained its platform.

The crisis motivated the people of India to stop, think, plan, and set goals to move forward with agility and alertness to survive and create something new on their own. At that turning point, freedom gave them the power to equip themselves, contribute, and thrive to a global talent pool in which they began to hold prominent positions in government, academia, and industry. The pandemic was costly but brought out the best in the Indian people.

I had experienced a few major crises in my own lifetime: 1) The energy crisis of 1979, 2) The Iran Crisis, 3) The hyperinflation of the 1980s where farmers were forced to borrow at a 25% interest rates, 4) The S&L Banking Crisis, 5) The Y-2K Bank considerations, 6) The Dot-com Bust, 7) The 9/11 surprise attack, and 8)

The Great Recession of 2008. In each case, we had learned lessons and came out of them stronger.

We are now faced with another crisis of a different kind – whose likes we have never seen before, it caught us by surprise. This invisible enemy is not someone standing before us with a sword drawn that we can attack. We remain powerless like the mighty Pharaoh of Egypt who could have easily wiped out legions of standing armies but he was dealing with intangible plagues without preparation to fight them nor the ability to physically confront them. He was brought to his knees and found himself helpless as he was unprepared.

In this new era, we need to get used to fighting these invisible viruses that are being unleashed into our realm of both physical and cyberspace. Our knowledge lags to confront them. There are good reasons to panic when a crisis confronts us without warning; we have no control over "time" to stop it or slow it down. This calls for open innovation to accelerate our knowledge to defend ourselves. We are seeing this happen right before our eyes as knowledge is flowing across industries to accelerate solutions. Let us not waste this crisis.

See also my other books:

The Road to Mori: Smart Villages of Tomorrow

The Untouchables: Three Generations of Triumph over Torment

How to think like the CEO of The Earth –
Restoring the Declining Balance Sheet of The Earth

FOREWORD
MESSAGE FROM THE CHAIRMAN

Anil Shah, MD, FACC, FSCAI
Interventional Cardiologist, Anaheim, Ca. USA
Executive Chairman, Smart Village Movement

While growing up in India, I witnessed extreme poverty in the slums of Bombay and the rural villages until I graduated from Medical School with an MD. I was blessed to come to this country and complete my fellowship in Cardiology at UCLA's School of Medicine some 40 years ago. Over the years, I had prospered as an interventional cardiologist and medical entrepreneur in Los Angeles and Orange County, California. My desire to help underserved people motivated me to continually explore effective and practical ways to address this daunting task. The GDP of India can never go up meaningfully and sustain itself unless 70% of the rural population is productive. I have great confidence in the DNA of the Indian population that given the opportunities and push, a significant economic development can occur, and more importantly, the happiness index can increase. In more recent years, I have been heavily vested in philanthropic activities related to smart village initiatives in India. As a physician, I was interested in the health and well-being of people living in substandard living conditions around the world and help those less fortunate than me.

A couple of years ago, I started adopting villages and have been tirelessly investing in infrastructure to provide for the basic needs of rural people. These activities brought me much joy and fulfillment as I began to share my prosperity to the underserved people living in villages. My passion has driven me to explore innovative models that can scale to more rural places in the world where 3.4 billion people live.

A few months ago, my search has led me to the Solomon Darwin's first book on the subject "Smart Villages of Tomorrow – The Road to Mori". It was here where I first learned about the concept of Open Innovation applied in creating, scaling, and sustaining Smart Villages. Professor Darwin returned my call almost immediately, though we are strangers to one another over the phone, our vision to help the underserved people blended immediately. Since then, we became brothers of the same heart. Seeing my passion and dedication to the cause, he immediately asked me to take charge as the chairman of the Smart Village Movement, an initiative of UC Berkeley, under the umbrella of the Center for Growth Markets.

Professor Solomon Darwin, the founder of the Smart Village Movement and his colleague Professor Henry Chesbrough, the Father of Open Innovation, came up with a specific and narrow definition for a Smart Village that will fit the definition for scaling through Open Innovation methodology. Among the many definitions that exist, their definition is unique that caught my attention. They simply state that a smart village is "a community empowered by digital technology and open innovation platforms to access global markets". The mission here is not to build infrastructure in villages but to build people and empower them by connecting them to the global ecosystem and markets through digital technology.

This book clearly articulates the benefits of digital technology: affordability, b) adoptability, c) mobility and portability, d) no learning curve, d) benefits outweigh the costs, e) user-friendliness, f) Information and knowledge access 24/7 on-demand, g) many free apps for practice use, e) time savings, f) convenience, g) access to markets, h) speed of transactions, i) cloud-based storage and many more.

These once lost souls in the godforsaken rural places can now be on-boarded onto Open Innovation platforms to thrive and build their dreams leveraging the digital technologies.

Learning about the Smart Village idea for the first time at the Haas School of Business last summer was the "Eureka Moment" for me. These methods seemed to be practical and based on research conducted on the ground. As you read through this book, you will begin to appreciate the Open Innovation principles and ecosystem approaches to solving problems on the ground in emerging economies.

It gives me great pleasure to write the forward to "How to Create Smart Villages". The book is meant to serve as a textbook on the subject for students around the world and also as a manual for the practitioners and government officials on the ground. I welcome you to join me in the Smart Village Movement to address the needs of 3.4 billion people whose potential can be unleashed to create a more equitable world for us to enjoy.

PREMISE:
DEVELOPMENT AND GROWTH
REQUIRE NEW APPROACHES

Venkatesan Ashok
Retired Ambassador, Government of India
Former Consul General of India, San Francisco

Nearly 70 percent of India, or 900 million people, live in over 600,000 villages. About 200 million of them live 'below the poverty line' or BPL as qualified by an economic benchmark and poverty threshold by the government of India. Poor infrastructure by way of physical, electrical, electronic and internet connectivity, coupled with inadequate healthcare, hygiene and nutrition locks rural populations in a vicious cycle of poverty, impeding development and growth and overall happiness.

"How to Create Smart Villages" illustrates how to eradicate poverty and achieve development through active involvement of villagers by listening to and analyzing their pain points. Learning from the extreme social and economic problems experienced by his family and community, Prof. Solomon Darwin, the "Father of the Smart Village Movement" has evolved an ecosystem to involve global companies to bring scalable innovative digital technologies on open innovation platforms to access global markets. The revenue generating models on which this process is based ensures sustainability of the program. This book has been written with experiences gleaned from the field in operations in 472 villages in Andhra Pradesh, and will be a continuing exercise with the Smart Village Movement now involved in 100 villages in Arunachal Pradesh.

Other states of India have also expressed keenness to develop similar programs. The book stresses that development cannot be sustainable when it is merely in the form of foreign aid or government doles; that only programs which create sustainable and scalable revenue models can succeed in the long run; and programs must integrate innovation and technology from academia with commercial viability of businesses, while operating with the support of governments at the local, state and central levels – the triple helix model of innovation. The book also shows how the efficacy of innovations from different companies and institutions can achieve greater synergy and delivery when operating on open innovation platforms which share knowledge and capabilities for the common good, rather than competing with each other. For rural development to be comprehensive and all encompassing, innovative technologies in all verticals – water, sanitation, hygiene, healthcare, connectivity, education, agriculture, energy, entrepreneurship, transportation, safety and security need to be simultaneously addressed. Increasing awareness through connectivity leads to empowerment of all, especially women and deprived sections of society.

In developing countries like India, it is only through providing employment and making our villages more attractive places to live in that we will be able to enhance the happiness index of rural populations and reverse the drift of populations from villages to our overcrowded cities. The Road to Smart Villages can lead to the dream of P.U.R.A. – Providing Urban Amenities in Rural Areas envisioned by late Indian President Abdul Kalam. Making Smart Villages work in India could serve as a model for the rest of the developing world.

PREFACE

"The alleviation of rural poverty is one of the defining challenges of our time. This book will take you on a new journey to this important destination."

– Henry Chesbrough, Haas School of Business, UC Berkeley

This book is written to help corporate executives, government officials, startups, and academic researchers to appreciate the value of creating Smart Villages. The book illustrates the benefits of the new Smart Village movement to the entire business eco-system while addressing the socioeconomic inequities that prevail in emerging markets, the home to a great multitude of nations, tribes, peoples, and languages. The huge diversity that exists between and among global markets demand digital tools that are affordable and user-friendly to disrupt the many barriers for mar-ket access. Tools alone are useless to empower rural people; they need easily accessible market spaces that transcend the natural and man-made barriers. Open Innovation processes and platforms are necessary to enable rural populations to directly connect end consumers by eliminating middlemen and the cost of inefficient redundancies and reinvention of wheels. Open Innovation refers to "a distributed innovation process based on purposively managed knowledge flows across organizational boundaries, using pecuniary and non-pecuniary mechanisms in line with the organization's business model".[1] The book articulates that the world is now ripe for exponential growth through Open Innovation processes and strategies illustrated by the success and failure of documented real-world cases.

This book is an aggregation of all the experiences gained during more than 3 years of operations in rural India executing the Smart Village idea. These experiences have been channelized into novel approaches for innovation in rural emerging markets such as India. Establishing and implementing the Smart Village idea doesn't mean heavy infrastructure deployment for one large group as seen in the Smart Cities concept. The Smart Village vision uplifts rural populations socio-economically in a widespread effort that allows them to become self-entrepreneurial through digital technologies and Open Innovation platforms with access to global markets. However, product and service solutions for rural populations in emerging economies are often unfitting or unavailable and cannot meet the specific demand. The Smart Village idea is therefore about business – enterprises devising and delivering affordable digital technologies that rural villagers want and are willing to pay for in order to resolve their needs. These affordable technologies must then be embedded in new open business models that technology suppliers can scale and sustain throughout Andhra Pradesh, and later, all of India. A huge market opportunity that India offers to these industry partners is its 650,000 villages where 70% of its 1.3 billion people live.[2]

New approaches are necessary to expand markets to the people of India. Collaborative activities from multiple stakeholders and Open Innovation mindset will create shared value for all participants: governments (state and local), corporations (well-established enterprises and startups), universities (local and abroad), and lastly citizens (from various areas and income levels).

The Smart Village vision was the outcome of crossing career paths from Henry Chesbrough and Solomon Darwin, several learnings from Smart Cities programs and on-ground research in rural areas of Andhra Pradesh, India. Darwin's awareness of the disastrous situation in his village in India where he grew up aligned eventually with Andhra Pradesh's Chief Minister Naidu's need to improve the situation in his rural constituencies, where thirty-five million of the 60 million residents live. Moreover, CM Naidu lost his last election in 2004 because he neglected rural populations of his state, focusing too much on urban development.

The vision of Smart Villages eventually began to emerge because of several political leaders prompting Darwin after presenting the concept to address the drastic challenges of rural India. The first action toward its realization was in June 2016, when the first Smart Village experiment was launched in collaboration with the Andhra Pradesh government to provide possible models and solutions as a research partner. This initiative is primarily funded by private organizations, and the state government providing leadership and a supporting role. In December 2016, the first prototype village was completed, in Mori Village, Andhra Pradesh. It validated two things: 1) readiness of the villagers to embrace digital technology to empower themselves and 2) willingness of global technology firms such as Google, Cisco, IBM, and Ericsson, among other corporate partners to invest in prototyping business model experiments in India. Given the success of the prototype phase, Minister Naidu requested UC Berkeley to pursue 472 villages as laboratories of innovation. The goal of this extension phase was to explore and create new business models where industry partners can scale and prosper by providing value to the poor, rural population. To date, more than 60 companies and startups from India and outside of India such as WIPRO, SAP, and Zero Mass Water, have chosen to deploy staff and equipment to the villages to support the goals of this project. In mid-2018, the initiative was additionally rolled out in the most northeastern state of India – Arunachal Pradesh followed by Meghalaya in 2019.

This book explains how to create Smart Villages through Innovating in rural emerging markets and how business and social impact can eventually be reconciled to empower the many underserved communities. It captures the processes, strategies, techniques, failures, successes, and learnings in developing various successful and unsuccessful models throughout the project over the course of two years.

The book starts with an introductory chapter on scaling Smart Villages. A glimpse into the future and how the Smart Village idea will be executed in 2020; it provides the reader the ability to connect the dots from the future with the past to understand its evolution from a prototype village towards a movement building on a scalable digital platform.

The evolution starts in part I by examining and answering the question *why* the Smart Village idea works. It highlights learnings and the weaknesses from existing approaches to not reproduce old mistakes but rather make new mistakes. If chapter 1 explains how this approach differs and learns from previous rural development initiatives, chapter 2 elaborates the evolution of the vision from Smart Cities to Smart Villages. The underlaying theoretical concepts the Smart Village idea is built on is explained in chapter 3. Part I of this book closes with chapter 4 – the overall idea of the Smart Village initiative in detail.

Part II of this book shifts from the theoretical feasibility of Smart Villages of chapters 1 through 4, to *why* the Smart Village idea works in practice and how it was demonstrated. Chapter 5 emphasizes therefore the huge need to address prevalent pain points of rural populations in India through a concept like Smart Villages, particularly when examining the situation in verticals including healthcare, education, and others. Chapter 6 is a detailed and chronological reflection of how the vision eventually became reality and highlights why the collaboration with Indian state governments has been so successful. Since the private sector plays a crucial role when innovating in rural areas to resolve prevalent pain points, chapter 7 concludes part II in showing why business enterprises are participating in the Smart Village program.

Part III of this book eventually shows *how* the Smart Village idea is being executed in practice. Chapter 8 therefore introduces how an organization can be built for executing such programs. Chapter 9 explains how the database for unlocking innovation and new value was created. Ultimately, chapter 10 provides a holistic Open Innovation Framework for Innovating in Rural Emerging Markets as a manual for tapping into the rural market of emerging economies. It is built on academic research along with the many learnings, failures, and successes faced on-ground. A real innovation case in the field of rural healthcare illustrates its application and provides detailed insights into the process – from identifying the pain points to piloting and pivoting a promising solution.

Part IV focuses on *what* successes and challenges emerged throughout the last years of executing the Smart Village idea. Chapter 11 describes aspiring success stories from innovating in rural India in multiple verticals such as agriculture, entrepreneurship, and safety and security. In chapter 12, the many-faced challenges, failures, and learnings are discussed. Roadblocks, such as barriers, weak links and bottlenecks are illustrated with multiple examples and on-ground insights. This part closes with chapter 13 providing responses from stakeholders alongside a reflection of the Smart Village idea.

The last part of this book, part V, provides an outlook into the future of Smart Villages. If chapter 14 lays out the increasing need for transforming into a sharing economy, chapter 15 closes this book with guidance on how to balance knowledge with ethics to create a sustainable economy.

There is a lot of research available about tapping into emerging markets, but little research exists about innovating in the rural markets (from a multinational, academic perspective) like in India. This book provides new findings, a first-time perspective, and detailed observations in the work; It focuses on the orchestration of innovation projects in rural emerging markets among state governments, business enterprises, universities, and populations. Many astonishing learnings are highlighted when operating and innovating in an unknown and demanding territory like rural India when lagging far behind from its urban areas. The experiences encountered while working in collaboration with governments, private sector companies, universities, and the local population provides new insight about innovating in rural emerging economies. The affiliated philosophy strives to share acquired knowledge with governments, corporates, NGOs, and philanthropists all around the globe to effectively learn from experiences and to let the 3.4 billion rural people all around the world thrive in the utmost sustainable way. The motive behind launching this book is therefore to share the expertise in order to replicate the Smart Village model to many other states in India and across the world. See the following exhibits for the overall value propositions on how each participant and stakeholder within the Smart Village ecosystem can benefit, explanations of Indian specific terms and definitions, and finally, the book's key takeaways.

Value Propositions

To Governments

Research & Consulting

- First hand research insights to better formulate policies.
- Accessing database of village pain points.
- Receiving recommendations on relevant pain points to address.

Meeting Needs of Villagers

- Getting proposals and proof of concepts for sustainable business models and ecosystems.
- Participating in orchestrating the Co-Innovation process with villagers, companies and universities for further scaling.

Economic Improvement

- Encouraging entrepreneurship in villages.
- Recognition for the state in academia, attracting young talents.
- Potential investment from Silicon Valley firms and Startups.

To Private Sector

Tap into the rural Indian Market

- Resolving relevant customer needs and have a first-mover advantage.
- Access to an efficient structure to test offerings in the villages and achieve a successful product to market fit.
- Developing business models for technology offerings based on data and feedback that can scale in India's untapped market.
- Information about government programs that enable or deter innovation and growth.

Access to an Open Innovation Platform

- Co-Innovation process with participating firms, universities and government to form collabora tions and partnerships to enhance offerings.
- Networking with the government for MoU and further scaling.
- Access to UC Berkeley Open Innovation network and expertise.

To Rural Populations

Empowerement

- Developing social and human capital to be socio-economically and independently uplifted.
- Access to better services (e.g. healthcare).
- Digital tools to increase income.
- Loan facilitation
- Being relieved from existing pain points through education, skill development and digital transformation.

Recognition and Participation

- Getting recognized in academic publications.
- Co-Innovation: giving feedback whether a possible solution really helps/is relevant.
- Ranking grand challenges to be addressed in terms of personal relevance.

To Academia

Relevant Research Opportunities

- Accessing real life challenges to be solved with academic research.
- Getting data for conducting in depth research.
- Receiving high international recognition when solving real pain points with research.

Access to an Open Innovation Platform

- Being connected to private and public sectors to collaboratively solve the rural needs.
- Extending research network with prestigious universities.

Introduction
Indian Specific Terms and its Explanations

Term	Explanation
1. Government Structure: Central Vs State	The Indian government has a federal structure, declaring it to be a "Union of States" where legislative, administrative and executive powers are distributed between the Union/Federal/Central government and the States/Territories of India. There are 29 states and 7 union territories.
2. District	A district is an administrative division of an Indian state.
3. Mandal	Subdivision of a district.
4. Constituency	Legislative district, a voting district consisting of serveral villages/places.
5. President	Ceremonial head of state of India and the commander-in-chief of the Indian Armed Forces.
6. Prime Minister	Leader of the executive of the Government of India and the chief adviser to the President of India and head of the Council of Ministers.
7. Chief Minister	Elected head of government of each of twenty nine states and two among the seven union territories.
8. District Collector (Magistrate)	Senior most executive magistrate and chief in charge of general administration of a district in India.
9. MLA	Elected representative of a constituency who then becomes a member of the Legislative Assembly (MLA).
10. Crore	Denotes ten milion in Indian numbering system (100,00,000) and equals 100 Lahk.
11. Lahk	Denotes one hundred thousend in Indian numbering system (1,00,000).
12. Rupee (INR)	Official currency of India.

Key Takeaways from this Book

1. The largest untapped market for growth lies in rural villages around the world

2. Open Innovation Framework is most effective for creating Smart Villages

3. A Smart Village is both scalable and sustainable

4. Scalability of Smart Villages can be achieved through Open Innovation Platforms

5. Sustainability is achieved through formation of ecosystems

6. The role of Governments, Universities, and Businesses are critical to success

7. Relevant data needs to be converted into knowledge to fuel business ecosystems

8. Open Business Models are required to achieve both scale and scope to expand markets

9. Social Capital formation is the disruptive force that abolishes unfair barriers and laws

10. Premier research institutions provide credible and agnostic validation of growth strategies

11. Creating Smart Villages is not a "Project" but a "Movement" driven by a vision of the many

12. The way forward for socioeconomic prosperity calls for wisdom the right use of knowledge

INTRODUCTION TO SCALING SMART VILLAGES

It was early summer 2018, the Smart Village team sat and reflected on the 1.5 years of operating the first Smart Village project across 472 villages in Andhra Pradesh. There was an intense discussion on how to move forward with the Smart Village idea – How can the Smart Villages continue to build and grow on its successful results, but moreover, its failures? It seemed that in order to scale the program to a wider level, a new strategy was needed. It was evident that despite the success of the project, the uncertainty of knowledge flows across projects, functional teams, and stakeholders (start-ups, corporations, governments officials, universities, and beneficiaries – the people on the ground) were all working in isolation. It is true that the success of the project derived from the ecosystem that had been created to address the rural needs of the villages.

However, the link between the ecosystem was disconnected. Moving forward, and expanding to Arunachal Pradesh meant that the current approach would limit successful coordination and management to effectively scale the Smart Villages. As a result of these bottlenecks, the next step was to take a look at the current business environment, which proved to be moving towards a platform economy. Disruptive companies like Uber, Amazon, and Facebook confirmed a new strategy – an evolvement towards a platform – one that would help accelerate and scale the Smart Village Movement, drive innovation outcomes and create impact for all its participants. Considering that the current Smart Village model was already working, why the need to move towards something new? As such, this chapter will explain and share the vision of how the Smart Village Movement will be executed in 2020. Now, let's look into the future by connecting the dots from the past.

Looking first into platform theory derived from industry success stories can explain the huge general need and potential for this approach in the digital age of our time. Shifting from emerging to developed economies such as the United States lets us quickly understand how some of today's dominant platforms were given birth to and why these platforms are so powerful.

In 2007 when Brian Chesky and Joe Gebbia realized that accommodation in San Francisco for conference attendees would be too expensive, they offered "networking in your jam-jams" meaning they would provide their private space for short term rental. Eventually, they attracted three guests and hosted their air mattresses to them, which made them realize that casual space sharing can provide affordable room rentals and is a lucrative business for hosts. In order to scale their idea, a platform where everyone can rent out their spare sofa or guestroom all over the globe was the logical way forward. They called their new platform "Airbnb" and the rest is history. This meant a disruption to one of the world's biggest industries and made them a giant enterprise without owning one single hotel room. There are plenty of other examples why platforms are disruptive and powerful to change industries and humungous to spearhead in the digital age – companies like *uber* in the traditional taxi business without possessing a single taxi car, or *Alibaba* featuring billions of articles to be sold on their eCommerce platform without owning any item of inventory.

These digital platforms all share a similar DNA: connecting people, resources, and organizations to exchange information, knowledge, and value in an interactive ecosystem. More precisely, it refers to enable value creation between external producers and consumers when having an open, participative infrastructure to perform matches and facilitate the exchange of services, goods, knowledge, expertise, etc. Thus, it is a dramatic shift away from the traditional system of a linear value chain ("pipeline") towards a platform structure, where different types of users are producers and or consumers at the same time, using the provided resources from the platform to create different forms of value. New sources of value creation and supply are being unlocked when resources can be used without having ownership. Moreover, data-based tools on digital platforms enable community feedback loops to ensure the right solution for future customers. The former straight line from producers to consumers is now shifted to value creation in multiple ways – whenever, wherever. Digitization removes barriers of time and space, it produces immediate and precise results. Thus, platforms invert the focus from inward to outward, meaning operations are centered around people, resources, and functions which are outside, replacing or complementing the existing internal ones of a traditional business. Platforms make it easier to scale since traditional gatekeepers that manage the flow of value from producers to consumers are eliminated, and network effects are pushing its growth in a new, formerly not to imaginable way.

Industry giants were mainly possible due to supply economics of scale. In the platform business, success and scale are possible when having network effects – demand economies of supply. This means that the value of a platform grows as more people are using it, which again attracts more users and again increases the value even more. In the *uber* example, such traction on both ends refers to the decrease of wait time for riders as well as downtime for drivers. A driver then can make more amount of money since he has more riders during the same working hours, even if the fares are lower, which again increases the demand of riders. A virtuous cycle starts because of two-sided positive network effects; drivers attract riders and vice versa leading to stimulating network growth. Thus, it is important to ensure traction for both – the supply and the demand side for successful scaling. However, there are also negative network effects, meaning when matches of supply and demand are not being balanced, it leads to bad user experience. If men approach women on a dating app in an unfiltered way, beautiful females are not happy because of the large unfiltered attention. Less attractive males are left alone since women of their choice are never responding. One the other hand, attractive women are leaving the platform and attractive men, who might have been a good match for them, are unhappy because all attractive women already left. A continuous decrease in the platform's value emerges. Therefore, a platform needs to implement a distinctive curation strategy to balance supply and demand efficiently and effectively. A platform sets hereby its very own governance conditions to all participants.[3]

To conclude the theory of developing successful platforms in the digital age, producers and consumers need to be pulled and attracted in a balanced way to generate two-sided network effects. Matching actors to one another then needs to be done carefully when implementing a powerful curation mechanism. Thus, a platform needs to perform three crucial functions; pull, facilitate and, match. In general, unlocking value beyond the obvious as a platform grows can be accomplished when the design satisfies interactions for large numbers of users but always leaves room for serendipity and the unexpected since users themselves will find new ways to create value on the platform. A clear defined overall value-creation mission is however critical, to not divert from the original vision of the platform.

Scaling with a platform approach seems ultimately the must do approach to succeed in today's business environment. These insights and knowledge about platforms were grasped by the whole Smart Village team, which let them pivot the platform concept to the context of the Smart Village idea to start a Movement for rural development by having a powerful digital tool to execute. The following explains how this will be effectively executed in 2020 under the general Smart Village vision and mission:

Smart Village:
Mission & Vision

"Smart Village is a community empowered by digital technologies and Open Innovation platforms to access global markets."

Solomon Darwin & Henry Chesbrough

Vision
To Increase the Happiness of the Villagers
Mission
Building Scalable Smart Villages

The Smart Village Movement Platform for Scaling

The overall mission and vision of the Smart Village Movement platform remain the same along with its fundamental innovation methodology (as explained later in this book). An interactive platform provides now immediate access to resources, actors, knowledge, and information to enable a collaborative value creation without barriers. Central to the Smart Village Movement platform are rural grand challenges derived from research to be solved in a collaborative, open way. The following illustrations explain the user flow for participating entities, such as universities, startups, corporations, people (rural citizens), and governments (state and central governments). First, to curate content and functionalities accordingly, participants can choose their respective entities (Exhibit 1).

Exhibit 1 – Smart Village Movement Platform: Entity Selection

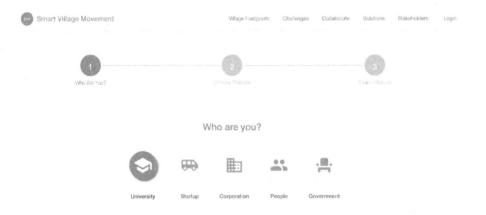

After choosing one's entity (step 1), the field of interest can be selected (step 2), this refers to the vertical an entity wants to get more information about and eventually, can take upon and solve

existing challenges with the available ecosystem and resources (see Exhibit 2).

Exhibit 2 – Smart Village Movement Platform: Problem Area Selection

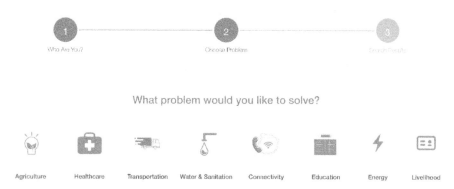

The platform now displays entity-specific relevant content in the field of the chosen vertical with respect to available grand challenges, possible technology solutions not being applied yet in the Smart Village ecosystem, existent collaborations within the Smart Village Movement, and prevalent key stakeholders (step 3) (see Exhibit 3).

Exhibit 3 – Smart Village Movement Platform: Search Results

Details can then be found in these sub-categories. Each presented *grand challenge* provides general details, specific pain points, a profile of the location where the challenge exists, the possible socio-economic impact a solution can create, affiliated business opportunity, available resources, and links to discussions and ratings regarding this specific challenge.

Possible solutions comprise existing technologies, research findings, business models, and innovations that are related to address rural challenges but are not yet applied within the Smart Village Movement. It serves therefore as a powerful solution repository and knowledge database in the field of development and innovation efforts in the rural emerging economy setting.

Collaborations show what existing projects with multiple parties have already taken forward within the Smart Village Movement and what impact was created. Moreover, it gives other participants an understanding of how their progress, learnings, and challenges have been and also provides them the opportunity to plug in and collaborate to perfect the solution if necessary.

Ultimately, key stakeholders, such as government departments, key bureaucrats, local politicians, etc. are listed, which are necessary to engage with in order to successfully come up with solutions, executing pilots and eventually achieve scaling. Only if signed up, participants are provided with full access and can directly reach out to other participants, and can submit their solution proposals to take their idea forward with the help of the Smart Village team and access all provided resources.

The platform enables a continuous engagement process from all different participants. Data and information can be extracted, consumers can become producers and vice versa; actors to eventually solve presented grand challenges. Gained knowledge during this process and accomplished outcomes are then to be repatriated back to the platform in the form of data, information, and accumulated knowledge. This process enriches the platform since more knowledge is being captured, making it again more efficient for its participants to solve challenges. The more data, knowledge, experience, and learnings are available, the easier it becomes for its participants to solve the rural grand challenges in an Open Innovation way. These network effects lead to an ongoing upwards virtuous cycle of value creation, which allows the platform to become very powerful in the domain of rural development.

Central to the platform is problem finding, framing, and solving. In order to find problems, data on rural India's pain points is being collected (more on data collection in chapter 9), and stored in cloud-servers to be analyzed by data analysts with partly automated data analytic functionalities. Eventually, analyzed data will be visualized for easy consumption for all of its participants, using data visualization libraries and capabilities to turn raw data into visuals. Presented grand challenges therefore build on collected and analyzed data to empirically prove their relevance. Moreover, challenges are getting ranked from villagers to additionally assess their relevance directly from the ground to prevent missing customer-centricity and alignment. Participants from various fields then can submit their solution proposals which get validated by a consortium of experts consisting of the Smart Village team and the advisory board from industry, government, and academia. Again, here curation plays a critical success factor to funnel out the most relevant, realistic, breakthrough, and promising ideas to hold up the quality and effectiveness of the platform, and ultimately make sure that value is being created when solving outlined grand challenges. Therefore, a semi-automated curation mechanism is applied. If getting approved, an intelligent matching mechanism using artificial intelligence recommends and connects viable resources, key stakeholders, companies, startups, and universities which might help to further enhance one's idea. Moreover, the proposal and progress can be discussed in discussion forums, and onground feedback from rural people can be collected. The Smart Village team operates then as the orchestrator as a key player, supported by the intelligence of the Smart Village platform and its comprehensive functionalities (see exhibit 4).

Exhibit 4 – Core Functionalities of the Smart Village Movement Platform

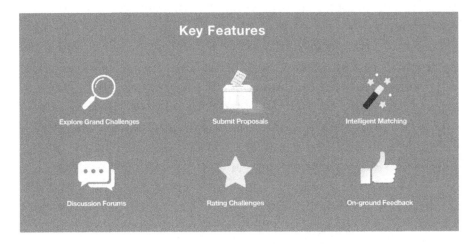

Discussion forums for student classes have also been implemented. Students can engage in the project and its findings, and they can also receive feedback from academics, industry practitioners, people from the ground, and the Smart Village team. To this date, project-based classes with students such as from the Lancaster Business School, UK, on creating Smart Villages were successfully organized and operated on the Smart Village Movement platform. It successfully demonstrated how academic activities can be powerfully leveraged as a contribution to Open Innovation solutions for rural emerging markets. These student projects to develop supply chains and business models for individual agricultural products from Arunachal Pradesh accomplished outstanding results, which were presented to the Chief Minister of Arunachal Pradesh. A full-fledged project proposal was developed providing project launch readiness when having signed up identified supply chain partners. The major success factor hereby was the platform approach which enabled students to quickly exchange knowledge with each other, it connected them directly to the farmers on ground in India to better understand the setting and receive feedback to evaluate their concepts. Ultimately, the platform provided them access to the government of Arunachal Pradesh and to relevant industry partners which could unlock new value and accelerate implementation readiness. An example of a project in the form of an opening statement can be found in the appendix.

Another core component is the project management tool that is being implemented, which builds on the Open Innovation framework for rural emerging markets as explained and illustrated in this book. This helps the participants connect, design ecosystems and business models, derive value hypotheses, execute pivots, accomplish a proof of concept, and eventually scale their solutions with ongoing customer feedback. Also, it keeps the participants track of their project, follow the recommended innovation methodology and brings transparency for all stakeholders, e.g. the state government. Entity-individual dashboards are therefore provided, which highlight the relevant information and functionalities for their respective interests and roles. Hereby, the platform can be customized specifically for a state government. It is this aspect that makes it a platform of platform approach. The main objective hereby is to train the government and eventually hand over the Open Innovation Platform. In particular, the government is able to manage its state-specific platform on their own after a while. In the end, the government stays engaged with Berkeley by continuing to exchange data and knowledge when remaining a platform of the overall Smart Village platform.

The Smart Village Movement platform itself is an Open Innovation endeavor. It is co-developed in collaboration with many startups and corporations as well as universities under the leadership of Arun Sharma, lead architect. Open Innovation partners in this process have been Mphasis, PayPal, NineSigma among others. In order to fulfill the needs of its users, a first beta version was rolled out in late 2018. Feedback to validate and improve the platform has been collected and support was received from academics, (many scholars and professors from UC Berkeley, Melissa Schilling from NYU Stern), senior industry executives (e.g. Jim Spohrer from IBM, John Chambers, ex-chairman Cisco), Silicon Valley startup thought leaders (Will Decker from Plug and Play) and government officials (Pema Khandu, Chief Minister from Arunachal Pradesh, Dr. Rajiv Kumar, Vice Chairman from NITI Aayog).

Ultimately, the Smart Village Movement platform is a virtual place, where academia, government and corporations, startups and multinationals, come together to co-innovate to solve grand challenges of rural emerging economies. The platform enables hereby a value creation in real-time as knowledge is being created and flowing across organizations, countries, entities, and people. Given its unique characteristics, the Smart Village Movement platform provides a dynamic environment (opportunity), which escalates and accelerates problem finding, framing, and solving for innovating in the rural setting of emerging markets in the most potent way. The platform automatically captures created data, information and knowledge, cutting edge research and investigation for analysis through a consortium of universities; it documents and scientifically evaluates which models for rural empowerment are working and which are not. Being a research project with no commercial interest, a resulting un-biasedness ensures the credibility of this platform, which is highly valued and received from state governments and the industry.

Scaling of the Smart Village idea needs to happen organically and needs to be driven by its very own energy and participants to create a win-win situation. Moving artificially and using advertising to create scale doesn't lead to success. Organic chemistry of collaboration of its participants who are self-motivated is required. This platform digitizing the Smart Village idea offers every entity its very own value proposition to drive and scale this movement. The grand challenges of today and tomorrow can only be solved when governments, industry, academia and, the people come together with willingness and passion to address the needs of humanity. This platform provides the needed tool for executing the Smart Village idea when facilitating ecosystem approaches, generating innovative ideas, and publishing research beyond any known boundaries.

In order to really understand how the whole Smart Village vision emerged, how the platform developed, and enhances and advances the vision for 2020, it requires a deep understanding of how to create Smart Villages in general. The following chapters therefore explain all its accomplishments, failures, all its excellent moments, and formidable moments, all its grandness, and imperfections and elaborate its underlying processes of why it worked in theory and how it works in practice. While reading the following sections, it is recommended to keep the outlook as a platform in mind to truly connect the future with the past – to understand and reflect on the unique evolution of the Smart Village idea from a prototype village towards a movement as it is built on a digital platform.

PART I.

Why the Smart Village Idea Works

CHAPTER 1

WHAT ARE THE LEARNINGS FROM PREVIOUS RURAL DEVELOPMENT INITIATIVES

Villages in India have received government aid through several programs over the years. Although these programs help villagers in the short term, they are not enough. They do not lay the foundation for sustainable economic development. Typical job programs, for example, do little to improve villagers' knowledge or skills. Moreover, once government funding for a program ends, there is little to sustain further at the village level. Creating economic opportunity would help the village and the government, which could potentially reduce expenditures on aid while improving villagers' lives. This creates a virtuous cycle, as greater knowledge and skills lead to higher income, which promotes an increase in health and well-being leading to further knowledge development.

Many companies have long histories of giving to villages in the developing world, but charitable donations often have no connection to the companies' mission or core competencies. Such as an oil company contributing money to promote health and wellness initiatives. As a result, the effects are not sustainable, and the companies have no incentive to expand their efforts beyond the charity provided. In many cases, governments and companies have not involved villagers in the design of their aid programs, so the programs often did not address villagers' actual needs.

These outcomes are not unique to India. Traditional aid programs have often led to unintended consequences, negative outcomes, and reduced economic growth, according to economist Dambisa Moyo, author of *Dead Aid: Why Aid is Not Working and How There is a Better Way for Africa*. Although the book addresses aid given to African countries, many similarities exist to aid given to individuals in developing countries. Aid, he argues, "has failed to deliver the promise of sustainable economic growth and poverty reduction … it has not lived up to expectations. It remains at the heart of the development agenda, despite the fact that there are very compelling reasons to show that it perpetuates the cycle of poverty and derails sustainable economic growth."[1]

One of the biggest problems with traditional aid is that it instills dependence. Finite, limited aid programs that address specific goals can help alleviate important problems, but much of the aid in low-income countries is pervasive and essentially continuous, Moyo writes, "without the inbuilt threat that aid might be cut, and without the sense that one day it could all be over, African governments view aid as a permanent, reliable, consistent source of income and have no reason to believe that the flows won't continue into the indefinite future. There is no incentive for long-term financial planning, no reason to seek alternatives to fund development when all you have to do is sit back and bank the cheques."[2] Aid can also harm otherwise successful local businesses and, paradoxically, create the need for more aid. Moyo cites the scenario of a mosquito net maker in Africa who employs ten people who altogether support as many as 150 people.[3] An influx of free mosquito nets from a well-intentioned aid program helps some people in the area, but puts the net maker out of business thus making the 150 people his business was supporting suddenly dependent on aid. The ability to provide more nets in the future now depends upon further philanthropic support, instead of local business people responding to local market incentives to supply them. To date, "more than US $2 trillion of foreign aid has been transferred from rich countries to poor over the past fifty years," writes Moyo, yet there is not very much to show for this effort.[4] One reason: aid programs are frequently evaluated in the short term, which is largely irrelevant to their effect on the target region's long-term problems. "Aid effectiveness should be measured against its contribution to long-term sustainable growth, and whether it moves the greatest number of people out of poverty in a sustainable way. When seen through this lens, aid is found to be wanting."[5]

Exhibit 5 Comparison Between Development-led Aid and Smart Villages Approach

Government-led Aid Initiatives	Smart Villages – Open Innovation-led Initiatives
During the period of substantial aid, local prices often inflated, pushing many basic items out of reach for the already poor.	Minimal staff in village, minimal impact on local prices.
Village residents acquired little to no skills that might help them to be more productive.	Strong focus on skills development and training.
Residents were still kept away from larger markets, so much of the value that they produced was captured by middle-men.	Digital technology platforms enable direct linkage to local, regional, national and even international markets.

Government-led Aid Initiatives	Smart Villages – Open Innovation-led Initiatives
Corruption was endemic, reducing the amount of money that actually reached the local residents, and creating political barriers that last long past the end of the aid itself.	Digital technology platforms enable much greater transparency and reduce opportunities for corruption. Open innovation connects all providers together into a coherent platform.
There was no way to scale any success beyond the immediate rural area.	Companies contributing talent and resources are looking to expand their markets, will scale once they understand what villagers want, and are willing to pay for.
Once the aid ended, little economic benefit remained.	The business models for the village and for the companies are sustainable, so market capitalist incentives will sustain the activities in the village, once government support is withdrawn.

Many of Moyo's conclusions about the effects of aid on African countries align with Naidu's findings from his Pada Yatra regarding the limited effectiveness of aid programs on rural Indians. Although the programs in Andhra Pradesh are not the same as the programs Moyo describes, Naidu does see a key parallel: the need to empower villagers to shape their own futures. As a result, he is seeking a solution that provides villages with information, training, and other tools people need to become successful entrepreneurs. The solution must focus on solving real problems facing villagers rather than on addressing what people outside the village assume are problems (excerpt from the 2017 White Paper *"Smart Village Ecosystems. An Open Innovation Approach"* by Henry Chesbrough and Solomon Darwin)

CHAPTER 2
WHY SMART VILLAGES AND NOT SMART CITIES

The vision of Smart Villages is derived from the Smart Cities concept to bring in digital tools for enablement and economic prosperity, but without having the need for heavy infrastructure. The main difference between Smart Cities and Smart Villages is that Smart Villages are a more widespread and organic effort, and goes along with the idea of building self-sufficiency rather than providing one-time infrastructure and citizen services to one large group.

The Smart Village vision could not have emerged without the encounter of Solomon Darwin and Henry Chesbrough, two individuals with different, yet complementary backgrounds Henry Chesbrough, Adjunct Professor and Faculty Director of the Garwood Center and Solomon Darwin, Executive Director of the Garwood Center for Corporate Innovation have been colleagues since 2012. Professor Henry Chesbrough first-ever coined the term of Open Innovation in 2003 and is consecutively researching on its many different applications in industry, public sector, and academia. He became the "father of Open Innovation" – making him the main expert for Open Innovation in Academia as well as in industry. Chesbrough has published many bestseller books and more than 280 research papers about Open Innovation so far, leading to more than 64,000 citations. Solomon Darwin has years of teaching and corporate experience, throughout his career, he has always had a strong affiliation with India for its development. Open Innovation sparked an interest in Solomon Darwin, and through Henry Chesbrough, he realized how important this methodology is for business, technology, including social collaboration in communities.

Open Innovation became a foundation for Solomon Darwin's work and teachings thereafter. Smart City frameworks were developed at UC Berkeley with respect to Indian urban development, Open Innovation was key for designing and developing concepts to be presented to the Indian government. Open Innovation leads to better stewardship for assets since capital requirements were heavy; It served as an easing vehicle to optimize resources and activities related to the implementation of Smart Cities. Finally, when prompted to ad0pt the Smart City concept to villages, both – Henry Chesbrough and Solomon Darwin developed the vision and concept for Smart Villages based on Open Innovation. The Smart Village idea flourished by bringing together their expertise and experiences, and as a result, the vision has impacted thousands of people in India, and many others around the world. Finally, they defined Smart Villages as "a community empowered by digital technologies and Open Innovation platforms to access global markets".

The deeming of a geographical unit "smart" first started with the idea of Smart Cities. It is already being implemented in places such as Dublin, Ireland, where the city applies analytics to data to help optimize a wide range of public services and works to engage citizens, business leaders, and scholars to improve city life.[1] Motivations for transforming Mori and villages like it into

Smart Villages are similar to those driving leaders in Dublin and around the world. Specifically, they encompass empowering villagers with access to smart and lean technology, transparent information, easy-to-use digital tools, resources to develop entrepreneurial skills, and direct access to global markets. IBM built one of the first smart cities in Rio de Janeiro in Brazil to use IBM's Smart Cities technology to coordinate city services in real-time.[2] Cisco worked on transforming Barcelona into a Smart City. Some of these models were not that promising and required enormous capital investment having infrastructure but not showing promised outcomes. In 2014, when Modi announced 100 Indian cities to become smart, the feedback was originally very positive. However, to this date, there is no Smart City in India.

In general, the situation in Indian cities is very tense. People leaving Indian villages face many challenges in their new homes. Migration also creates challenges for the Indian cities to which villagers relocate. Some cities are growing rapidly and unable to accommodate the additional population. For example, the population of Hyderabad, a midsized city approximately 500 kilometers inland of Mori, nearly doubled from 3.6 million in 2001[3] to 6.7 million in 2011,[4] putting the 2011 population density at 47,274 persons per square mile.[5] By comparison, in 2010 New York City's population density was 27,012 persons per square mile, and San Francisco's was 17,179 persons per square mile.[6] As of 2015, approximately 170 million Indians lived in urban slums, largely due to a lack of affordable housing.[7] Infrastructure in rapidly growing cities is strained in other ways. Traffic, for example, can easily stretch what would normally be a 30-minute trip within a city such as Bangalore to two hours or longer. In essence, some large cities are reaching their population limits and diseconomies of scale are setting in. At the same time, villagers often need basic tools, such as information about market prices for their farmed produce, to become more prosperous, whereas city dwellers tend to have more complex needs. Simplicity can help keep costs low for companies developing products and services. Villages are also close to being green fields – that is, the general lack of infrastructure and services means fewer constraints exist on those entering the market. For example, distributed energy generation innovations like small-scale solar are not competing with clean, stable power sources in villages.[8] Instead, they often compete with a lack of access, inefficient and unreliable power systems, or pollution-emitting generators.

Ultimately, in the case of emerging economies such as India, where the urban areas are flooded with people since the villages lack so far behind in their development, the concept of Smart Villages could create a much bigger impact for the Indian economy and people than building a few smart cities.[9] Moreover, for industry partners, tapping into this market means an enormous business opportunity when offering the right products and services to the villagers. By comparison to emerging economies, economic growth in developed countries is much lower. In both 2014 and 2015, U.S. GDP expansion was approximately 2.42 percent. The Japanese economy contracted slightly in 2014 and grew by .47 percent in 2015. In Germany, GDP grew by 1.6 percent in 2014 and by 1.69 percent the following year.[10] In all, about 1.5 billion people in the world live in wealthy countries with highly developed economies, and about 5.5 billion people live in emerging-market economies, such as China and India. The GDP of highly developed countries totals approximately $40 trillion; if GDP grows at an annual rate of 2.5 percent, the potential new value to businesses is approximately $0.8 trillion per year. The GDP of emerging-economy countries is lower than that of the rich countries: it totals approximately $30 trillion.[11] However, assuming 7.5 percent growth means new value to businesses each year and is approximately $2.3 trillion – nearly triple the potential new value in rich economies (see Exhibit 3) *(excerpt from the 2016 HBR Case "Prototyping a Scalable Smart Village to Simultaneously Create Sustainable Development and Enterprise Growth Opportunities" by Henry Chesbrough and Solomon Darwin).*

Exhibit 6 – The Relationship Among Value, Price, Basic Strategy and Innovation

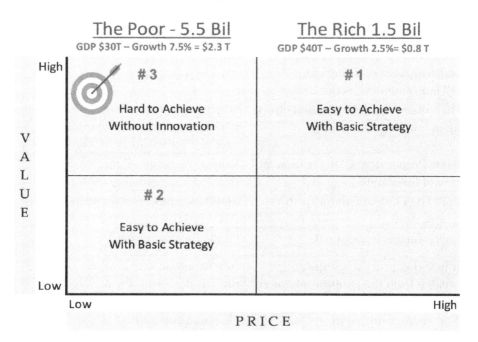

For countries, the investment in Smart Villages is ultimately better than that for Smart Cities as it is much easier and cost-effective. Moreover, the scale of making villages "smart" to foster economic prosperity in emerging economies offers a huge potential to drive the GDP of a country as described above. When first announcing the Smart Village vision, it was irreversible taking upon the Smart Village initiative – the noble vision immediately inspired and convinced.

Exhibit 7 – Comparison Between Smart City Approach and
Smart Village Approach in Emerging Economies (EE)[12]

Smart City Approach (EE)	Smart Village Approach (EE)
Requires a lot of expenses for infrastructure	No infrastructure expenses required
Technology becomes obsolete very quickly which keeps up ongoing infrastructure investments	Technology doesn't require annual updates; long duration possible
High effort to retool, restructure and reorganize existing cities -> Time- and money-consuming	Infrastructure is not prominent, no need to restructure
High planning and execution efforts when building smart cities	Organic development by village population, community building is easy as it is the nature of mankind
Value Proposition: GDP creation and ease of livelihood	Value Proposition: Empowering people for economic growth
ROI: High investment for medium output	ROI: Low investment for high output
Public Image: Impersonal	Public Image: personal
Innovation process is static and isolated from the public as planned among relevant stakeholders.	Innovation process is organic and directly done with the people.
Non-community-based	Community-based

Former Chief Minister Naidu clearly agreed to the advantages of Smart Villages over Smart Cities for his state. Meeting the stated objectives will not require substantial infrastructure development or large outlays of money. Rather, it will require uninterrupted internet connectivity, community engagement, and skill-building. With these resources, villagers can identify and pursue entrepreneurial paths to economic independence. Being very convinced about the impact from Smart Villages over Smart Cities, an MoU (Memorandum of Understanding) between UC Berkeley and the

Andhra Pradesh government was signed to experiment with the potential of a first Smart Village prototype in Mori. Moreover, presenting a paper on Smart Villages to the President of India after talking with CM Naidu on rural empowerment created even more traction.

CHAPTER 3
WHAT IS THE UNDERLAYING DESIGN PHILOSOPHY

Creating Smart Villages is a novel approach addressing the needs and pain points of rural populations in emerging economies with an entrepreneurial approach and providing growth opportunities for the private sector at the same time. This can create benefits for the many stakeholders and reduces the dependency on e.g. government aid programs, as mentioned before.

Businesses are therefore asked to the stage to contribute to resolving societal challenges. However, an open approach is hereby needed and pooling in capabilities and resources to accelerate innovation, grow operations, and establish partnerships and new innovation ecosystems to achieve positive social change. Open Innovation accounts consequently as the central framework for the Smart Village design philosophy, embedded with other relevant, existing concepts and approaches mainly from academic business research, such as the triple helix concept, the shared value approach, social capital, and leadership framework to build the effective bedrock for its execution. Learning from existing research and building upon that makes it possible to do new mistakes within this unexplored, unique endeavor rather than reproducing old, known mistakes.

The Role of Open Innovation

Open Innovation as a term was first coined by Henry Chesbrough as "Open Innovation means that valuable ideas can come from inside or outside the company and can go to market from inside or outside the company as well. This approach places external ideas and external paths to market on the same level of importance as that reserved for internal ideas and paths to market during the Closed Innovation era."[1] Therefore, it is based on the concept of harnessing knowledge flowing from the outside in one's own innovation processes and allowing unused knowledge to flow outside for others to use in their innovations. Typically, companies take a closed approach to innovation. That is, a company employs a research and development team that generates and refines ideas into products and services for end markets, be they consumers or other businesses. In Open Innovation, companies both take in external ideas and make their own ideas available for others to build upon.[2] For example, a company may license technology from another company and develop it into a new product. Or, the company may enter into a joint venture or other agreement with an external firm to co-develop the idea into a product or service. Firms leveraging Open Innovation may also make their unused patents or ideas available to outside companies or other entities interested in developing products or services. These unutilized outcomes refer to so-called spillover effects and were long viewed as a major cost component in a firm's R&D process and were generally judged as unmanageable. Open Innovation instead proposes that these spillover effects can be purposefully managed and specified when being transformed in inflows and outflows of knowledge.[3] Therefore, Open Innovation allows organizations to capture greater value by utilizing their key assets, various resources, ideas, and knowledge or position which is not only in their own operations but also in other companies' businesses.[4]

When companies bring external ideas into their development processes, they save money and time by only paying for the technology they need and avoiding the early stages of research, which often involve dead ends.[5] When companies share their ideas, they can earn royalties and even construct value chains that otherwise would not exist. For example, Procter & Gamble achieved this with its Swiffer Dusters, which it licensed from Unicharm in Japan, and turned into a billion-dollar brand in the rest of the world.[6] In some cases, an idea may not be directly relevant to a company's core competencies but could prove valuable to partners or key suppliers. Ultimately, Open Innovation makes research and development a more economically sustainable activity that carries less risk. Moreover, competing companies and complementary industry sectors converge to exchange knowledge and provide unique customer solutions. Such ecosystems are difficult to imitate, leading to competitive advantages for participating parties. From the transactional cost perspective, collaborations generate scale, which effects and minimizes risks by sharing investment costs. Moreover, collaborations diversify the product and service portfolio by combining diverse, complementary expertise and resources. This leads to an accelerated speed to market[7] and to better and more innovative solutions.

This concept is described as a Minimum Viable Ecosystem (MVE) approach through Open Innovation, where innovation is being accelerated through complementing partners with different characteristics. Having all participants aligned with the overall vision of the innovation project and that there are individual benefits, the overall value proposition can be created collaboratively. In this sense, benefits are to be long term and sustaining for driving their commitment throughout. Ultimately, multidimensional perspectives on the individual business models as part of the high-level business model will attract and sustain the ecosystem approach.

Open Innovation in the Context of Smart Villages

The companies participating in Open Innovation within the Smart Village program are seeking to innovate new products and services for the bottom of the pyramid. Mori village is an ideal testbed for these companies to use in their explorations. These villagers have many needs and few resources. Therefore, business models thriving in Mori, (40,000 villages in AP, more than 650,000 throughout India, and millions across the developing world) will likely root in numerous other villages as well. The rural world is a large and rapidly growing market, making these experiments well worth trying for the participating companies if they can be linked together coherently. There is a further ecosystem effect that continues to emerge in the Smart Villages project. The presence of one company in the village makes it more attractive for subsequent companies to also locate a contact person in the village. The result is a vibrant ecosystem of possible products and services for local villagers. Note that no single company or organization could martial all these disparate resources. It takes an ecosystem of organizations, all seeking to understand villagers' needs and their willingness to pay to obtain this Open Innovation ecosystem. By facilitating collaborations among various relevant companies and creating an integrated solution for the rural population, the overall costs for the customers of these digital technologies (i.e. the rural farmers) decrease. Also, a reduction in complexity, greater awareness, and education will be fostered and therefore, the adoption of digital technology and modern concepts will increase among rural populations. This leads to improving financial stability, self-sustainable empowerment, and an increase in well-being and happiness.

The pilot stage of the Smart Villages project succeeded in attracting more than 40 companies and organizations to Mori village. These companies were not providing charity, however. They were making small business development investments to learn about the needs of rural villagers for products and services they can provide or could provide. Importantly, these investments will reveal what villagers valued enough to pay for it directly with personal income. This is a kind of business model discovery that we see in Lean Startup approaches[8] to business model innovation, which is being applied in the innovation process and will be further explained later.

Participating companies are providing resources to the village for little or no money upfront, but each participating company sees an opportunity to expand their sales to rural villagers, as a result of the Smart Villages initiative. Their participation is more like business development for the bottom of the pyramid than it is another round of charitable donations to the poor. It is an example of Open Innovation, both for the companies and also from the perspective of Chief Minister Naidu. Previous approaches were government-led, with less input and support from the private sector. Moreover, the private sector participation was primarily charitable, rather than business-driven.

The Triple Helix Model

Because of globalization and the spread of digital technology, innovation is happening faster than ever and can originate from any point on the planet. Companies can no longer depend on their current products and services based on today's technology. They must begin to innovate and co-innovate in order to develop the technologies of tomorrow. Innovation cannot happen in a vacuum and businesses need the help of government and academia. These three key stakeholders need to be equal partners. They need to leverage the triple helix model where there is open communication and collaboration between government, academia, and business. Each has a role to play. It is therefore important to first understand the dynamics of a framework, which seems to be prevailing in most of the countries but differs vastly around the globe. Consisting of government, academia and business, these roles, their interdependencies, and how they interact with each other are indeed determining the foundation for a county's innovativeness. A strong framework explaining this dynamic and recommending ways of optimizing it is the *Triple Helix Concept*[9].

Exhibit 8 – Triple Helix Model of Innovation

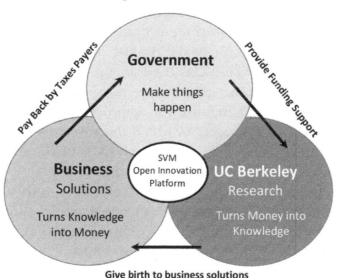

Give birth to business solutions

The government is a key player and needs to be the catalyst and provide incentives for innovation and co-innovation as well as remove any regulations that get in the way and disable the innovation process. The government needs to provide incentives for innovation in the form of funding and grants for research, and special tax incentives at the local and regional levels. Their policy toward the schools needs to be one that facilitates an open exchange of information. This means that even if funding comes from the government in the form of public education, they need to have the same hands-off policy that privately-funded colleges and universities have with regard to research projects. The key to the level of research that occurs in academia is directly related to the level of freedom from government interference they have to pursue the research they – or their business partners – deem worth pursuing. The laws governing the patents and use of research that was done with government funds by a university or college need to be viewed through the modern lens of Open Innovation.

The role of government in the development of Silicon Valley companies is an example. Knowledge of many of the basic technology was created when Government invested in funding to these universities. As an example of the results, 70% of the early Ph.D. theses in the sciences were classified as top secret. Downstream from the innovation, the government provided investment and tax incentives to commercialize the knowledge and create jobs. Jobs that generated taxpayers by which the government gets paid back. The caveat is that for this work, all parts of the circle need to be relatively equal which most countries are unable to achieve because of their cultural, political, or ideological mindset.

Academia must support an open exchange of ideas and be the risk-taker in experimenting and researching areas that might not have any immediate or obvious return-on-investment of time and money. The labs in the universities and colleges need to focus on ideas and projects and provide the education and resources needed for basic research. Senior managers and executives also need to be educated by schools about ways to be more open and innovative, and the movement of personnel between businesses and schools is an important part of the transfer of knowledge. There is also the opportunity for co-op programs between the schools and the businesses where they can work and learn together. In the Knowledge Economy, in which innovation is increasingly a function of the knowledge created through research done by universities and colleges, academia plays a more co-equal role than ever before.

Business does what it does best and monetizes and commercializes the ideas that come out of the research academia produces and is helped to market by government rules and regulations. Business can provide funding for projects in academia as well as establish strong and lasting relationships with a university or college. Businesses can also enter into a partnership with a university or college and create an ongoing research program. The Triple Helix Model gives Open Innovation leverage to solve the world's most pressing challenges, including global health, water, energy, environment, food, education, security and poverty. The Open Innovation process provides cost-effective and sustainable solutions, capturing the work and support of government, academia, and business.

The triple helix model assumes that research and the resulting innovations are part of a developed economy in which economic growth is a function of a market-based economy where the innovations can find consumers. It also presupposes that the role of government is to protect the resulting innovations by providing laws for intellectual property. Until recently, the triple helix model, overlapping the government, academia, and business, only worked in countries where all three stakeholders were able to freely operate and would not be viable in a developing country like India.

What was missing was co-innovation where the people are a fourth dimension in the helix structure. The Smart Village Movement Open Innovation platform brings together all the parts needed. *(excerpt from the 2017 book "Smart Villages of Tomorrow: The Road to Mori" by Solomon Darwin).*

Understanding the elaborated Triple Helix Framework for Innovation provides a generic level of the design philosophy being applied to execute the Smart Village idea.

The Concept of Shared Value as a Private Sector Opportunity

Another perspective that informs the design of this initiative is that of Shared Value. Shared Value, as Porter and Kramer define it, does not involve a company sharing the value it has already created; that is, it is not redistribution. Rather, "it is about expanding the total pool of economic and social value.[10]" Shared value is an approach to innovation in which companies look for ways to grow and sustain their own businesses and create societal value by addressing society's needs and challenges. This approach adds value to the society in which the organization operates, which in turn expands the market for the organization to provide its products or services going forward.

By way of explanation, Porter and Kramer contrast the shared value approach to the fair-trade movement, which focuses on paying higher prices to farmers for the same crops, a form of redistribution. "A shared value perspective, instead, focuses on improving growing techniques and strengthening the local cluster of supporting suppliers and other institutions to increase farmers' efficiency, yields, product quality, and sustainability. This leads to a bigger pie of revenue and profits that benefits both farmers and the companies that buy from them."[11] Porter and Kramer cite studies of cocoa farmers in the Côte d'Ivoire that indicate fair-trade increased farmers' incomes by approximately 10 to 20 percent, but shared value investments increased their incomes by more than 300 percent.

"Thomson Reuters has developed a promising monthly service for farmers who earn an average of $2,000 a year. For a fee of $5 a quarter, it provides weather and croppricing information and agricultural advice. The service reaches an estimated two million farmers, and early research indicates that it has helped increase the incomes of more than 60 percent of them – in some cases tripling incomes."

– Porter and Kramer, 2011

For companies, the first step in pursuing shared value opportunities is assessing their products and services in terms of how they address or create societal needs, benefits, and harms. Companies can also identify sources of shared value by changing their perspective on their relationships with suppliers. "The traditional playbook calls for companies to commoditize and exert maximum bargaining power on suppliers to drive down prices – even when purchasing from small businesses or subsistence-level farmers," according to Porter and Kramer. However, marginalized suppliers' productivity and quality levels often plateau or begin to fall. Companies can reverse this trend, thereby ensuring access to inputs and potentially reducing the total environmental impact of their products, by helping suppliers gain strength. For example, obtaining reliable supplies of coffee is essential to companies like Nestlé, which includes Nespresso. Many coffee growers run small farms and face many constraints, including low productivity, poor quality, and environmental degradation.

"To address these issues, Nestlé redesigned procurement. It worked with its growers, providing advice on farming practices, guaranteeing bank loans, and helping secure inputs such as plant stock, pesticides, and fertilizers," Porter and Kramer write. Nestlé also began measuring the quality of the coffee produced at the point of purchase, a change that made it possible to pay quality premiums directly to growers. As a result, yields and quality increased, as did farmers' incomes. "And, the environmental impact of farms shrank. Meanwhile, Nestlé's reliable supply of coffee grew significantly. Shared value was created."

Another benefit of shared value, especially as opposed to corporate charitable giving, is that it can scale. Indeed, even for social enterprises – for-profit companies that aim to have a positive impact on the world – placing a priority on financial results is correlated with successful scaling.[12] A social enterprise with stagnating revenues is limited in its potential social impact because it is limited in size and growth potential.

Shared Value in the Context of Smart Villages

For the people of Andhra Pradesh to benefit from the prototype being created in Mori, scalability of the intended social and financial benefits is essential. For the public sector, a scalable prototype could eventually alleviate some of the need for policy interventions in cities and abroad, such as building millions of new housing units or assisting thousands of migrant workers. It also has the potential to strengthen economic growth in India and even to help transform the entire developing world, which is home to millions of villagers. For the private sector, scalability is equally key. The revenues from any one village are simply too low to justify the costs of investing in technology and other solutions. However, the total opportunity within India and other developing countries is potentially large. Designing a prototype that can successfully scale is therefore crucial to the private sector's participation, which is in turn crucial to the success of the smart village concept. Companies that fail to build shared value in their markets will sooner or later impair their ability to grow to become impaired. Companies must seek to grow the pie in order to be able to sell more of their own wares. Companies working in Mori village possess extremely use-ful skills and knowledge that can help grow this pie, whether it is Ericsson helping to manage water with sensors, Hiro delivering health care through its specially designed bicycles, or IBM provid-ing farmers with better weather data to help them know when to plant, when to fertilize, and when to harvest. In short, the people in Mori village became a more connected, more knowledgeable, and more capable supplier to many more markets than it was previ-ously able to address. For example, an electrocardiograph (ECG), a machine used to record heart activity, costs thousands of dollars, and requires reliable electricity. A full-sized machine would need to be transported by truck to its destination and would need to be operated by a skilled technician. A highly educated cardiologist or other medical professional then interprets the results. Many vil-lages lack not just the funds to purchase such equipment for the local hospital, but also everything else necessary for the machine to serve its purpose, including easily passable roads in and out for the delivery truck. To address this need, General Electric created the MAC 400, a simplified, low-cost ECG that runs on batteries and is small enough and light enough to be portable.[13] Since intro-ducing the MAC 400 in 2007, GE has expanded its line of low-cost ECGs by refining the design to better meet the needs of villagers and villages. By 2011, total sales in the MAC line exceeded 10,000 units[14] (excerpt from the 2016 HBR Case *"Prototyping a Scalable Smart Village to Simultaneously Create Sustainable Development and Enterprise Growth Opportunities"*).

Social Capital

Transforming villages in emerging economies requires many efforts that need to be effectively channelized to their populations characterized by various social structures. When individuals have better access to social networks and are better integrated into social structures, the efficacy of empowerment increases. Therefore, it is important to understand the concept of social capital to be unleashed and to be built on. In general, social capital can be created from a network of strongly interconnected elements and is seen as an advantage for society. Whereas society can be seen as a market to exchange goods and ideas by people to follow their interests, certain people or groups of people are doing better when receiving higher returns on their efforts. Thus, the interests of some people are better served than others. An explanation of human capital in the context of emphasized inequality in society gives more understanding about social capital. People who are doing better are seen as more skilled, intelligent, and more able in general. Social capital complements this theory contextually when referring to overcoming inequality in society with the ability of people to be well connected to other individuals. This results in gaining trust, being obligated to support each other, and in the end, creates a dependency on mutual exchange. An individual holding a certain position in such an arrangement characterized by exchanges can be seen as an asset, which refers thus to social capital.[15] Prominent definitions of social capital are from Bourdieu (1980) stating "social capital is the sum of the resources, actual or virtual, that accrue to an individual or group by virtue of possessing a durable network of more or less institutionalized relationships of mutual acquaintance and recognition"[16] and refers to resources resulting from social structure. Moreover, Coleman (1992)[17] defines social capital "by its function, it is not a single entity but a variety of different entities having two characteristics in common: They all consist of some aspect of a social structure, and they facilitate certain actions of individuals who are within the structure. Like other forms of capital, social capital is productive, making possible the achievement of certain ends that would not be attainable in its absence." Ultimately, highlighted perspectives of social capital have all one common ground: social structure can be an asset that can create competitive advantages for individuals and groups. The better connected, the higher the returns will follow.

Ultimately, embracing and organizing social capital leads to the creation of a movement, but how can communities move to scale and take action? A movement consists of a mobilized population driven by a shared vision and mission. Building relationships, embracing social capital creates a self-sustainable community to take action for a common objective is an optimal way to claim rights, vote people out of the office, be heard, and become empowered.

The power of groups leveraging social capital as they grow can be seen in the example of sharing economy platforms, such as AirBnB. In 2013, the city of New York couldn't distinguish between hosts acting purely commercially when renting out their flats and apartments through AirBnB to avoid tax payments and private tenants, sharing their space occasionally. Compliance with the existing law was difficult since the law addressed the mechanism of the traditional hotel industry rather than the dynamics of sharing economy platforms. The General Attorney ultimately issued the subpoena for the records of more than 15,000 hosts in New York city – threatening the privacy of members and the overall business model of AirBnB. Many community members raised their voice and over 20,000 users signed an online petition to stop the subpoena and change the existing law.[18] In the end, the attorney general's office refiled the subpoena with narrower demands to secure the privacy of Airbnb's users.[19] Despite both sides needing to find a solution that adapts to the sharing economy model and thus develop a compromise, this example shows nicely the power of social capital and communities.

Social Capital in the Context of Smart Villages

Increasing social capital is therefore likely to happen if villagers face a rich network and a variety of different entities which can be leveraged to increase the availability for opportunities and eventually increase advantages and returns. Disregarding cultural influences and resulting social structures, villagers ultimately need access to new opportunities for significantly increasing their accessible personal network and entities and thus, their social capital. Moreover, when establishing social capital as a crucial foundation, human capital can be more effectively developed to create more able individuals who can thrive. Building self-sustainable communities to accelerate the empowerment of underprivileged groups with a strong socio-economic focus can then be achieved. However, transforming villages and building social capital that lets villagers identify and pursue entrepreneurial paths to economic independence takes new approaches rather than traditional ones government-led development assistance (as described above regarding dead aid). Leveraging Open Innovation practices and the triple helix concept combined with digital technologies are able to excel in the availability of opportunities for villagers significantly and helps with building social and human capital in the rural setting. Encouragement and support for community development are hereby critical, as we see when farmers are establishing cooperative entities and pool their economic power for achieving higher prices and accessing new markets. This way of organic empowerment and development opens up unlimited opportunities for village populations and has the power to disrupt prevailing systems, hierarchies, or mindsets in a self-sustainable way.

"Social Capital is more powerful than Financial Capital; one fights for justice and the other demands profits."

– Emma Brunat, Visiting Scholar, UC Berkeley

Leadership Framework

Execution of Open Innovation requires the right leadership, and the creation of Smart Villages requires a new mindset. That mindset requires more than the ability to organize and manage it requires a paradigm shift in thinking and approach. Smart Village leadership requires the ability to have a vision and to galvanize everyone to make that vision a reality. Rapidly adapting to changes as they happen is not easy, yet it is the key to success. These new leadership capabilities, incorporating these Open Innovation approaches, is a dramatic change from traditional approaches and is a critical requirement needed to expand markets in this digital age.

Professor David Teece, from the Haas School of Business, makes a good comparison of this paradigm shift. In the past, the balance sheet view emphasized a focus on assets owned to develop a product. That was the way product development was traditionally viewed. The new way is to get access to assets rather than ownership of assets. Uberization is not new in villages.

This approach is important as we move into the digital knowledge economy because the value of technology and intellectual assets evaporate very quickly, unlike physical assets which we can touch and feel. Ownership is less valuable than access. Today is all about access to more soft and mobile assets that a company may not even own. And this makes the differences between old and new approaches very apparent.

The traditional way of doing business requires the ability to manage a large organization and effectively operate a hierarchical chain of command. The old way of leadership required more traditional capabilities including operating, administrating, and governing. This type of leadership is all about "doing things right" which is easily imitated and managed. The new approach, suited for a Smart Village prototype, requires different capabilities in leadership. It is all about quickly adapting and orchestrating a rapid deployment and redeployment in response to the changing environment. The new way calls for much more dynamic capabilities adapting, integrating, sensing, ceasing, and transforming. In short, being able to successfully and continuously pivot. This is a big difference in leadership styles and one that was made clear as the Smart Village evolved *(excerpt from the 2017 book "Smart Villages of Tomorrow: The Road to Mori by Solomon Darwin).*

"When I was growing up, my village had only one of everything. One family owned a stone grinder, and another owned a flour strainer. We circulated them around instead of each family buying their own. In rural villages, assets "sweat" from being in almost constant demand. This eliminates the need for investment costs and lowers the risk."

– Prof. Solomon Darwin, Haas School of Business, UC Berkeley

Exhibit 9 – Theoretical Design Philosophy for the Smart Village Idea

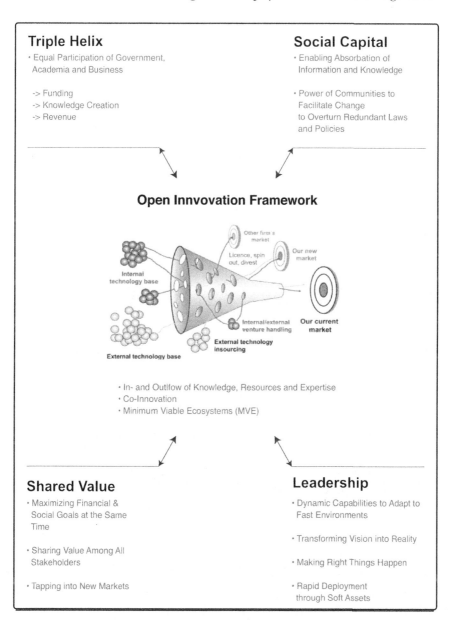

Triple Helix
· Equal Participation of Government,
  Academia and Business

  -> Funding
  -> Knowledge Creation
  -> Revenue

Social Capital
· Enabling Absorbation of
  Information and Knowledge

· Power of Communities to
  Facilitate Change
  to Overturn Redundant Laws
  and Policies

Open Innvovation Framework

Other firm's market
Licence, spin out, divest
Our new market
Internal technology base
Internal/external venture handling
Our current market
External technology insourcing
External technology base

· In- and Outlfow of Knowledge, Resources and Expertise
· Co-Innovation
· Minimum Viable Ecosystems (MVE)

Shared Value
· Maximizing Financial &
  Social Goals at the Same
  Time

· Sharing Value Among All
  Stakeholders

· Tapping into New Markets

Leadership
· Dynamic Capabilities to Adapt to
  Fast Environments

· Transforming Vision into Reality

· Making Right Things Happen

· Rapid Deployment
  through Soft Assets

CHAPTER 4
WHAT IS THE SMART VILLAGE IDEA

The smart village idea is to empower villagers with access to (1) smart and clean technology, (2) transparent information, (3) easy-to-use digital tools, and (4) resources to develop entrepreneurial skills and direct access to global markets. That process will not require substantial infrastructure development or large outlays of money. Rather, it will require uninterrupted Internet connectivity, community engagement, and skill-building, along with Open Innovation practices to link these activities together:

1. Communication channels and open platforms within and outside the community.
2. Practical education and apprenticeships for self-development and to further their skills.
3. Tools and technology that empower will enable them to carry on their entrepreneurial activities.
4. Energy resources that are dependable and affordable to power their homes, shops, and schools.

5. Connectivity, affordable digital wireless connectivity that will save them costs and time and provide an invaluable connection to one another and the rest of the world.

The meaning of the term "smart village" follows the definition developed by Professor Solomon Darwin and Henry Chesbrough that states, "a smart village is a community empowered by digital technologies and Open Innovation platforms to access global markets." Specifically, Darwin emphasizes that a smart village meets six criteria:

i. **An Ecosystem**: The village leverages its resources, as well as those of surrounding villages, distant places, and other entities to generate revenue and lower its costs and risk.
ii. **A Platform:** The village allows external and internal businesses to exchange resources to profit for economic development.
iii. **A Brand:** The village creates an identity and becomes known for its unique value.
iv. **A Community**: The village is a self-organized network of people who collaborate by sharing ideas, information, and resources to build a strong ecosystem. If and when projects fail, the community remains and rebuilds itself.
v. **A Business Model:** The village creates value for its people and others outside the village by utilizing lean and cost-effective state-of-the-art technologies. The village captures some of the value it creates for itself.
vi. **A Sustainable Unit**: The village operates using a triple-bottom-line, focusing on people, profit, and planet.

The working definition of a Smart Village became one that focuses on a community empowered by digital technologies and Open Innovation platforms with access to global markets. These Smart

Villages are a means of empowering people with access to tools, resources, real-time transparent information, using uninterrupted internet connectivity. Professor Darwin's vision of what a Smart Village needs includes six criteria that are critical for it to be successful. To decide whether or not a village has become a Smart Village, there must be an ecosystem, an economic development platform, a brand, a community, a business model, and a sustainable unit.

An Ecosystem

As an ecosystem, the Smart Village must leverage its resources, as well as those of surrounding villages, distant places, and other entities, to generate revenue and lower its costs and risk. Our human body is an ecosystem in which all individual organs work in perfect co-operation and coordination with each other creating, destroying, recycling, and deploying substances when needed to sustain itself. This is done by producing and sharing resources that each other needs, using common distribution channels like the circulatory system for distribution, and the nervous system for communication.

Many ideas are being pivoted in the Smart Village of Mori. In villages, we are working with the taxi services to provide additional services as they drive around the village. When they are done picking up and dropping off passengers, we are also having them pick up groceries and supplies from local merchants and drop them off at doorsteps of people on their way for a small fee. Here all members of the ecosystem -the taxi firm, the passenger, the merchant and customer who order the groceries or goods, the cell phone app company and the telecom service -all benefit. Time is saved, costs are consolidated or eliminated, the risk is shared, the speed of service is improved, a higher number of transactions are generated, and for some new revenues and services are created. All this is now enhanced with digital technology that offers platforms where the apps can reside on mobile devices offering the convenience of ordering on-demand whenever wherever and however these services are needed. See the illustrated healthcare case in chapter 10 serving the rural population with an ecosystem approach. Ultimately, ecosystems from many verticals emerge to one big ecosystem (see following Exhibit).

Exhibit 10 – Smart Village Ecosystems

SVM Ecosystem:
Participating
Companies

Logistics & Transportation
Hero Cycle
Meebuddy – Wipro
Maruti - Trringo

Safety & Security
Digital Twins
3rd Eye
Johnsons Control
Tyco

Farming & Agriculture
Tech Mahindra
IBM Weather
Bighaat - Argikal
Napanta - Agrinos
KisanSaathi

Energy & Connection
Enel - Indian oil
Hygge - Ericsson
Atum - Cygni - Airtel
Reliance Jio
Tarana wireless

Water & Sanitation
Ketos H2O
Zero Mass Water
Recykal
Earth enable
Mr. Clean

Health Care & Public Health
Dr. Reddy's Labs
Healthcubed
Gramin Health
SPRY - StaTwig
Zipline - Apollo

Education & Livelihood
Sales force - Nvidia
Microsoft Amazon
Wipro - SAP
3D Manufacturing
Adobe

Education Ecosystem:
From Access to Job
Placement

1 Access
Smart Village
University
Assessment
Mentorship
Corporate
Programs

6 Job Placement
Salesforce
Microsoft
Google
Adobe - IBM

2 Basic Skills
Khan Academy
Prathom
Amazon - SAP
Brightmind.io
LearnOnMobile

Students
(Smart Village
University)

5 Certification
Microsoft- Nvidia
Salesforce
LinkedIn
Million Sparks
Teacher APP

3 Creative Skills
Abode
LinkedIN
Microsoft

4 Technical Skills
Technical Skills
Salesforce - SAP
Amazon - Google
Nvidia - Microsoft
IBM - Oracle
LinkedIN

An Economic Development Platform

To become an economic development platform, the Smart Village needs to allow external businesses access to its resources for both the businesses and the villagers to profit. This is the basis for the Co-Innovation approach to be viable. Village Digital Mall is a platform now being tested and developed by PayPal. Local rural merchants can put their products online to sell directly to households around the world for higher margins eliminating a host of intermediaries. Here, everyone in the ecosystem benefits using this platform. All this happens by one click from a customer sitting on a couch in his living room in any part of the world. For example, the customer shops on his computer and selects a product. That one click triggers a series of text messages to the village merchant in India, the platform owner who fulfills the order, and to the transportation company. All this was impossible before seamless processes and networks were developed to orchestrate these activities. A more detailed explanation about the Village Digital Mall can be found in the appendix.

A Village Brand

As a brand, the Smart Village must learn to create an identity and become known for its unique value. For example, the weavers of Mori, who have perfected a unique art and producing for materials for thousands of years, need to brand their products and sell recognizable and need to sell recognizable and desirable vintage hand-loomed sarees "Made in Mori."

A Village Community

With connectivity and desperately needed access to information, the Smart Village is enabled and empowered to be a community that is a self-organized network of people who collaborate by sharing ideas, information, and resources to build a strong ecosystem. When projects fail, the community remains and rebuilds itself.

The Smart Village community is more than any project or program. The community is a group of people who adapt to changes in the marketplace and seek new ways of survival. A while back, demand for rice export went down, but demand for shrimp farming went up. The community was able to adapt and switch their investments and form new ecosystems to meet this demand. Now with the availability of digital technologies, this can happen more efficiently empowering the whole ecosystem and thriving social and human capital.

A Business Model

To become a business model, the Smart Village must create value for its people and others outside the village by utilizing lean and cost-effective state-of-the-art technologies. The village business model is composed of the sum of its business activities taking place within itself. This means the village should offer an efficient digital infrastructure to its business to generate profits and cut costs by promoting and supporting platforms and the formation of ecosystems. For example, the first thing we did in Mori is to provide internet and cell phones to every household to provide global access to everyone to begin to communicate, set up a business, and make transactions. This is the first step in laying the foundation to build business models. An individual business in a village will need to address the pain points of its customers to create value.

To create value, it needs to leverage its ecosystem around it to be profitable. It needs to secure resources, generate activities and form partnerships, in a cost-effective manner, to address the needs of its customers. The village, with its many businesses operating within it, should capture some of the value it creates for itself in terms of profit or taxes. Thinking in terms of a business model makes villages more sustainable and self-contained. This reduces its dependence on the state and the central governments and reduces the emigration of its human capital to cities. In this era, we need to adapt our village business models by incorporating digital technologies to create value.

A Sustainable Unit

Finally, the Smart Village grows to be a sustainable unit. That means that the village operates using a multiple-bottom-line approach, focusing on people, profit, the planet, partnership, and prosperity. All aspects of the bottom-line need to be part of the equation and equally considered for a balanced and sustainable future to happen. This means that we need to develop models that will not destroy our planet. Profitability and scalability of businesses should not be the enemy of sustainability. Therefore, we align with the UN sustainability goals since we defined our scope based on that as described before. The school kids in Mori at the Smart Village exhibition proposed that their village roads should not allow petrol or diesel vehicles to travel within the village. They also proposed to ban the local cashew processing factories that produce excessive carbon emissions. A sustainable unit is governed by good policies and technologies that improve the happiness and health of local people, generates economic profit, promotes a green planet, provides equitable profit sharing to its ecosystem partners and builds a prosperous community where people do not seek to emigrate elsewhere. All this is possible with today's technology.

Social and human capital can emerge when converting a village meeting these criteria and processes which can unleash hidden entrepreneurial potential. Ultimately, making a village smart is intended to enable villagers to improve their employment, per capita income, standard of living, and their happiness level. The process is also intended to enable villagers to become economically independent while simultaneously creating business opportunities for firms bringing their products and services to the village. In turn, government expenditures in the area can go down or be redirected to new, higher-value projects.

This definition matters, because it underlies the design of the Smart Villages initiative. The target recipients are the villagers themselves, and the digital technologies are the delivery vehicle for the services in the initiative. Note, that unlike Smart Cities, there is little public investment in infrastructure, beyond digital connectivity in the village.[1] To date, we estimate that roughly US $6.5 million has been spent in Phase 1 & 2. About 80% of these funds are from the private sector, with the AP government supplying about 20%. In turn, about 95% of the funds spent stay in Andhra Pradesh, with about 5% going to UC Berkeley for research and evaluation of the project's performance.

It is important to note at this point that the Mori Smart Village is not a place, but an idea. It is not a location, but an objected destination to reach. Mori was the first attempt or realize this idea. That village represents villages everywhere, all 650,000 in India alone and over a million in countries around the world.

Smart Villages are about making life better for the people living in these rural communities and raising their happiness level. However, if that was the only reason, Smart Villages would not succeed. In the disparate worlds of business and at academia, companies need to venture into new markets to continue growing, and the 3.4 billion people living in the villages of the world are an enormous untapped market.

A Smart Village would raise the happiness level, improve the standard of living and way of life, and build a new way of life. It needs to be sustainable. To have a sustainable future, the community would also need to learn how to create *and* capture value, to be an economic development platform with a brand that identified their work. That means the digital technologies need to connect to the easily available knowledge and markets around the world. From the gained experience, it is understood that academia and government alone could not get the job done. It requires a business model, one that incorporates the expertise and experience that businesses have in developing, manufacturing, marketing, and selling products and services. The business model was the door to the enormous untapped markets the villages represented. The model needed to be based on Open Innovation to bring together all the parts of Smart Village, an idea that was practical and sustainable whose time had come *(excerpt from the 2017 book "Smart Villages of Tomorrow: The Road to Mori by Solomon Darwin)*.

Excursus: The Regression from Data to Happiness

The Smart Village Idea would be a dramatic change for the villagers, to let go of the way they worked and lived for their whole lives. Talking with them reveals that they were more than ready for the journey. To help them understand what would be involved, there were many important connections between where they were, and where they wanted to go. The answers were not to simply add technology or information. There was a logic in my mind that defined the road to a Smart Village. That logic became the guidelines I shared about what it takes to create a Smart Village. The regression from data to happiness became a simple set of steps to follow.

Data is useless unless it is converted into Information. We live in a world in which data has become the basic currency. In the past, it might have land or things, but now it is data. And data is just that, a lot of little bits, ones and zeroes in a digital world, and it leads to facts and then becomes information. Data alone is useless it becomes information.

Information is useless unless it is converted into knowledge. Once data is transformed into information, it needs another step to make it useful. Information needs to be found, curated, read, understood and transferred as knowledge to make it useful to people. Information to help the weavers find markets, the rice farmers to preserve precious water, the shrimp farmers to avoid disease. Information was a key, but information alone is useless. Information needs to be turned into knowledge.

Knowledge is useless unless it produces something useful, and that means in a Smart Village, a useful way of doing things. This can be a new approach or a new technology that helps to improve the way work is done or how people live. Knowledge is useless unless it flows in society. The old idea that "knowledge is power" and that it needs to be hoarded is destructive and disabling to a smart society. The new idea that "shared knowledge is the real power" needs to take hold. A Smart Village is an open society in which knowledge flows freely from one person to another, connecting their minds, enriching their lives, providing the basis for sharing, collaborating and communicating. Knowledge needs to be transformed into technology.

To take it step further, technology is useless without a business model. Unless there is a business model that involves the potential users in a way to help that technology be valuable and useful, places a monetary value on the technology, and locates a market in which it can be found and sold, the technology is useless. Without a business model to make the technology into a useful product or service, the only purpose it will have will be as a display in a technology museum.

Even the business model is useless unless it is sustainable and scalable. Once the technology has a business model, the next step is for that model to be sustainable. Sustainable means that the model needs to be able to go forward in time and be as useful tomorrow as it is today. That means it can be repaired if needed and easily replaced when needed. Scalability is useless if it becomes the enemy of sustainability. The downside to scalability is that the business model and the technology it offers can be scaled too much, it can grow too fast. When that happens, it becomes a problem for sustainability because there are issues with quality and reparability, and the shelf life and usefulness of the technology is limited. Plus, scalability can get in the way of the long-term goal of continuous improvement if the short-term goal is to keep making as many things as possible. Both sustainability and scalability need to work together for the business model to be dynamic and successful.

Ultimately, the point is to improve the happiness index of people. Data can be transformed into knowledge, and the resulting technology can be made useful by a scalable and sustainable business model, yet none of is worth very much unless it adds to the happiness of the people. In the final analysis, it is the happiness of the people that must override everything else. And that happiness is tied up in the ability of the community to be part of the process that takes them from all the data to happiness *(excerpt from the 2017 book "Smart Villages of Tomorrow: The Road to Mori by Solomon Darwin).*

PART II.

How the Smart Village Idea was Demonstrated

CHAPTER 5

WHY ARE SMART VILLAGES RELEVANT FOR VILLAGERS

Villages represent an extremely large – and largely untapped – source of potential economic growth. In India, approximately 70 percent of the population of 1.31 billion people lives in the country's 650,000 villages. On a national scale, India's economy is growing quickly. In 2017, India's Gross Domestic Product (GDP) grew by 6.6 percent and is forecasted to reach a growth rate of 7.327 for the year 2018.[1] China, which has approximately one million villages, also has high but slowing GDP growth. In 2017, the economy expanded by 6.9 percent and is forecasted to grow at 6.503 percent in 2018.[2]

In 2012, N. Chandrababu Naidu, Honorable Chief Minister of the state of Andhra Pradesh in India, began a Pada Yatra, a series of visits to his rural constituents. He wanted to understand their concerns, their challenges, and their goals so he could find ways to improve life for the approximately 35 million rural residents in the state. Two years and 3,000 kilometers later, the Pada Yatra concluded, yielding key observations. Chief among them was the fact that welfare and other government and development programs had helped improve villagers' lives, but to varying degrees and not to the extent expected. Two other key insights arose from the tour: villagers want and need to be empowered in order to encourage participation in any development program, and village populations are shrinking. Residents are moving to urban areas or other countries with comparatively better infrastructure and job opportunities, and this emigration leads to labor shortages and a brain drain in the villages.

The Pada Yatra also identified two reasons for the underperformance of government programs: these programs too often focus on one aspect of village life rather than taking a holistic view, and government departments frequently struggle to effectively coordinate their efforts.

One of the primary motivators for Naidu's tour was his party's defeat in the state's 2004 elections, which Naidu attributed to a severe drought and anti-incumbency sentiment. In 1999, Naidu had led the party to a decisive victory in both houses of the state legislature. Over the next five years, Naidu and his party worked to develop the state by transforming the major cities into showpieces for foreign investment, particularly in key sectors including information technology, biotechnology, and outsourcing services. Although Hyderabad and other urban centers thrived under the leadership of Naidu and Telugu Desam Party, the drought and rising debt among farmers led to an increase in suicides. The large rural population saw the party's policies as failing to address their needs. In 2004, Naidu retained his assembly seat, but the Telugu Desam Party went from being the second-largest party in the coalition government to a small minority.

In 2014, the Telugu Desam Party, again led by Naidu, returned to power in the state legislature, and he regained his position as Chief Minister. That same year, the state split in two. The northwestern part of Andhra Pradesh, including Hyderabad, formed the new state of Telangana, and the rest of the state retained the name of Andhra Pradesh.

After reviewing the results of his tour, Naidu became committed to finding innovative ways to improve life in the 38,000 villages in Andhra Pradesh. During the Pada Yatra, constituents expressed their desire for improvement along five dimensions: poverty (with the goal of creating a poverty-free society), social justice, farmer welfare, youth employment, and proper governance (excerpt from the 2016 HBR Case *"Prototyping a Scalable Smart Village to Simultaneously Create Sustainable Development and Enterprise Growth Opportunities" by Henry Chesbrough and Solomon Darwin*).

Building on the learnings from the AP government, the Smart Village team started to research on relevant verticals, which need to be addressed during their pivotal upcoming mission. Determining these verticals was achieved in compliance with the United Nations Sustainable Development Goals (UN SDGs) for India from 2015[3] since UN's scope aligns highly with the vision of Smart Villages. Focus group interviews with villagers and government departments were conducted along with considering various other available sources of information. Ultimately, the seriousness of needs, potential of addressing these with digital technology and business model innovation, and the on-ground feedback led to setting the scope for the Smart Village project in the following 9 verticals:

1. **Healthcare**
2. **Education**
3. **Agriculture**
4. **Safety & Security**
5. **Energy**
6. **Livelihood**
7. **Internet & Communications**
8. **Transportation**
9. **Entrepreneurship**

Pain Points of Rural India

Having determined the scope for extensive research, many surveys have been conducted to dive into the specific pain points from the given villages in above-explained verticals. Ultimately, life in the village presents residents with constant challenges, including lack of access to basic resources such as healthcare, sanitation, and clean water. For example, there are very few toilets in the village, leading to open defecation, which leads to active mosquito breeding. In turn, the mosquitoes spread malaria and dengue, a virus that is a leading cause of illness and death in the tropics and subtropics and for which there are not yet any vaccines to prevent infection. Initial research has shown that in villages, basic necessities like water, security, waste disposal, education and healthcare are complicated by high levels of corruption. Villagers are missing access to correct information to create value for themselves and are lacking simple tools and basic training that will enable them to prosper in a self-sustainable way. Moreover, pain points differ among various districts, mandals or villages for multiple reasons. In the most southern district of Andhra Pradesh, Chittor District, for example, the climate is very demanding and water is scare compared to the more northern Krishna District having a more balanced climate. Not till analyzing collected data across the 472 and comparing them individually through a village footprint, differences were in detail apparent.

In the following, determined verticals are explained from a rather high-level perspective to highlight their general relevance for the smart village project by using existing research as from the UN SDGs and other sources, which is then further elaborated in more detail with the own conducted research from the 472 villages. It is to give a broad overview of the critical situation in rural India with a focus on Andhra Pradesh. Thus, this book doesn't assure the integrity of all prevalent pain points. However, the general footprint survey with over 10,000 responses could provide a more comprehensive understanding to bring light in the dark what is really happening on-ground in the villages. Additionally, village profile case studies were created for each village, to get to know more specific pain points, the unique village situation, and data in terms of economic status, culture, or demographics. This effort served as the initial overall foundation for further, more specific research and ultimately for the whole project execution.

1. Healthcare

Despite continuous progress, the health indicators are far from a desirable benchmark. India struggles with the benchmarks such as life year expectancy (14 years lower than the OECD average of 80 years), child mortality rate (43.2 deaths per 1,000 live births compared to an average of 33 per 1,000 live births of lowand middle-income countries (2010-15)), patients to doctor ratio etc. There is still a major imbalance in the availability of the resources between rural and urban populations. India lags way behind the various benchmarks set up by World Health Organization. Unavailability of quality services at primary healthcare centers and essential medicines is prevalent in most of the rural parts of India. India has one of the lowest public-to-total expenditures on health in the world. Only 5 percent of the country's GDP is used for healthcare spending. Only 33 percent of the total health expenditure is used for public expenditure on health, which is significantly low compared to the world's average of 63 percent.[4]

Healthcare access in the village is limited and, for many villagers, cost-prohibitive. One Mori resident described the situation: "Healthcare is expensive. Since we are uneducated, we cannot question what the local village doctor says. Several people in villages like ours choose to approach godmen [spiritual healers] to cure their ailments. I have heard of cases where people's health has gone the detrimental route due to improper diagnosis, poor care, and lack of proper healthcare facilities." *(excerpt from the 2016 HBR Case "Prototyping a Scalable Smart Village to Simultaneously Create Sustainable Development and Enterprise Growth Opportunities" by Henry Chesbrough and Solomon Darwin)*

Although villages in Andhra Pradesh do have more or less access to government hospitals, few private hospitals, PHCs (Primary Healthcare Centers), a fairly comprehensive RMP (Rural Medical Practitioners) network, ANMs (Auxiliary Nurse Midwifery) and Asha workers (medial auxiliary workers) to provide health services, the ineffectiveness can be concluded from the dramatic results of the survey conducted on 40,000 rural households; only 33 percent of the surveyed audiences tend to be satisfied with the existing infrastructure. Affordability is still a major concern, with every 2 of 3 persons reporting it to be unaffordable and too expensive. Some of the shocking statistics demonstrate the unavailability of pharmacy for every 1 out of 3 people in rural Andhra Pradesh. Moreover, the inability of pharmacies to deliver the required drugs and medicines adds to its complexity. Reports state the dominance of RMPs in rural healthcare: 80 percent of the surveyed audience prefers RMPs over government or private hospitals, which reflects a situation where mostly illegal and questionable methods are being used to serve the rural population in terms of healthcare. In fact, the survey reveals that inaccessibility and delayed treatments being the major factor for consulting RMPs over official health-care providers. Considering the scenario of medical availability in rural India by given numbers and seeing the bad healthcare situation on-ground talking to villagers and collecting data, a huge emphasis on this sector is of utmost importance to make a significant contribution to the health of rural Andhra Pradesh.

2. Education

Education is the foundation of any country's future and plays an even more critical role in emerging economies for sustainable growth. However, many developing countries, including rural India, are struggling to catch up and are lacking in many areas.

Reports have suggested that the learning level of children/students especially enrolled in primary schools are significantly low. For example, the Annual Status of Education Report (ASER) indicates that of all the students in India enrolled in Standard VIII in 2014, still about 25 percent could not read a Standard II level text. [5] Moreover, it is estimated that only 2 percent of the existing workforce in India applied formal skill training and that only 15 percent of the existing workforce is meant to have marketable skills. This stands in a huge contrast when considering that 90 percent of the available jobs in India are considered skill-based and in turn require indeed vocational training and proper education.[6] Viewing this from the more rural perspective, a large population is believing in education to be a formula to increase their income (60 percent). However, access to skill centers is minimal. The conducted survey among the 472 villages shows that only 18 percent of people have access to skill development centers. Furthermore, bus transportation within the village is often erratic, making it difficult for students/learners to regularly get to educational institutions on time or access them in general.

As of 2014, every second school in India was not meeting the pupil-teacher ratio (PTR), which requires one teacher for every 30 students.[7] Moreover, in addition to missing access to schools, delivery of quality education is lacking: 65 percent of the 40,000 surveyed audience didn't value the existing education system in rural Andhra Pradesh. Young adults who wish to pursue careers in medicine, engineering, law, or education must emigrate to cities and spend hours traveling to attend colleges. There are no higher institutions for education within village proximity for around 80 percent of people. This emphasizes the unequal opportunities that rural population has compared to urban areas.

A challenge, especially for youth. is that it is required to be able to speak English in order to enter into professional education programs. However, no instruction for children in e.g. Mori village from grades one to five are conducted in English. These factors lead to dissatisfaction for the higher education system as English has become a barrier to entry and has caused an increasing number of drop-outs due to this huge knowledge gap.

"I have been applying for jobs for the past 5 years but faced rejection due to my bad communication skills. There are no jobs available locally so I had to sit in the shop which is run by my father and two elder brothers."

— Venkat, a resident of Mori, India

Despite the enormous efforts from the Indian government and affiliated advancements in the education sector, the results are not as expected and reveal huge gaps to be filled. The desired impact is not yet observed: reluctance from teachers in adapting to changing technology and walking the extra mile to impart world-class education seems to act as a major roadblock among many other challenges. A lot of work needs to be done to provide access to efficient education in the country, especially in the rural setting, where the situation is even tighter and of utmost need.

3. Agriculture

Sustainable agriculture and food security in India are facing a major threat today. High rates of soil erosion because of indiscriminate and excess use of fertilizers, insecticides, and pesticides have depleted the quality of productive soil over the years. Improper use of inorganic fertilizers and inefficient irrigation practices have resulted in deterioration of soil fertility. In rural India, farmers are losing faith in agriculture and shifting to other means of income for livelihood. Low priority to agriculture, high input cost, no control on market, and society's perception of farming as a poor livelihood option are major contributors to this trend. A major population of the farmers has raised their concerns over the involved risk and low return from farming and have shown willingness to adopt other professions for self-sustainability.[8] However, presently, 70 percent of the population of Andhra Pradesh, 35 million people, live in villages and agriculture is the main source of income in rural areas and contributes to a major portion of the state GDP (30 percent))[9]. The majority of the population (60 percent)[10] thus still practices agriculture, which emphasizes the huge dependency on this vertical, since shifting to other professions, e.g. more skilled jobs is rigid as relevant skills are missing among farmers.

In a survey conducted with over 40,000 farmers in Andhra Pradesh, the Smart Village team got to know the disastrous situation that farmers themselves perceive. It is about time to address these needs – otherwise, many farmers lose their source of income and their will to live. The following pain points are highlighted with respect to the general crop cycle: Education for Farmers, Pre-Harvest, Growth & Maintenance, and Post-Harvest.

Education for Farmers

The majority of farmers are presently using the obsolete knowledge of fellow farmers or ancestors as a source to educate on themselves on farming practices. Additionally, education offered by the Government is limited to only 25 percent of the farmers. Along with not having access to relevant programs and high expenses in terms of costs and time, the perception about the ineffective and inconsistent education on farming is a major reason (for 40 percent of asked farmers) for an overall dissatisfaction with courses offered on farming. Although the government is facilitating multiple programs on modern farming, a large number of farmers (88 percent) are unsatisfied with the available education programs.

Pre-Harvest Phase

The government is providing soil analysis and advisory for each farmer, but only small numbers of farmers are using this service (27 percent). Still, 31 percent of the farmers are lacking access to soil analysis and advisory to determine the best crop type and seeds to use according to the soil properties. This means technology involvement is relatively rare, which can lead to misinformed crop planning and eventually to decreased yields. Besides this, every third farmer is facing seed costs they report as too high and lacks subsidized agricultural inputs due to non-transparent access to resources or an overly difficult procedure to procure these inputs. Moreover, farmers lack relevant agricultural gear and are not able to purchase new equipment as costs are too high for a fourth of the farmers. In order to compensate for high operational costs or to afford new equipment, 52 percent of the farmers are dependent on the government in the form of subsidies or loans. Every third farmer faces the problem that the loan approval consumes too much time and paperwork. Furthermore, high interest rates for loans (22 percent) and missing availability of small loans with relevant payback periods (18 percent of all asked farmers) impede economic growth for small-hold farmers. Overall, almost 90 percent of all farmers are dissatisfied with existing pre-harvestsolutions with respect to soil analysis and advisory services, acquiring agricultural inputs, access to agricultural equipment, and getting farming loans.

Growth & Maintenance Phase

When it comes to sustaining the consistent growth of the crop, irrigation plays a crucial role. Almost two-thirds of the farmers are currently getting their water supply through canal irrigation, whereas one-sixth are irrigating their fields through water pumps in the studied area. However, a significant number of the interviewed farmers are still relying on rainfall as the only source for irrigation (20 percent). In general, large numbers of farmers (41 percent) are presently struggling to irrigate their fields in an efficient manner because of ineffective irrigation systems. Furthermore, inconsistent water supply is negatively affecting the growth of the crop (18 percent). For example, Mori has a system of gates that release water through canals to farmers, but farmers say the water is not released when they need it, and sometimes no water is available. The large majority of the farmers (80 percent) are thus dissatisfied with the existing irrigation solutions.

In order to prevent diseases and to monitor the crop to better predict and increase the overall yield, farmers take informal advice from fellow farmers (47 percent) and only 20 percent of farmers get regular guidance from agricultural offices. Very few farmers are using digital technology for crop monitoring and disease prediction. Consequently, every fourth farmer lacks proper advice on disease prediction and yield monitoring. In addition, maintaining and increasing yield requires the application of multiple products as well as the performance of various activities. Therefore, every fourth farmer faces the difficulty to monitor their crop and every third farmer to know what type of fertilizer and pesticide to use. 80 percent of the interviewed farmers are dissatisfied with the existing solutions for crop monitoring and disease prediction/prevention in general.

Post-Harvest Phase

After harvesting, farmers struggle to exchange their produce for a fair monetary income. Almost every second farmer is dealing with middle man issues, low market prices, and inaccessible markets. Missing market access prevents farmers from increasing their overall benefit. Currently, government (25 percent) or middlemen (57 percent) are the most common buyers for agriculture produce. In addition, the village's lack of cold storage facilities means a large share of what farmers do produce ultimately goes to waste. Thin margins mean farmers – 80 percent of whom lease rather than own the land they farm – often struggle to make any profit after paying for supplies such as seeds and fertilizers. This leads to an overall dissatisfaction among the farmers (92 percent) *(excerpt from the 2017 White Paper "Smart Village Ecosystems. An Open Innovation Approach" by Henry Chesbrough and Solomon Darwin)*.

In general, some farmers are growing higher-margin crops such as lentils, peanuts, sesame, and avocado, and the environment is well suited to growing these. However, harvesting these crops is labor-intensive, and emigration makes finding a sufficient number of workers difficult. Compounding the labor shortage are government programs. For example, a job program in Mori employs residents to dig canals, perform maintenance work, and other tasks. Although this program provides some value to the village, it is not a source of sustainable, demand-based employment growth. It also discourages residents from going to work for farms, where they would earn lower wages for more physically demanding work.

Other farmers harvest shrimp, a high-margin product, from manmade ponds in the village. Salt is added to the water in these ponds for the shrimp, which increases the salinity of the soil in the village. Excess salts in soil hinder the growth of crops by limiting their ability to take up water.[11] Digging the shrimp ponds, which must be deep in order to be effective, also draws seawater into the aquifer, further salinizing the soil and reducing yields for other crops, such as rice. Although shrimping near rice fields is banned in order to prevent salinization damage, according to a survey of villagers, it is still practiced *(excerpt from the 2016 HBR Case "Prototyping a Scalable Smart Village to Simultaneously Create Sustainable Development and Enterprise Growth Opportunities" by Henry Chesbrough and Solomon Darwin).*

Urgent need for education on modern farming techniques, the introduction of advanced technology, the necessity of ecosystem approach, and rural-urban linkages need to be realized to overcome drastic challenges in this vertical.

4. Safety & Security

"Two tribal girls gang raped in Andhra Pradesh, village authorities try to hush up crime" [12]. *"Peaceful villages jolted by faction killings in Kadapa district"*[13]. *"Over 8,000 dead in accidents on Andhra Pradesh roads this year"*[14]. Those terrible headlines are quite common and refer to the rising criminal cases, road accidents, and safety issues against women and beyond which in turn pose a great challenge and danger for citizens. The rising crime rate in Andhra Pradesh, emphasizes to strengthen security measures in the state. Increasing crime cases against women with an illicit relationship, property disputes and personal vendetta being the major categories for murder in Andhra Pradesh (1,123 cases in 2016) along with cruelty by husbands with 6,466 cases in 2016 followed by kidnapping and abduction (992) and suicide (405) indicate the terrible reality. [15] The advent of social media, interconnectivity, and the diffusion of smartphones make such horrible incidents more and more public and demonstrate the reality of the village scenario. Such drastic cases seem to be just the peak of the iceberg of what is really happening in the dark.

The survey conducted in the 472 villages can furthermore deduce the lack of an overall ecosystem providing simple tools to improve the safety and security situation in the villages. Out of the many installed street lights, only a few seem to be functional leading to distress and perceived discomfort among villagers. Besides working light during night-time, surveillance cameras can radically improve safety issues when making public places more transparent. This not only prevents and reduces crime but also can have positive side effects on public defecation or aggressive road behavior. Of the surveyed audience, 80 percent state that in their area, surveillance cameras for security are completely missing. Furthermore, the helpline tool offered by the government has been launched for reporting grievances for efficient governance and to increase safety and security. However, only 50 percent of the rural population is aware of the service being available. In the end, the conducted research in five districts shows that every fifth citizen of the asked audience feels unsafe due to the previously mentioned reasons. Technologies improving safety and security through more transparency, accountability, and potential to change people's behavior in the villages of India is to be urgently realized to address the dreadful condition.

5. Energy

"Neighbors rushed to help douse the fire, but we couldn't save anyone," Vidhate, 45, said of the blaze four years ago, which he blames on an overturned kerosene lamp. "My children were burned alive before my eyes".[16] People still rely on kerosene lamps for lighting and also for cooking since having no access to electricity or other safe sources of energy. While the government is making decent progress in meeting its 2020 deadline for the 100 percent electrification of the villages, the majority of rural Indians still don't have power supply to their houses. Despite official data stating that the majority of the population has access to electricity, looking closer to the definition of "electrified" reveals a huge gap: Only 10 percent of village households need to be connected to coin a village electrified. It is therefore assumed, that only 7.3 percent of all villages across India has 100 percent household connectivity. Moreover, the design and implementation of providing electricity often are then poor when contractors just aim to fulfill the requirements in order to qualify the village as electrified.[17] Related to having access to electricity in villages, access to clean cooking is critical since cooking with biomass comes with high health and environmental risks. In spite that the share of the overall Indian population relying primarily on sources of energy as biomass in order to cook fell from 66 percent in 2011 to 59 percent in 2015, still, 830 million people in India lack access to safe sources of energy for cooking, such as LPG.[18]

For one thing, one part of the country of India is making a huge leap in implementing the finest of technologies like Blockchain in the electricity transmission sector where on the other side there are millions of homes without a grid connection and access to clean cooking.

In general, the Indian energy sector faces serious issues, which Sagebiel, J. et al. summarize in their book *Enhancing Energy Efficiency in Irrigation. A Socio-Technical Approach in South India* from 2016[19]:

- supply shortage, leading to power cuts and low-quality electricity;
- unsustainable and market-distorting cross-subsidies;
- large-scale theft and non-payment of bills;
- inefficient and overstaffed utilities, suffering from a high degree of corruption;
- rural villages without access to energy services;
- an incentive-distorting tariff system that cannot cover costs.

Analyzing the condition, determination of the scope of work, and corporate partners dealing in the energy sector, the Smart Village team included it as a sector to work upon. Simple technologies, such as solar-based self-sustainable solutions can make the difference to ensure a safe, worth living situation.

6. Livelihood

Despite livelihood being a general vertical embracing the many segments required for a worth living situation in the village context, the critical areas specifically defined to livelihood for the smart village program are water and sanitation, financial inclusion, eco-friendly environment and applying values for a better together such as people's participation, the dignity of women, social justice, gender equality, cooperation, self-reliance, transparency and accountability in public life, etc. Peace and harmony for any individual are hence overall core deliverables to be assured. This approach opts for ongoing consideration of environmental-friendly practices within all efforts. Moreover, in order to accomplish described basic values for village societies, programs need to be designed in compliance with elaborated values to in turn foster their application on-ground. Ultimately, changing values for better is a product of many efforts throughout the program and comes from the holistic character of the smart village program rather than from distinct, vertical-wise initiatives. In the following, issues related to sanitation, financial inclusion, and eco-friendly environment are being focused on in terms of livelihood since having overall great feasibility for innovation via technology and business models for addressing these, respectively.

Sanitation and Water Availability

Sanitation and water availability play a critical role in achieving a better livelihood. These are closely linked together and can only be achieved if addressed jointly. Therefore, existing water bodies need to be used sustainably while the quality of water is to be kept at standards. Also, maintenance, in turn, is dependent on how industry, agriculture, and public disposes of water, which are major sources of water pollutions. Uncontrolled industrialization and urbanization exacerbate these issues. India has an ambitious target of providing universal water and sanitation coverage by 2020 and achieved almost universal coverage of drinking water.

However, India is far from providing water in a quality consistent with international norms as well as giving universal access to a piped water supply. Lack of proper institutional arrangements, bacteriological and chemical water contamination (e.g. fluorides and arsenic), or even social exclusion of backward communities are major bottlenecks for accomplishing this. Moreover, a shocking 60 percent of the rural population lacks access to toilets, which requires, in turn, big infrastructure investment along with programs to create behavioral change for improvement. Also, rivers, canals, and lakes are often used as dumping grounds for sewage, solid and liquid wastes. River Ganga, on the one hand, provides water to more than 40 percent of the population of India in 11 states. However, over 2,900 million liters of sewage is led into the river every day.[20] In a brief summary, only 49 percent of people living in rural areas are using safely managed drinking water services (2015)[21]. When seen from absolute numbers, 63 million people living in rural areas of India don't have any access to safe drinking water, 770 million people still don't have access to improved sanitation and around 70,000 children aged under 5 years are dying from diarrheal diseases every year, which is caused by unsafe water and poor sanitation.[22] Such disastrous numbers show that India is far from having villages where basic needs like safe water and sanitation are self-evident – no, they are in utmost need.

Financial Inclusion

Financial Inclusion is essential for providing the poor a central platform in order to save money and earn interest. In fact, it serves as a channel to access formal loans to avoid the dependency of resorting to informal moneylenders and paying unfair interest rates. Also, other financial services such as pensions, insurances, and funds from welfare programs can be directly accessed.[23]

According to the National Bank for Agriculture and Rural Development (NABARD), 88 percent of rural households are estimated to have a savings account (2017) with an average annual savings of around $ 240.[24] Modi pushed policies to bring 310 million people into the formal banking system since 2014. The 2016 demonetization, where 86 percent of India's cash was pulled of, forced many Indians to get a bank account. However, it is estimated that in 2017, nearly half of Indian bank accounts were inactive, which is one of the highest shares in the world. Among the many issues causing this outrageous result, low financial and digital literacy, cash shortages, and issues with transferring welfare benefits can be named. The public faith in electronic payments decreased and the demand for the physical currency was reinforced. Growth of bank branches and ATMs hasn't kept up and eventually due to all these issues, villagers are stuck in long queues to get cash when welfare programs are directly linked to accounts.[25] Moving away from the formal banking system due to an insufficient working system needs to be urgently addressed since the benefits of financial inclusion are tremendous. Microcredit and micro-insurance solutions and new channels to obtain cash from people's accounts are only a few out of many models within the scope for improvement through digital technology and innovative business models, since too many current issues exist to attract the poor to use the formal system at this point.

Eco-friendliness

"Living in rural India showed me the many cultural differences on a daily base. Especially the mindset regarding environmental concerns differed vastly from mine.

I once had a vibrant discussion about buying coffee in a large glass versus in little, small plastic bags. My colleague didn't understand my conviction to avoiding plastic. Not only seems this a major difference, but seeing trash laying all over the place outside – such as little plastic bags – showed me the effects of consumption without considering the whole product lifecycle.

However, throwing away its own trash is not seen as negative in the places I experienced. When I asked a small shopkeeper where to throw the trash, he pointed out to the street. It is not about blaming people but rather bringing awareness about this topic."

– Werner Fischer, Former Research Director SVM
and Research Scholar at UC Berkeley

Eco-friendliness in villages comprises the many activities for having a clean, healthy environment. The situation related to cleanness is bad in India as untreated waste can be found almost everywhere. A combination of growth, urbanization, and the embrace of consumer capitalism spurred this negative development. Disposable goods consumption rises and limits India's capacity for waste handling. Despite India having a long history of frugality and recycling, the advent of the large availability of goods to consume, designed in a disposable fashion, broke with these historic values – called the *kabaadi* tradition. Moreover, one of the critical factors for the waste crisis in India is its caste system preventing intrinsic waste management from the population itself. A large number of people are predisposed to the idea that touched, tainted, used things need to be thrown away from one's personal space. This is to happen as far and quickly as possible, even if it has external effects on neighbors, public sanitation etc. Also, caste leads to a widespread perception that it is not in its own responsibility but in the hand of someone else's. The very bottom of the caste system, such as scavengers, are the ones to take care of the waste and are historically treated without dignity – justified by the caste they are born in.[26] Understanding the deeply rooted problems in Indian society shows the need for sensitive changes to move towards a more holistic approach to tackle the waste problem in India. Framing programs that integrate culture along with society and complementing these with innovative technologies can and need to make the difference for improving India's livelihood.

7. Internet & Communication

Despite having a strong focus on programs and technology interventions for addressing prevalent pain points, which require no heavy infrastructure investments, basic connectivity is a prerequisite for this program to enable empowerment through digital technologies. This approach very much aligns with many programs executed in India for facilitating and leveraging internet & communication for multiple segments. Examples are 'Digital Village', an initiative introduced in February 2017 by the Indian government that aims to bring free Wi-Fi to 1,050 villages or the *Digi Gaon* program as it is colloquially known, to provide telemedicine, education, and skills through digital technology. Moreover, the government of AP launched its AP FiberNet program in Mori itself, to include villages in the new age of communication, which paved the way for the inclusion of Internet and communication in the scope of work for the Smart Village project. However, by the end of 2017, only 186 million Indians used internet in rural areas compared to the 295 million urban users. That means on average, only 1 out of 5 rural Indians have internet access. Also, limited access on-the-go in rural areas is decreasing the usage per day because of bad connectivity, quality of services, and the affordability of internet services.

"I bought a smartphone as I was fascinated by its features but because of the poor network, I am unable to use it to the fullest. Call drop rates are high, internet support is poor and at times there's no network."

– Ramlal, a resident of Sompalle, India

Sadly, 64 percent of rural and 59 percent of urban women are unable to go online in general, highlighting the huge gender gap in India for digital inclusion.27 The survey conducted in the assigned 472 villages in Andhra Pradesh shows that 80 percent of the surveyed audience is deprived of Internet connection. Despite the efforts of the Andhra Pradesh government, penetration into rural areas is considerably low. AP Fiber launched by the government is, for example, struggling to provide internet to every household. Only every 1 out of 10 villagers has a wired internet connection which therefore increases the dependency on mobile internet providers. Airtel and Reliance Jio are the top internet providers with 40 percent of the surveyed audience recognizing as their Internet provider. However, bad connectivity and slow speed internet are the major problems, and inconsistency of the internet and low bandwidth act as another roadblock for users of mobile internet services. In general, more than 70 percent of the people surveyed are dissatisfied with the existing infrastructure and services related to internet and communication – both, wired and mobile. Therefore, the smart village project encourages private sector providers to complement the existing system with innovative technology – such as using free optic space or whitespace technologies. The progress of the project and beyond hence is relying on reliable basic internet connectivity in villages.

8. Transportation

Poor road quality and under-funded existing road maintenance leading to the deterioration of roads, congestion at barrages due to high traffic demand across certain regions and unavailability of proper public transportation are causing serious problems in terms of an efficient and safe transportation system. Moreover, every year, more than 150,000 people are killed in traffic accidents in India, which translates to around 400 fatalities every day. It seems that India didn't catch up with international safety features to make them mandatory for carmakers yet although it is planned to pass a law in 2018. Global NCAP tests are not mandatory which gives carmakers the incentive to reduce the safety features to a minimum when exporting their models to India. Most lower-priced cars are not even equipped with airbags and if, they most likely just have a driver's airbag. Also, penalties for offenses like drunk driving or speeding and its enforcement need to be more effective. 67 percent of road accidents in India are caused by speeding.[28] In terms of the availability of public transportation in rural areas, villagers face a huge disadvantage compared to urban areas.

"Frequency of public transport is very low, at times it is challenging to commute to nearby places. There's only one bus that goes to Amravati (State Capital of Andhra Pradesh) from my village; resulting in over-crowded and uncomfortable travel."

– Raju, a resident of Mori, India

Only 25 percent of the surveyed audience from the 472 villages is satisfied with the current state of transportation in Andhra Pradesh, stressing on the inefficiency of the system. Commuting to different places is challenging as 50 percent of the surveyed villagers don't own personal vehicles since missing affordability and public transportation is insufficient due to low frequency, which affects 40 percent of regular commuters adversely. Thus, there is massive inaccessibility for poorer communities in terms of mobility. Eventually, villagers should face equal opportunities to get around like in urban areas, which of course is a huge challenge. Considering additionally the disastrous road safety situation in India, novel models along with advanced technology need to be urgently applied. Ideas like enforcing traffic offenses with digital technology from citizens themselves or bringing in an *Uber* carpooling model can make a significant impact.

9. Entrepreneurship

The rising rate of jobless individuals implies that there is no direct relationship between sustained investment and economic growth when it fails to assure adequate employment for the majority. The Economic Survey 2013 has cautioned that by 2020, India could be faced with up to 16.7 million 'missing jobs'.[29] Emphasis on employment generation needs to be given that economic development can be synchronized with quality employment generation to provide an ideal development scenario in India.

Approximately 30 percent of Indians, 309 million as of the 2001 census, are internal migrants, meaning they have moved from their hometowns to another location in the country.[30] The state of Andhra Pradesh is one of the leading sources of migrants, with many moving to Maharashtra, the state that is home to the cities of Mumbai, Pune, and Nagpur.[31] The Census of India 2001 estimated that internal migrants made up 31 percent of the population of Indian cities with at least one million residents. According to the

United Nations Educational, Scientific and Cultural Organization, these migrants face many constraints, including: "lack of formal residency rights; lack of identity proof; lack of political representation; low-paid, insecure or hazardous work; limited access to state-provided services such as health and education, and discrimination based on ethnicity, religion, class, or gender."[32] A much smaller number of Indians, approximately 11.4 million, emigrate from the country.[33] Many Indians go to the Middle East, where they too face a variety of challenges. Historically, oil-rich Persian Gulf countries have offered laborers from India and other countries opportunities to work in the construction, transportation, and other industries.[34]

In fact, as of August 2016, there were an estimated three million Indian workers in Saudi Arabia alone. But recent plunges in oil prices, from around $100 a barrel to around $40 a barrel, have disrupted the economies of these countries and the lives of migrant workers. In Saudi Arabia, private companies are shutting down; the government is running large budget deficits, and workers are not getting paid. Complicating matters is the fact that Saudi Arabian employers hold workers' passports and do not allow employees to leave the country without permission. When companies cease operating, retrieving passports can be a time-consuming and extremely difficult process. In the summer of 2016, to help the estimated 10,000 laid-off migrant workers in Saudi Arabia – some of whom had not been paid in months – the Indian government provided food aid and other assistance. The country's junior foreign minister, V.K. Singh, also visited Saudi Arabia to help coordinate efforts to repatriate those Indians who wanted to return home.[35] The situation in Saudi Arabia is not the first time the Indian government has needed to assist migrant workers. In 2015, officials evacuated more than 4,000 Indians from Yemen due to armed conflict between a Saudi-led coalition and local rebels.[36] Back in the villages of Andhra Pradesh, emigration creates shortages of not just labor but also of educated and skilled workers. With opportunities lacking at home, many of the people with the most potential to improve village life are leaving. This trend exacerbates many problems, including the lack of teachers and local doctors.

"There is urgent need for doctors, yet very few are willing to work here. My family is still living in the city. They are unable to settle here due to a lack of basic education, healthcare, and sanitation facilities. My income here is also meager in comparison to what I would have gotten by working in city hospitals or as a private medical practitioner."

– Venkat, a Doctor practicing in Razole, India

The lack of good economic opportunities alsopresents villagers with challenges. For example, one villager described his work: "I used to work as a daily wage worker in gruesome conditions at a textile mill, were working full-time, I earned 30 Rupees [approximately 45 U. S. cents] a day."[37] Furthermore, mechanization and automation have destroyed many jobs in the handloom, pottery, handicraft, and goldsmith industries. For those people still employed in the handloom industry, wages are low, and unsold inventory is mounting. Disguised unemployment is increasing, contributing insignificantly to the aggregate output. Farming, shopkeeping etc. are the areas with high rates of disguised unemployment. There are various seasonal employment schemes run by the government, but corruption and politically biased agenda act as a roadblock in successful implementation *(excerpt from the 2016 HBR Case "Prototyping a Scalable Smart Village to Simultaneously Create Sustainable Development and Enterprise Growth Opportunities" by Henry Chesbrough and Solomon Darwin).*

The overall income satisfaction among age groups emphasizes the resentment among especially the younger generation (see exhibit 11).

Exhibit 11 – Income Satisfaction by Age Group[38]

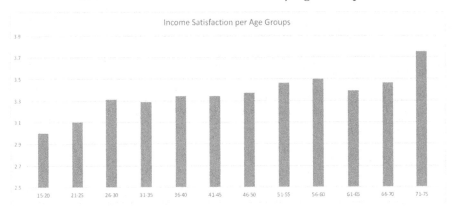

The previously mentioned areas of concern and other village conditions have caused many residents to leave, seeking better lives in some of India's large cities and in the Middle East. Yet, they are likely to face substantial challenges in their new homes. Taking into consideration all the facts mentioned above, A program to foster rural entrepreneurship was urgently needed. A village accelerator program called Prarambham meaning "startup" in the Telugu language, was initiated to generate rural Entrepreneurs in an effective and sustainable way.

Story 1 –Prof. Solomon Darwin and his Relation to Rural India

"I grew up in a small village in Andhra Pradesh, India. Back then my village was a clean and peaceful place with many hardworking people who labored in the field. I left my village as a teenager to the United States along with my father who was offered a position as a scientist at the University of

California. I returned to my village many times to find that there was little to no improvements. In many ways things have gotten worse. The canals that I once swam and fished in are full of pollutants and plastic waste along with animal and human excretions. The roads are more crowded with autos and buses with a lot of noise and air pollution. Despite the number of schools that have come up, including the one I started, there is a high level of youth unemployment. I noticed that year after year farmers stopped growing their crops, as costs exceed revenues and suicide among them has gone up. Many, who left the village to the Middle East to earn a better living through menial labor offer, have no incentive to go back to their family to work or improve their lives – many suffer from ailments of addictions and spend free living. I was told by my Chinese colleagues, the same is true in the villages in China with the migrant workers. Based on a survey done by my students and validated by a prior survey done by the AP government, the basic necessities like water and food, security, waste disposal, education and healthcare complicated by high level of corruption are the major issues.It is ironic that there have been many new advances in technology, new business model innovations and exponential growth in information and knowledge since I left my village as a teen. All this progress did not offer much benefit to the rural populations where most of the people in world live.

Our educational systems have failed us – they have not kept in synch with the changing landscape resulting from technology since the industrial era. Education is all about the flow of knowledge – or access to knowledge as it is created. Knowledge gives humans the power of invention and innovation to explore opportunities in creating value for them.

Knowledge is useless unless it flows in real time. Knowledge, I believe, that once it is created, must become a social good to benefit society across the silos and global barriers. When knowledge is held captive by the privileged class of a few – then inequity and injustice prevails."

Prof. Solomon Darwin, Haas School of Business, UC Berkeley.

Scaling technology solutions to a large number of villages, which are located in different areas come with challenges. Due to diverse cultures, demographics, and ultimately, needs, scaling strategies need to be elaborated in detail to gain the expected success. Meeting the stated objectives will not require substantial infrastructure development or large outlays of money. Rather, it will require uninterrupted Internet connectivity, community engagement, and skill-building. With these resources, villagers can identify and pursue entrepreneurial paths to economic independence.

CHAPTER 6
WHY GOVERNMENTS PARTICIPATE

The Smart Village project eventually became reality and has been established and orchestrated in collaboration with Indian state governments Andhra Pradesh and Arunachal Pradesh. This chapter is to chronologically reflect the process for such participation and what takeaways can be derived from this journey to succeed in partnering with the public sector in emerging economies such as India. In this context, there have been four parts, which individually mark accomplishments in progressing the Smart Village Idea with respect to partnering with Indian state governments: (Phase 0) successfully accessing and approaching the government for this initiative, (Phase 1) signing the first Memorandum of Agreement to create the Smart Village prototype in Mori, (Phase 2) extending the project to scale up the Smart Village initiative to 472 villages in 5 districts of Andhra Pradesh and (Phase 3) eventually launching the project additionally in the state of Arunachal Pradesh.

Phase 0: Accessing and Approaching Government

To promote an idea to key stakeholders within the public sector, it cannot be achieved instantaneously without prior efforts and relationship building. Access is limited and difficult to get. Among other factors, a viable balance of relevant, credible experiences and a valuable network of businesses would be primarily needed in order to be considered for accessing and approaching high-level government officials.

The main journey paving the way for the Smart Village idea began originally in 2013 when the Smart City idea was an arising concept, it had become very prominent, and was spreading across cities throughout the world. Private and public sectors started talking about its possibilities and indicated great interest in this concept. Companies invested and still invest in building Smart Cities. Moreover, the Indian government announced in 2014 the plan to develop 100 Smart Cities and to allocate Rs 7,060 crore (around 1 billion USD) to the union budget (federal government). US President Obama met with Prime Minister of India, Narendra Modi in mid-2014 and announced to help India in developing three Smart Cities – Allahabad, Ajmer, and Visakhapatnam.[1] When assigned by the dean of UC Berkeley to take forward an initiative for Entrepreneurship between the Indian Institute of Management (IIM) Allahabad and UC Berkeley under the chair of Prime Minister Modi, Darwin's engagement for Smart Cities eventually evolved. At the time, Henry Chesbrough's academic ecosystem was highly invested in Smart City research. Chesbrough encouraged Solomon Darwin to pursue this idea, which was eventually developed into a course titled "Building Smart Cities, Leveraging Open Innovation", a special course for engineering and business students. For the first time at UC Berkeley, engineering and business students worked together to develop a framework for these three cities using Open Innovation.

Coincidently, the city he partly grew up in, Visakhapatnam, was one of the selected ones to become a Smart City in collaboration with the US-Government. He took his students to Visakhapatnam for them to experience how Smart Cities were being created. Prime Minister Modi and Chief Minister Naidu (Andhra Pradesh) were also interested in seeing how a Smart City could be developed from scratch – the so-called green cities. Therefore, students developed proposals for both approaches.[2] The outcomes were presented to M. Venkaiah Naidu, the Minister of Urban Development at that time (now Vice President of India) in May 2015.[3] Going through the presentations, he prioritized the proposal for Visakhapatnam. Solomon Darwin then took the initiative to partner with Andhra University in Visakhapatnam, which is the oldest University in Andhra Pradesh. As partners, they inaugurated an Open Innovation center, where different ideas on Smart Cities were conceptualized and developed by Indian students and later partnered with UC Berkeley faculty and students. Within this initiative, Darwin invited several US-American companies to India to explore opportunities for the Smart City project. For the inauguration of this new innovation center in January 2016, he was aiming to invite the Chief Minister of Andhra Pradesh and was able to approach the District Collector of Visakhapatnam, who put a notable request to the Chief Minister. It was an astonishing moment when Chief Minister Naidu indeed attended the inauguration, giving Solomon Darwin the unique opportunity to approach him for new proposals and discussions.[4]

Phase 0: Success Factors

Being able to access and approach the political head of state like Chief Minister Naidu in India is for most people almost impossible. Furthermore, initiating fruitful discussions for partnering requires many prerequisites in this very specific scenario. The challenges encountered were difficult access, limited time of key government individuals, and the sheer competition among multiple actors aiming to partner with the public sector. The following highlights are key takeaways for successfully overcoming those barriers.

Offering Relevant Experience and Value

Offering an extraordinary experience and value which perfectly fits in the government's scope of work is critical in establishing collaborations with the public sector. In the case of India, especially Andhra Pradesh, specific needs in terms of economic development through foreign investment, innovative technologies and, business innovation are determining the fields of interest. Extensive experience with Silicon Valley technology companies, multilateral corporations, and business research especially in corporate innovation from both – Henry Chesbrough and Solomon Darwin led to an outstanding offered portfolio that was relevant to the state government of Andhra Pradesh. As experts in Open Innovation, Henry Chesbrough and Solomon Darwin regularly consult and advise senior executives, multinationals, and governments around the world, which helped them develop a renowned reputation and credibility. Moreover, Henry Chesbrough provided strong academic expertise and guidance for Open Innovation among multiple actors including governments. Solomon Darwin offered strong experience in bringing western companies to India to tap into emerging economies effectively.

Pooling this relevant expertise was a convincing value that was highly recognized by the Indian government. To address the needs of the governments in emerging economies, it is important to offer countryspecific experience since the settings across countries differ vastly.

Since 2013, Darwin collaborated with companies like IBM, Phillips, Dell, and others by providing a platform that would allow these companies to explore new opportunities in developing countries with the focus on urban India. This quickly developed his expertise on how large and global firms can expand their markets to emerging economies by adapting their business models and technologies – an experience that fell concretely under the agenda of the Indian government. As a result, his and Chesbrough's experiences were requested to push forward initiatives like the Smart City program. Indeed, when the right fit of offerings exists, traction for collaborative activities strongly emerges. In the Smart City context, Professor Darwin along with Henry Chesbrough offered a wide network of necessary information and communication technologies (ITC) from foreign (mainly US-American) companies. Therefore, with regards to the Smart Village idea, the technology and business background very much aligned well with Naidu's mission to improve his rural constituencies with new, unconventional ways. The first steps to getting attention, starting the conversation, and moving forward become feasible with relevant and credible expertise, country-specific context, and offerings, such as a network of relevant companies aligned with a government's scope. Thus, the first step to defining a vision, and moving forward with an idea that aligns with the government's scope is to have the credible and reliable experience that is supported by a strong network of relevant companies.

Offering Viable Networks

Providing access to viable networks is essential, but needs to go hand in hand with valuable brands, unique technologies, and organizations/stakeholders which are highly relevant for the public sector. Indian state governments are looking for partnerships across the globe, especially with a focus on innovative technologies from

Silicon Valley. Providing a viable network to governments facilitates access, increases its own reputation, and fosters the overall value creation for initiatives like the Smart Village project. Being part of the Haas School of Business at UC Berkeley, a large network of private sector firms naturally exists. Particularly, the Garwood Center for Corporate Innovation hosts the Berkeley Innovation Forum (BIF), a biannual membership forum founded by Henry Chesbrough in 2006. BIF consists of over 40 large global corporations that participate from all around the world. Companies like Cisco, NASA, Siemens, Mitsubishi present corporate challenges, latest trends, and technologies; business models and cases concerning innovation and Open Innovation are discussed.

Moreover, the Garwood Center for Corporate Innovation hosts the World Open Innovation Conference (WOIC), an annual international conference that bridges the gap between theory and practice. WOIC brings together renowned business practitioners and academics from all over the world to solve industry challenges through Open Innovation where there is a mutual exchange knowledge and expertise across industry and academia. Henry Chesbrough and Solomon Darwin direct and moderate many more international Innovation conferences and forums. They chair quarterly Chief Innovation Officer round tables in the Silicon Valley and consult and advise international brands like Google, Hewlett Packard, IBM, and Dell, among others. All efforts lead to a larger business ecosystem, creating a network which results in many opportunities to collaborate with multiple actors from the public and private sectors, and longstanding relationships with companies. This results in a generally higher willingness to participate in proposed business opportunities based on trust and established credibility.

Understanding the Prevalent System and Culture with a Dual Mindset

Approaching and working with Indian politicians and bureaucracy requires a deep understanding of Indian culture, Indian mindset, and the specific economic ecosystem. In order to operate in India, it is necessary to understand how to achieve accomplishments in India. Otherwise, all efforts will not create anticipated outcomes. Moreover, to some extent, it is required to align with the Indian culture and its values. Therefore, having an Indian project leader is beneficial to successfully accessing the government and getting projects approved quickly, which will be closely executed with the government. Professor Solomon Darwin could therefore easily approach the government in an effective way because of his Indian origin and his former experience working with the government and the private sector in India.

However, understanding perfectly Indian culture and the system is only one part of the story. Emerging economies tend to appreciate the involvement of western companies as well as western leadership. In a globalized world, emerging economies also need to understand how the systems in developed countries work. Professor Solomon Darwin has been living and working in the US for more than 30 years, which complements his Indian profile when bringing his western experience, leadership, and network, which makes him a perfect candidate to work within this scenario. Ultimately, establishing government projects in emerging economies necessitates expertise, knowledge, and technologies from developed countries, which requires a dual mindset. In an optimal case, the project's spearhead is not only from local origin to fully understand the respective system, but also has a deep understanding of western systems, culture, leadership, and business.

Establishing Relationships

Establishing trustful and long relationships is crucial to access government. There is almost no chance for foreign organizations or companies to enter India and immediately start operations. To date, the Indian government system is not built like that; it is designed so everyone from a higher level has to start from the ground level and has to work for decades to rise up.[5] Even having an excellent reputation, experience, or valid resources, it is tough for a foreign organization to enter the Indian system without having established relevant relationships with the government in advance. Having set up a missionary society with an NGO status, Professor Darwin brings in 30 years (1988) of experience in working with the Indian Government. He has built long and trustful government relationships within his efforts to provide cost-effective education and healthcare to the rural area of Andhra Pradesh and beyond. Because of the nature of getting promoted within Indian government structures, many former politicians he was dealing with on the district level are now in a state-level position.

Moreover, through the Berkeley network, Professor Darwin received access to high-level bureaucrats and politicians beyond the scope of Andhra Pradesh. Prime Minister Narenda Modi came to the Silicon Valley to chair an MoU (Memorandum of Understanding) between UC Berkeley and IIT Allahabad for Entrepreneurship and met Professor Darwin and Henry Chesbrough. Also, UC Berkeley's Haas School of Business handed over an award for Distinguished Contribution to Leadership in Open Innovation, established by Henry Chesbrough, to the president of India, Honorable Pranab Mukherjee, where Solomon Darwin was leading this effort. This effectively shows the strength of the Berkeley network and opportunities to access key individuals. Moreover, when having access to the many high-level persons within the public sector, it increases its credibility among the public sector itself. Eventually, the strong network eased the process to access the right stakeholder from the Andhra Pradesh government for the Smart Village proposal considerably.

Understanding Leadership within Government

It is critical to understand the leadership within the government and to identify advocates for the proposed initiative. Stakeholder mapping is therefore crucial to effectively approach government. Chief Minister Naidu immediately aligned with Professor Darwin's vision to empower people with digital technology. Moreover, the Andhra Pradesh government experiments and implements a wide range of technology solutions for its people. Consequently, many key stakeholders were convinced from the beginning and became advocates for this project, which eased moving forward.

PHASE 0 SUMMARY:

Accessing and Approaching Government

Key Activites for Unlocking Government Collaboration

Derived General Success Factors

Expertise & Experience

- Chesbrough & Darwin are experts in innovation.

- Supported Smart City initiatives since 2013; consulted western companies to tap into urban Indian markets.

- Offer relevant expertise & experience which is valuable for governments.

  -> Country specific context is needed

Viable Networks

- Offered Silicon Valley business and technology network.

- Offered Berkeley corporate network.

- Offer viable networks to goverments for easing and accelerating their partnerships outside India.

Dual Mindset

- Darwin has 30+ years of western experience as corporate executive in the US and being from Indian origin.

- Understand prevalent culture & system with a dual mindset.

  -> Have Indian and western understanding

Relationships with Government

- Darwin established long term relationships with Andhra Pradesh (State Gov.).

- Affiliation with Prime Minister and President of India (Central Gov.) through UC Berkeley.

- Establish relevant relationships with both - state and central governments as early as possible.

Understanding Government Leadership

- Mapped key advocates favourable of technology for rural development.

- Understand leadership among governments to identify project advocates.

Phase 1: Proposing, Signing and Developing the first Smart Village Prototype in Mori

Indeed, having access to key government stakeholders provides opportunities for collaboration, nevertheless, it also means the beginning of a complex journey for accomplishing and sustaining a partnership deal. The starting point here is a relevant project proposal followed by a formal process to establish a partnership. Eventually, agreed deliverables need to be showed to the state government for sustaining the deal.

Leveraging all prerequisites (described in Phase 0) made Solomon Darwin and Henry Chesbrough considerable candidates for future partnerships. Finally, Solomon Darwin and Chief Minister Naidu had private talks during the inauguration of the Open Innovation center at Andhra University in Visakhapatnam in late 2015. Central to these talks was the discussion on how to adapt the Smart Cities concept to a rural setting. Eventually, both concluded that building a few hundred Smart Villages in Andhra Pradesh would create a much bigger economic impact for the state and the people. Prior to that serendipitous conversation, Professor Solomon Darwin had been envisioning a village where technology would create a better future for its people. His idea was to set up a prototype village in Mori, the village he grew up in – he wanted to continue his legacy and foster entrepreneurship like his grandmother did when selling lace abroad to the UK back in the day.[6] The initial agreement between Chief Minister Naidu and Professor Darwin was to begin in Mori, where Darwin would bring in companies to test their technologies in India's rural setting. The idea was for these companies to later adapt their technology when co-innovating with the villagers. To oversee the academic research activities and advise participating firms on innovating in Mori, Henry Chesbrough brought in his academic expertise and provided guidance on Open Innovation among contributors.

Eventually, the Smart Village approach would mean a completely new application of Open Innovation in rural emerging markets and therefore, an undiscovered field of academic research of how Open Innovation operates in rural communities and the rural Indian market setting.

Chief Minister Naidu was very much convinced by this idea and comprehensive package, Solomon Darwin was offering at that time. Moreover, this aligned with similar approaches Naidu planned to address after the findings of the Pada Yatra. After that, formal processes needed to be followed to prepare for the MoU (Memorandum of Understanding) signing. This involved the assessment of needed government funds, determination of the deliverables, and detailing the proposal from the Smart Village side to address organizational, financial, and strategic matters. After finalizing the proposal, the Chief Minister was fully convinced and signed the MoU in June 2016. The government had the role of providing funds needed for the Smart Village operations and serving as an advisor, facilitator, and supporter for this project. The agreed objective of the Smart Village initiative between Professor Darwin and the government of Andhra Pradesh was therefore to explore innovative opportunities to make villages smart and to present outcomes by the end of December 2016. This would then serve as a foundation to further evolve this novel approach beyond the Mori prototype.

Initial recruits came to Mori and field visits, discussions with companies and introductions to government officials were happening. The main focus during June through December was to test technologies on the ground and to co-innovate with villagers. Therefore, an event to introduce and to start the co-innovation phase was conducted in September 2016, where all partner companies were invited to display their existing technologies for the villagers. Companies received immediate pivoting feedback from villagers.

Because the respective District Collector of East Godavari, responsible for Mori, and the Revenue Division Officer (RDO) came to that event, remarkable public attention arose. Eventually, all the villagers from Mori and the villages nearby attended that event to see various demonstrated technologies and to give their inputs. The scope for the remaining time until December was to test and implement relevant technologies in three co-innovation iterations with the villagers.

Finally, on the 29th of December 2016, the Smart Village prototype in Mori was presented to a broad audience. The smart village prototype showed that traction among the village population was created, several technologies were implemented, and corporate executives came to the rural village to present and test their technologies. It proved that people in rural villages are ready for technology and are willing to use it and that Silicon Valley companies are coming down to a village level. Chief Minister Naidu came to Mori on that day and was overwhelmed to see that 80 corporate executives[7] from top companies came to such a remote village to deploy and innovate relevant technologies. Additionally, speeches from high government officials and prominent companies like Google, or IBM were given to over 40,000 attending people. Having rural inclusion for internet on their agenda and seeing the potential of digital technologies from the Mori pilot, the government committed to equipping the whole Mori village with internet fiber connectivity and declared Mori to be the first digital governance village in the state of Andhra Pradesh on this day.[8] Naidu saw the huge potential of the Smart Village idea and the broad scope that needs to be covered and invited the whole Smart Village team to discuss the next phase on the upcoming day – a project extension was on its way.

Picture 1 – Chief Minister Naidu with US-India Smart Village Team in Mori 2016

Phase 1: Success Factors

Proposing the right idea to accomplish an official partnership agreement with the government along with funding to execute an initiative like the Smart Village project and keeping government involved and engaged throughout the project and beyond requires significant efforts as elaborated in the following.

Offering a Relevant Proposal

The MoU proposal, which clearly highlights the vision, the relevant need, and the detailed way forward for the smart village approach is critical for its success. Moreover, it was supported by research to underlay all conclusions and recommendations. Therefore, a complete village profile of Mori was created, which involved available demographic data, research findings of prevalent pain points, and insights from local community meetings.

Sustaining Continuous Government Involvement & Engagement

Sustaining continuous government involvement and engagement is critical for the overall participation of all included stakeholders. The participation of government, public, and corporations seem to significantly complement each other. However, the government plays the most critical role when attracting the local population in rural India for public events to in turn spread broad awareness among people. Therefore, high profile individuals are necessary to attract public attention – conducting an event without important political key stakeholders will not be successful. During the first co-innovation event, the District Collector attended, which lead to the participation of all the political leaders from the broader area of Mori.[9] People got to know that high politicians and government officials would attend and followed that call. When Chief Minister Naidu attended the final presentation in Mori in late 2016, over 40,000 people came to the remote village. While it was important to engage companies in local village events pertaining to the smart village project, this particular event proved to place a higher value on government officials. The highlighted story below (story 2) describes this peculiar set-up.

Story 2 – The story of Lakshmi and her Relationship with the Government

"I am Pallapothu Lakshmi, a resident of V.V.Meraka, a Panchayat beside Mori. My husband works seasonally in a gas filling station, ends up making money which is not sufficient to meet our daily needs, thus I had to step up to share the burden from his shoulders and support my family. I have been running a small snacks stall. Together we were able to earn two times meal for our family but the times have changed now. As the children are growing up, there needs have grown up too. Rising inflation, high cost for education, expensive medical facilities and increasing cost of living has made us helpless, there is no go to for people like us. Me and my husband have been looking for alternative means to earn some money to be able to provide some quality education to our children and give them a future that every child in this country deserves.

I was always inclined towards the efforts and measures that government has taken to improve the quality of life in Andhra Pradesh. Inspired by the efforts of our previous governments, I joined Development of Women & Children in Rural areas (DWCRA) in 1995. My association with this group assisted me to avail a loan that helped me equip my business and saved my business during the tough times. Being an active member and a leader in the DWCRA, I got the privilege to attend several government meeting and gatherings of the local leadership. I even got several opportunities to attend events like Janmabhumi, where our CM Sri. Nara Chandra Babu Naidu addressed thousands of people of Andhra Pradesh and talked to them to listen to their miseries and woes. I have been attending his events since very long, only to listen to CM. I take pride in calling myself a disciple of Shri. Chandrababu Naidu garu. He has been inspiring people of Andhra since ages and craze for him is evident in all his meetings. People gather in thousands just to capture a look of their hero. As a part of DWCRA, we also showcased products made by the lady members of our community like Mori Sarees and Cashews, informing him and asking for the solutions to our pain points. He listened to us with compassion and promised that his government will address all our pain points.

CM sir is my role model, I am very much aligned to his vision and highly appreciate his efforts in the state of Andhra Pradesh. I always look forward to attend his gatherings and being a DWCRA member, I am always informed of his visit to our nearby place. His support and encouragement to lakhs of helpless women like me have strengthened us to come out of our comfort zone and question government officers. I'm very thankful to the Smart Village team and specially to professor Solomon Darwin, because of him CM Naidu visited our village on 29th December, 2016 and all the DWCRA women were also invited to attend the meeting. More than 40,000 attended this event to support the efforts of Professor Darwin and to listen to their hero, Nara Chandrababu Naidu. We asked for his support on these issues, as I firmly believe government can definitely eliminate negativities from our society. I am assured that government will soon help families like mine to have a good quality life, provide security, health facilities, new employment opportunities and good education for our children."

Pallapothu Lakshmi, Resident of Meraka Village
near Mori, Andhra Pradesh

In contrast to the government being the significant factor for attracting people, the much-needed participation from both, government and corporations, depends mutually on each other. Since the government determines the legal framework and can act as a major scaling partner for companies, the latter ones have a big incentive for participating in a project, with the government as the main collaborator. Tapping into new markets requires not only in-depth knowledge about the market, the on-site presence, or co-innovation efforts, but also access to the government for regulatory clearances and scaling opportunities. When CM Naidu, among many other higher government officials, attended the December 29th round table conference at the Mori prototype presentation event, many corporations were able to establish individual collaborations with the Government of Andhra Pradesh. Out of intimate talks, CM Naidu decided which technologies to go forward with since the technologies were already tested in Mori. The most notable program which came out of this event was the collaboration with Google Free Space Optics as a data transmission solution for Andhra Pradesh.

At the same time, it is excessively difficult to make high government officials come to such public events, especially to events like the December 29th event in a small and remote village like Mori, which posed several political and non-political challenges for CM Naidu. Missing infrastructure and security and the fact that Mori is located in an area where the opposition party outnumbers became a big issue. It was not clear that CM Naidu would come to the December 29th event. All these factors became obsolete when CM Naidu saw the list of top companies coming to that event. He was amazed at how many global brands were coming to a remote area in rural India. He simply couldn't say no to such an opportunity to meet all these important actors to elaborate possible ways forward for an inspiring rural development initiative. CM Naidu saw an opportunity he realized that multinational companies are interested in Andhra Pradesh as a state with the potential to create innovative solutions at the rural level.

Exhibit 12 – Agenda for the December 2016 event.

Agenda for December 29, 2016
Scalable Smart Village Prototype - Mori Village
Executive Briefing with Hon. Chief Minister, Nara Chandrababu Naidu
Innovative Technology Solutions and Business Models for Rural Andhra Pradesh
Moderated by Professor Solomon Darwin, University of California, Berkeley

8:30 AM	Shuttle Pick-up at Dindi Resorts to Smart Village Co-Innovation lab, Riverside Campus
9:30 AM	Executives will be seated in the Conference Room (late comers will not be allowed due to security)
9:35 AM	Executive briefing by Professor Solomon Darwin
10:00 AM	**Chief Minister Arrives at Mori**
10:05 AM	Welcome by Mr. Arun Kumar, District Collector, East Godavari
10:10 AM	Overview and Results of the Scalable Smart Village Project - Professor Solomon Darwin
10:25 AM	**Session 1**: Smart Connectivity
	AP Fiber Update: Sambasiva Rao (5min)
	Google: Mahesh Krishnaswamy (5min)
	Discussants: Sambasiva Rao (CEO AP Fiber) and Ashis Baby (Sabse) (5 min)
	NASA: Dr. Greg Schmidt, Director - Inspiring the next generation in Space Sciences (5 min)
10:45 AM	**Session 2**: Smart Farming
	Kaneka, IBM, C-Fog, Ericsson + Appscape + Sensorex, Skylark Drones (10min)
	Discussants- Alan Walker, Srivats Kamisetty, Sridhar Gadhi, Sanjeev Rattan, Suresh Vempati, TR Mughilan
	Q&A (10min)
11:05 AM	**Session 3**: Smart Village Accelerator Program: Manav Subodh (Smart Village Director, UC Berkeley)
	5 Heroes & Cygni, Sahaj, Janalakshmi, Agrikal, Hella (10min)
	Discussants- Prof. Terry Beaubois (Stanford University), Venkat Rajaraman, Santhosh Dash, Venkit Eswaraan, Harish Rayaprolu, Rama Shankar Pandey (5 min)
11:25 AM	**Session 4**: Safety and Security
	Tyco Internaltional, Lingel Door & Windows (2min)
	Discussants- Santosh Muzumdar, Mario Schmidt (3 min)
11:30 AM	**Session 5**: Smart Healthcare Solutions
	Care Hospitals, 1M1B, Tata, BlueKare , Intitute of Transformative Tech-Berkeley, Hero Cycles (10 min)
	Discussants- Dr. Soma Raju, Dr. Swati Subodh, Col. Ravi Goli, Nupur, Neeraj Chandra (5 min)
11:45 AM	**Session 6**: Smart Energy Solution
	Tech Mahindra and Lumax (5min)
	Discussants- Raju Wadalkar, Vineet Sahni (5min)
11:55 AM	**Session 7**: Smart Education
	Cisco, Neurominders, Google Chrome (10min)
	Discussants- Vikram Kumar, Mia Finnestand, CP Vishwanath (5min)
12:10 PM	**Session 8**: Next Steps - Professor Solomon Darwin
	Lessons Learned through the Smart Village Project
	Next steps: Smart Village Accelerator for Razole Constituency – 58 Villages or beyond
12:20 PM	**Hon. Chief Minister's Remarks**
12:35 PM	Vote of thanks: Mr. Arun Kumar, District Collector offers closing remarks - Program Ends
12:40 PM	Chief Minister inaugurates the Smart Village Accelerator
12:45 PM	Hon. Chief Minister addresses the media
12:50 PM	Hon. CM tours UC Berkeley Co-Innovation Work Space, Mori Campus
	CM Inaugurates: Hella Automotive Center - Creating New Jobs in Rural Andhra Pradesh
	CM Inaugurates: Ericsson Farmer Training Center - Empowering Farmers for the Digital Age
	CM Inaugurates: Tech Mahindra Micro-Grid As A Service - Energy Surplus Program for new revenue generation
	Program Ends

To conclude how to sustain government involvement and engagement, there is the need to provide a complex ecosystem of involved participants, in which the government itself plays a crucial part and from which it absorbs value. To some extent, all three parties, the private and public sectors, and citizens, complement each other. If one party misses, the whole ecosystem might collapse. If there would be no companies, the government would not show up and thus people would not come. However, in the setting of India, the role of the government seems to be the most critical and dominant player to create the biggest vacuum if missing. Thus, incentives like highly ranked business executives and a large population attending need to be provided.

PHASE 1 SUMMARY:

Proposing, Signing and Developing the First Protoype

Key Activites for Unlocking Government Collaboration

Derived General Success Factors

Relevant Proposal	
• Submitted a proposal showing the unique project value and how to accomplish this.	• Highlight vision, mission, impact and needs to be resolved in the MoU proposal.
• Created village footprint from on-ground research.	• Emphasize real value for the government and defining deliverables for both sides.
	• Proof proposal with research.

Government Engagement	
• Conducted inauguration event with highest bureaucrats and politicians from the district along with industry partners and rural population.	• Ignite excitement and awareness among the government and leverage this to attract rural population. Without the government, people won't sign up.
	• Invite industry partners since participation of government and industry depends mutually on each other.

Traction	
• Presented outcomes of prototype to top tier government officials, like CM Naidu, along with over 60 international corporate executives and 40,000 villagers.	• Showcase value for the government in terms of industry participation, impact and traction among the population to get them hooked for partnership extensions.
	• Without relevant industry participation, high level government officials won't show up.

Phase 2: Extending the Project to 472 Villages

Working in partnership with the public sector for an initial prototype can be understood as a probation period with favorable terms and conditions. Succeeding and extending such a partnership to a larger scale would add more complexity to the many different aspects, such as the collaboration with the government.

Immediately after the December 29th 2016 event, the extension phase proposal was submitted in Amaravati (capital city of Andhra Pradesh), which led to a personal discussion with Chief Minister Naidu on how the Smart Village initiative moved forward. Eventually, CM Naidu confirmed the next phase and committed resources and support for the Smart Village project for one more year. Again, an MoU was determined which was submitted at the end of January 2017. From the learnings of the Mori prototype, the original proposal has targeted an extension of the Smart Village initiative to 19 villages in the nearby constituency of the East Godavari district, Andhra Pradesh, where Mori is located. Since the government and political leaders were convinced about the feasibility of scaling, a series of government-prompted extensions followed (see the following figure), which brought some unforeseen challenges due to the vast differences in demographic, cultural, and socio-economic status.

However, despite some challenges, this meant an enormous opportunity to take the project to another level and the Smart Village team was ready and excited to take upon this new endeavor. The final MoU with the finalized scope and the release of the given budget was soon signed and operations started in May 2017. In order to establish relationships with local leaders, the team initially visited every district collector (highest official of a district), respective MLAs (elected representative of a constituency), and even Member of Parliaments from the district (representing the district on a national level). The Smart Village district directors continued personal meetings on a regular basis with their respective local government leaders. On a district level, each district got assigned a nodal government officer for the Smart Village team to interact with. On a state government level, there were several important contact persons for the Smart Village team.[10]

Extension Phase:
Motives for 472 Villages

Initial Proposal: 19 Villages

• Smart Village team proposed a small
extension to 19 Villages in the same area
(East Godavari)

1st Extension: 59 Villages

• Bordering district of West Godavari was
added since gov. required a larger scope.

2nd Extension: 150 Villages

• District of Krishna was additonally added
to even further enlarge the scope and was seen
as relevant since the new capital city is in this
district.

3rd Extension: 300 Villages

• District of Chittoor was added for political
reasons since CM Naidu's consistuency is
located there.

4th Extension: 472 Villages

• District of Srikakulum was added for political
reasons to showcase potential in this relatively
backwarded District.

The complex public sector stakeholder structure eventually caused some additional challenges in terms of reporting, communication, commitment and alignment explained further in chapter 12.

The overall objective for the extension phase was to adapt technologies and business models to the given market of 472 villages. However, this did not mean that the Mori prototype would be fully recreated in 472 villages. The new scale was offered to have laboratories in different areas and districts to explore various opportunities for future scaling. Over 60 national (Indian) and international companies participated in phase 2 to test traction on village-level markets of India. Over 20 co-innovation projects successfully built the base to adapt existing business models to the new setting. Additionally, a Hackathon was conducted in Vijayawada along with an Open Innovation Forum India in August 2017 (see picture 2), where industry partners, key government officials like Chief Minister Naidu, and over 2,000 students attended to discuss challenges for rural development and to come up with innovative solutions. As the "father of Open Innovation", Henry Chesbrough addressed the participants and emphasized the importance of collaborative activities across domains for resolving urgent needs with increased speed to market.

In November 2017, over 20 companies and startups related to agriculture presented at the Agri Tech Summit in Vishakhapatnam an ecosystem concept where their solutions holistically merge to address farmer's pain points. This event was hosted by the government of Andhra Pradesh. A white paper about this approach[11] was handed over to key government officials and Bill Gates, who was the guest speaker at this summit. Furthermore, relevant technology solutions were showcased in the District of Chittoor in early 2018 at Kuppam hosted by the local government with the focus on technology solutions to foster rural development.

After one year of extensively exploring, adapting, and implementing technologies, establishing an entrepreneurial program and skill development program across the five districts, the extension phase finally concluded in mid-2018. Efforts for re-election started to slow down the overall government involvement, which put the project on hold for the time being. Recommendations for promising projects were handed over to the government, which paves the way for the state if choosing to scale these after the re-election.

Picture 2 – Chief Minister Naidu with US-India Smart Village Team in Vijayawada 2017

Phase 2: Key Takeaways

As government-funded projects like the Smart Village initiative evolve and eventually scale over time, dynamics and relationships become more complex. In order to sustain collaboration with the government on a higher scale, the following success factors reflect the experience which are closely linked with affiliated challenges.

Scaling Comes with Responsibility

Scaling comes with the responsibility to positively impact people beyond the actual project time frame. Long term commitment to execute and foster initiatives is needed. Although funding might be restricted to a specific date, sharing the long-term vision and perspective with the government is crucial. Innovating in the rural setting evolves organically and takes time. The funding partner like the government needs to be sensitized that novel innovation initiatives are not short-term impact projects but ways of exploration to create new ways of economic development. When first signing the MoU with the government, the scope was clearly to explore ways of creating Smart Villages to foster self-sustainable economic growth. All involved parties aligned with the long-term focus of the smart village vision. This scope continued when signing up for phase two to scale this approach to 472 villages.

Scaling Government Engagement

When scaling up projects from the prototype level in collaboration with the government, ongoing involvement and engagement are crucial. Necessary accountability and responsibility consequently increase and complexity arises. All government key stakeholders need to be integrated into the process of organizational development, operations, and the underlying approaches for the project. Eventually, the relationship with the government is crucial for overall project success. Proactivity and encouragement from the government evolve when the project core team engages with their government contact persons frequently. Not only can the government facilitate broad opportunities and resources for various causes, but being a funding partner, there are obligations with respect to committed deliverables. Such obligations involve transparency of all operations with continuous reporting and updating. Therefore, to maintain integrity, a transparent account-ability structure needs to be established, which additionally fosters relationship building with the government.

When establishing or developing the organizational structure, this needs to be considered from the beginning. Moreover, the scope of the project is required to complement the government's scope rather than disrupt it. To ensure this, conducting ongoing mutual education on expectations, existing projects, and future scope is critical. CM Naidu therefore chaired the executive board and key government stakeholders have been on that board to ensure a transparent structure from the beginning. Additionally, relationships with local political leadership and with key contact persons from the government were also established. Knowledge exchange happened in a continuous way. To continue the engage-ment, it was necessary to showcase the projects. efforts in public. It is about continuously proving its own value towards the govern-ment. Signing an MoU for one year doesn't mean receiving sup-port and commitment from the government throughout the whole time. Therefore, events were hosted and attended as mentioned above. Of course, the success criteria in terms of events as elabo-rated earlier are essential here as well. Lastly, given advice and encouragement from the government was appreciated and taken into consideration to foster the overall progress. However, many challenges emerged, which are described later in this book.

Reflecting and Reacting to Politics and Bureaucracy

Detailed understanding of the present political system and the government's bureaucracy in assigned areas and beyond is critical. Since politicians are following their strict agendas to fulfill electoral promises or even campaigning, in-depth awareness is essential to assess given advice or support to align with its vision. As people are very sensitive about political convictions, associations with political parties can backfire among the population from the given area. Therefore, the Smart Village initiative emphasized its role as a research project which clearly falls under academia and is seen to be neutral and thus does not fall under politics or other convictions.

PHASE 2 SUMMARY:
Extending the Project to 472 Villages

Key Activites for Unlocking Government Collaboration	Derived General Success Factors
Long Term Commitment	
• Continuously emphasized the long term vision, which is beyond the given project timeline.	• Be aware of the footprint you will create. Starting such initiatives always comes with a long term commitment towards the population.
	• Sensitize government that innovation requires time in erms of its efficacy and impact.
	• Keep on emphasizing the value for government of complementing their scope.
Extended Engagement	
• Engaged with stakeholders from the government on all given levels and established relationships.	• Work closely with all relevant levels - local government to state government.
• Established a structure to update, educate and to receive feedback from the government.	• Design and establish an accountability and feedback structure to keep both sides mutually updated on agreed deliverables. Absorb and apply feedback to move faster.
• Showcased efforts via organizing a student Hackathon and an Open Innovation Conference in India. Attended summits to present outcomes.	• Present your outcomes on a regular base to proof your value. It might require to do it in public or to condcut its own events.
Reflection and Reaction	
• Reflected the political system in eetail and always emphasized the central project role as a neutral research project.	• Understand the system, especially its politics driving it.
	• Assess given advise and support from gov. in terms of its implications, e.g. affiliation with a political party.
	• React adequatly if public would perceive your initiative wrongly.

100

Phase 3: Scaling to North East India – Smart Village Movement Launches in Arunachal Pradesh in 2018

In June 2018, another chapter of the Smart Village project began when signing an MoU with the state government of Arunachal Pradesh to additionally execute the Smart Village initiative in the most north-eastern state of India. 100 villages across 60 constituencies throughout the state will be the scope for research and will be serving as laboratories for technology and business model interventions for addressing rural, unmet needs.[12] Arunachal Pradesh bears new formidable challenges and differs vastly from Andhra Pradesh when having a small population of only 1.255 million but being one of the largest states by size.[13] A new local core team was formed in July 2018[14] to start operations in August to initially assess the situation in terms of challenges and how the Smart Village Movement can address these. The team is led by Shreya Evani, former project director of Andhra Pradesh, now overseeing both states. Taking all previous learnings into consideration, the project could be launched in a very confident, renewed, and more efficient manner.

The Smart Village initiative eventually grew to a more mature level and was hence relabeled as a Smart Village Movement, since being spread among two states and working with multiple companies and universities across the globe. To that date, many key persons and faculties from European, American and Indian universities such as Cambridge, Oxford, MIT, and Indian Institute of Technology Guwahati have signed up to support and collaborate within this movement. Traction steadily rises in a progressive way. An IT platform is being developed to ease and accelerate projects among state governments, startups, corporations, universities and, eventually rural people as emphasized at the beginning of this book. In 2019, the state of Meghalaya signed up for Smart Village implementation. Further extensions are planned. The following chapters are mainly focusing on the extension phase in Andhra Pradesh rather than Arunachal Pradesh and Meghalaya, since it laid the foundation for any upcoming extension.

Picture 3 – Chief Minister Pema Khandu with Indian Smart Village Team in Itanagar 2018

Phase 3 Takeaway: Incorporating Learnings and Adapting to the New Situation

Learning from mistakes and experience to be continuously incorporated, especially when re-launching in a new state is essential. Knowledge management has been a critical part of furthering the single village pilot to ultimately having simultaneous operations in two different states of India. Throughout the process, learnings from various fields and challenges have been documented.

Moreover, learnings from working along with the Andhra Pradesh state government, establishing the permission for failing, and being adaptable in different settings were essential not only during the extension phase in Andhra Pradesh but also when launching the project in Arunachal Pradesh. Therefore, continuous knowledge capturing is vital and its application requires a culture of allowing self-criticism. Besides learning from mistakes and challenges (elaborated in Part IV) faced in Andhra Pradesh and formulating strategies to prevent these especially when starting from scratch in Arunachal Pradesh, adaptation to the new state in the North East was crucial. Therefore, a 6-month assessment phase was negotiated with the state government to really understand the new scenario in personal and scientific ways before executing interventions on-ground. An open culture to co-create a proposal with the state Government and incorporating its learnings from reflection is important. Also, the different culture was embraced and adopted in the strategy for rolling out the project and most of the new team was therefore recruited locally. It is critical to signal the state government that this program is fully pivoting to the new setting. However, the fundamental smart village framework, described in this book such as the vision, design philosophy, organizational structure, and the innovation process was of course preserved and only slightly adapted to the new scenario. Changes mostly occurred in terms of the project timeline, scope of interventions, and government collaboration relationship.

PHASE 3 SUMMARY:

Project Launch in a New State

Key Activites for Unlocking Government Collaboration	Derived General Success Factors
Learnings	
• Captured effectively learnings throughout the project and applied these before launching in a new state. • Project proposal built on these learnings; a 6 month assessement phase was finalized - together with the state government.	• Implement knowledge management from the beginning and leverage gained learnings to continuosly learn and improve, especially when re-launching in a new state. Allow a constructive culture of self critisim and failure. • Explain new state government your learnings and co-create the proposal with gov. along with incorporating essential success factors.
Adaptation	
• Adapted to the different culture and setting; the new team was hired mostly locally.	• Absorb differences in terms of culture, demographics and needs and apply these to your strategies. • Signal state government your intention to fully adapt to the new state when recruiting mainly locally.

CHAPTER 7
WHY BUSINESSES ENGAGE

The unique character of the Smart Village idea involving the private sector for piloting and pivoting technologies and business models requires a vibrant ecosystem of practitioners. The main objective is to adapt one's business model and technologies to accelerate new markets and create value for the rural population. Partner companies are required to sustain a relevant ecosystem, consisting of the public sector, academia, the private sector, and the people. This chapter provides an understanding of the success factors to attract businesses and to understand their motives in doing so. In order to attract national and international companies and startups to such an initiative besides the business potential to expand to rural markets following success factors are highly recommended to consider as they were utmost critical for success.

Guidance, Business Model Consulting and Resources

In order for companies to explore opportunities in rural India and successfully expand markets, guidance is required. Companies need to consider the many factors that contribute to working in an emerging economy, including understanding business models, available resources, the existing challenges of tapping into a market with low purchase power, high-risk uncertainty, and the unfamiliar social aspects. Guidance is therefore utmost important to let potential companies understand the tradeoff between social and financial goals. Research indicates that when scaling a social enterprise, company management must make tradeoffs between financial and social goals.[1] Leaders at Endeavor, a non-profit that supports entrepreneurship around the world, studied more than 50 social enterprise companies in its network to understand what differentiated those that successfully scaled from those that did not. The analysis found that "entrepreneurs' approach to tradeoffs plays a critical role in their ability to scale."

In fact, the larger the number of necessary tradeoffs, the more difficult it is to scale the enterprise, and the more frequently the company prioritizes social goals over financial ones, the more difficult it is to scale the enterprise.[2] Specifically, "those who prioritized financial goals over social goals were much more likely to experience high rates of growth and have greater social impact. Though the sample was relatively small, the trend was quite strong. The more likely entrepreneurs were to favor financial goals, the faster their companies grew." Endeavor admits the research is limited; after all, the entrepreneurs interviewed all come from one organization that uses a specific selection process. Still, the researchers conclude that it is important for companies to "design business models that align financial and social goals as closely as possible to minimize tradeoffs and reduce friction," and when tradeoffs must be made, to "prioritize financial goals over social ones to maximize the long-term sustainability of the business."[3]

Although the concepts of social enterprise and shared value are not entirely the same, some similarities exist. In particular, both seek to create value for both the business and society. Differences also exist: for example, most of the companies participating in the prototyping are not social enterprises but instead driven primarily by profits. Furthermore, many of these companies already operate at enterprise scale, so the question is not about the company scaling but the innovations themselves *(excerpt from the 2016 HBR Case "Prototyping a Scalable Smart Village to Simultaneously Create Sustainable Development and Enterprise Growth Opportunities" by Solomon Darwin and Henry Chesbrough).* In this context, it is important to understand the nature of innovation which is needed for simultaneously creating financial and social impact. The concept of sustainability-oriented innovation brings these factors together. Sustainability oriented innovations (SOI) are defined as "realized ideas that improve environmental and/or social performance compared with the current situation."[4] SOIs can improve environmental and/or social performance and simultaneously foster competitive advantages. This also highlights new advantages beyond adapting technologies and business models to address the needs of rural markets; it also can replace harmful market incumbents by radically innovating new products and services.

However, sustainability-oriented innovation can be an expensive process and can involve high degrees of uncertainty and risk. There is an added complexity of potentially opposed dimensions regarding sustainability and increased stakeholder demands. Also, there might be either scientific uncertainty or even incomplete information.[5] Ultimately, it is important to guide participating companies on elaborated tradeoffs and risks and how the shared value concept along with sustainable innovation can become a strategy to win in the rural markets. Investing resources to develop an innovative high-value product for the rural setting and selling it for a price that reflects the market doesn't necessarily create profit in the short term. Financial and desired social goals can be eventually addressed when planning and executing in the long term.

Tapping into emerging markets comes consequently with initial investments but can lead eventually to vast strategic advantages –

e.g. cost or quality leadership in the respective market. Moreover, first-mover advantages can arise when providing innovative and disruptive solutions for the market.

In this context, to eventually adapt existing or novel technology and business models to rural markets, business model consulting needs to be provided. This eases the process and ensures the overall success for partner companies and ensures to win in rural emerging markets through getting expert knowledge and consultancy (it is explained in detail in part III of this book). The provision of data analytics, the overall research-based methodologies, and the excellence in academics and executive advisory from the University of California, Berkeley were highly valued by partner companies. Due to the no-cost policy, it served as a big incentive to be part of this project. The starting point of the consultancy marks the overall market potential backed up with research-based data and information on the individual company level. The enormous size of the rural markets in emerging economies is likely to provide vast scaling opportunities for novel and tested innovations, which clearly address corporate objectives. By having information and knowledge about pain points from a large number of villages, which can be extrapolated to the state level, needs from a large, representative population can be addressed from private sector companies. This serves as a knowledge database to derive market demand in rural markets and to take upon strategic decisions.

For companies participating in initiatives to foster sustainable economic development, it is crucial to address described challenges to eventually achieve desired financial and respective social goals. Therefore, companies require resources such as information, methodologies, and a workforce on the ground to decrease uncertainty and risk, among other challenges. 67% of the surveyed companies and startups[6], which actively participated in the smart village process, perceive that the risk to tap into the rural market in India is very high (respectively 24% as high). Moreover, 71%

found the deployment of technology with a team on-ground as an essential incentive for participating in the program to innovate in unknown terrain. Also, every third company and startup stated that market research and consulting services along the offered innovation process where the smart village team acts as an orchestrator to let companies match the rural market was a major incentive to participate. This would be essential to take upon the efforts in tapping into the rural market in India. Moreover, on-ground manpower complements information and knowledge to eventually effectively deploy technologies and to extract feedback from customers (co-innovation process). Co-innovating in given villages not only provides the relevant product feedback to lower the risk of non-acceptance among the future customers but also creates broad awareness for the novel technology or business models among rural populations. It is not surprising that word of mouth is a strong marketing channel within the village setting.

Public Visibility

Public visibility is a critical factor for companies and startups participating in initiatives like the Smart Village project. Multiple channels and associations can be utilized by these to create broad awareness for their products and services and strengthen their brand value among the public. During the Smart Village project, the association with the University of California Berkeley and the given members of the Berkeley Innovation Forum, BIF (over 40 strong and innovative corporations; global brands) served as big incentives for achieving public visibility (50% in terms of the company network, 33% in terms of UC Berkeley among the interviewed companies and startups). Moreover, it is astonishing that the association with the government of Andhra Pradesh was also a major incentive to participate (43%) among asked 21 participating companies and startups. However, the biggest factor for public visibility (57%) was being associated with the smart village initiative as a good corporate citizen. Moreover, when announcing the first Harvard Business Case about the Mori prototype, many companies asked to be featured in this publication. Ultimately, companies tend to strongly consider public visibly in their decisions to participate in initiatives like the Smart Village project.

Access to an Open Innovation Platform

Partner companies are more likely to participate when they have access to a dynamic Open Innovation platform, consisting of an ecosystem of corporations, startups, universities, governments, and rural populations. Kennedy et al. (2016) highlight that sustainability-oriented innovations (SOIs) require special organizational practices to enable the innovation process when aiming for successful SOIs. These include "technology super-scouting throughout the value chain, search heuristics that favor radical sustainability solutions, integration of sustainability performance metrics in product development, championing the value chain to build demand for radical sustainability oriented product innovation, and harnessing the benefits of Open Innovation".[7] Therefore, being part of an Open Innovation platform, technology scouting, championing the value chain and ultimately utilizing benefits of Open Innovation can be profoundly facilitated. Moreover, Kennedy et al. "recommend that firms with a proactive sustainability strategy should consider adopting an Open Innovation approach, as the two seem synergistic."[8] In fact, collaboration with other companies and organizations to form an Open Innovation ecosystem is central to the innovation approach to tap into rural emerging markets.

Having provided a vibrant Open Innovation platform, many Open Innovation collaborations emerged during the smart village project. In addition, companies from outside India require local support or even a local partner to tap into the Indian market as described before. When participating in the smart village corporate network, foreign companies could indeed increase their speed-to-market by having access to local partner companies. In fact, Ketos, a smart water solution provider from USA, was able to find a partner to manufacture in Andhra Pradesh when exchanging with other corporate partners. Ultimately, out of 21 participating companies and startups, 5 made collaborations with others, respectively. The smart village Open Innovation network provided access to the energetic Silicon Valley ecosystem. Beyond potential collaborations with such tech firms, access to relevant investors played a significant role when attracting partners, especially startups. Lastly, access to the government serves as a major incentive for companies to participate. The potential access to the state governments served as an essential incentive for 48% of companies and startups (respectively 30% in terms of access to other companies and startups for getting new business opportunities. 4 out of 21 surveyed companies and startups made collaborations with the AP government through the Smart Village program.

"It is hard to access the government based on the work done by a start-up like us. The knowledge and practical implementation thought process gap of a start-up entrepreneur and seasoned bureaucrats is highly differentiated. It is very difficult to build the bridge between these two. The Smart Village Platform very successfully destroys this barrier and builds an ecosystem where the startups and Governments can collaboratively work very efficiently."

– Naveen Kumar, Founder & CEO
of NaPanta (Indian Agriculture Startup)

SUMMARY:

Why Businesses Engage: Success Factors

Guidance, Consulting and Resources

• Guide businesses on the tradoff to integrate social goals, but to also focus on financial goals
for the long term sustainability of their business. Innovation is therefore the crux for creating sustainable
social impact along with competitive advantage and long term business success.

• Consult businesses on their business model on how they can win in rural emerging markets. Show on
individual company level their enormous market potential in rural India to take upon strategic decisions.

• Provide businesses resources such as market research, on-ground team to deploy solutions,
an overall innovation process along with villagers and insight information about the rural ecosystem
to overcome the complexity, risk and uncertainty of rural emerging markets.

Public Visibility

• Offer multiple communication channels and brand associations to increase businesses' public visiblity,
credibility and brand strength, via global player companies (e.g. Google), renowned universities
(e.g. UC Berkeley) and state governments (e.g. Andhra Pradesh).

Open Innovation Platform

• Provide access to a relevant ecosystem consisting of corporations, startups, universities, governments
and customers to accelerate the innovation process.

• Let businesses complement their own core expertise with partners throughout their value chain when
harnesting the benefits of open innovation.

Motives behind Tapping into
Rural Emerging Markets

When companies are participating, the question quickly arises: are they simply promoting social impact for marketing purposes or are they truly perusing to innovate and creating a sustainable and profitable business model that can create social impact simultaneously?

Since raising the question of the role that business has in society, and the responsibility it has for its economic, social, and environmental impact, Corporate Social Responsibility (CSR) awareness emerged. Among many existing definitions, Jane Nelson defines CSR used by the Harvard Kennedy School of Government at Harvard University as the following: "Corporate social responsibility encompasses not only what companies do with their profits, but also how they make them. It goes beyond philanthropy and compliance, and addresses how companies manage their economic, social, and environmental impacts, as well as their relationships in all key spheres of influence: the workplace, the marketplace, the supply chain, the community and the public policy realm."[9]

In general, CSR can be seen as an approach where resources from businesses are invested in being a good corporate citizen. Examples involve giving money to social causes, reporting on social and environmental impacts, or engaging employees in community service. In contrast, the shared value approach (Creating Shared Value; CSV) from Porter and Kramer is about changing the core business with respect to strategy, structure, people, processes, and rewards to be able to deliver triple bottom line returns. Therefore, CSR focuses on doing initiatives separately from the business whereas shared value focuses on integrating social and environmental impact in its business model to drive economic value.[10] Multinational corporations are steadily increasing their CSR and Shared Value efforts on global problems. In the BRICS (Brazil, Russia, India, China, South Africa) and frontier markets, companies are addressing hunger, poverty, inequality, unemployment and climate change. In fact, such emerging market businesses are adapting the shared value approach to form smart, sustainable and profitable business models.[11]

Within the Smart Village project, more than 90% of all interviewed corporate and startups partners stated that their aim for participating in the initiative was beyond CSR and therefore aligned with the shared value approach. Only 5% saw their participation as a CSR initiative. They stated that their main objectives for participating were to tap into the rural market, addressing pain points, and to obtain new business opportunities through the Berkeley/ Smart Village network.

Corporate partners participate primarily because they have a unique opportunity to address the many objectives they have in a holistic way. Doing a meaningful project for society and creating new business value enables them to go beyond self-interest without compromising their business needs. A strong business case along with excellent business model consulting that helps companies to tap into emerging markets provides companies a long-term business opportunity that fulfills financial and social goals. Moreover, being part of a vibrant Open Innovation platform can create and strengthen novel business opportunities beyond a company's business case and brings high public visibility. Lastly, social needs in emerging economies are met, which can improve a corporation's public reputation (CSR) and beyond and lets a business enterprise tap into new, highly scalable markets (with creating shared value, CSV).

PART III.

How to Execute the Smart Village Idea

CHAPTER 8
HOW TO ESTABLISH A SMART VILLAGE ORGANIZATION

Building an organization to operate in a demanding setting like rural India requires an unique approach. In the following, the organizational development is explained with a focus on the extension of the Smart Village pilot in Mori to 472 villages in Andhra Pradesh, India.

Originally, for the first prototype phase in Mori, Professor Darwin put together an advisory team to conceptualize the upcoming Smart Village project in detail. Beyond that, the advisory team would support related future efforts. It involved a broad spectrum from Industry experts to Professors.[1] Manav Subodh, Innovation Accelerator Expert from UC Berkeley became the project director and established the organization by hiring relevant talents and establish the organization.[2] Moreover, many students from Andhra University and other Indian Universities volunteered to research existing pain points in villages. Since being in prototype-stage in one village, the team and organization were very small.

After having determined the final count of villages to operate in the extension phase, Professor Darwin advised establishing an organization, where at least one intern in each village reports to their respective Mandal directors (county directors), who in turn report to their respective district directors. The newly established core team, consisting of 5 district directors, the project director and the director of corporate relations[3], got intensively trained from UC Berkeley faculty and several advisors. After recruiting 34 Mandal directors and training them, 500 interns were in turn recruited and also trained from respective Mandal directors. Within a span of two months, an organization of 550 people in five districts got established and trained to start operations for the smart village initiative. The initiative was chaired by CM Naidu, an executive board from UC Berkeley, including Solomon Darwin, the primary project advisor/visionary leader and Henry Chesbrough, chief advisor on Open Innovation and academic research, and Andhra Pradesh Government representatives, the formal reporting and accountability structure was finalized (see the following exhibit).

Exhibit 13 – Smart Village Organization for Phase 2

Organizational Chart
UC Berkeley – AP Govt.

HONORABLE CHIEF MINISTER - Chairman

EXECUTIVE BOARD – UC Berkeley & AP Govt.

SMART VILLAGE TEAM

SRIKAKULAM DISTRICT COLLECTOR			EAST GODAVARI DISTRICT COLLECTOR			WEST GODAVARI DISTRICT COLLECTOR			KRISHNA DISTRICT COLLECTOR			CHITTOOR DISTRICT COLLECTOR		
Villages	Mandal Province	Village Interns	Villages	Mandal Province	Village Interns	Villages	Mandal Province	Village Interns	Villages	Mandal Provinces	Village Interns	Villages	Mandal Provinces	Village Interns
54	2	108	13	1	26	15	1	30	23	2	46	48	1	96
89	2	178	11	2	22	13	2	26	14	2	28	64	2	128
42	2	84	16	2	32	20	2	40	31	2	62	38	1	76
43	2	86	08	2	16	14	2	28	33	1	66	60	2	120

Smart Village Team

Berkeley Faculty = 2
Berkeley Fellows = 10
Province Directors = 34
Village Interns = 570

Others: Berkeley and Stanford Faculty and college volunteers

Establishing a successful organization plays a very critical factor in the overall success of the project. As the scope of the work was 472 villages in 5 districts, laying a strong foundation was essential. Hiring is one of the most important processes in an organization, great people deliver great services, deliver great results, and eventually build a great organization. As simple as it sounds, doing it right in the rural setting in emerging economies is incredibly difficult. The Smart Village core team had a mammoth task of hiring employees given the time constraint of the project. As per the signed MoU, the allocation of the funds for the organizational structure and running was in accordance with the above figure. Involving highest government officials and politicians in the organizational structure was designed for establishing a clear accountability structure for the project. Direct reporting and monitoring were intended to be accomplished to assure easy communication and high commitment for the vision from both sides. However, there were many challenges in this regard as highlighted in part 4.

After the successful completion of Phase 1 with a small team, there was a high fluctuation of participating core team members. Effective advertising and social media campaign attracted enthusiastic applicants to the project to hire new talents. The main focus was on hiring candidates with passion and aspiration to contribute to rural development. Cultural diversity was emphasized and applicants from various fields were considered. In the following, the development of the organization and its unique requirements for operating in 472 villages in rural India is explained in detail.

General Work Values for Participants

Being the Smart Village organization built from scratch and operating with a novel approach in the tough setting of rural India, special values are required from employees. Lean and agile work methodologies are of utmost importance as the project operates in a very dynamic way where job roles and responsibilities change fast. Moreover, dynamic capabilities to adapt to the very fast changing environment is required.[4] Having a lot of independence for work, relations within the organization need to be built on trust to ensure efficient outcomes. Moreover, bringing together mindsets from different cultures and countries, conflict resolution and high tolerance is important. Lastly, innovation requires out of-the-box thinkers who aspire to disrupt existing models with new approaches and technologies rather than copying existing models and technologies. Intrinsic motivation is a major success factor to drive the project to success.

Establishing the Core Team

Building the core team was the most challenging hire as the project's progress and achievement of the milestones along the way was dependent on the quality of the core team – their knowledge, skills, competence, attitude, and aptitude. The following approach was followed for recruitment throughout the Smart Village recruitment drive.

The working scope of the Smart Village required professionals with expertise in various selected sectors. As there was the inclusion of 9 different verticals, efficient hiring of professionals in those areas was needed to ensure the optimization of human resources. Moreover, 5 district directors were needed to manage operations district wise. The need for a data scientist, web developer, corporate relations expert, and research expert was also realized. Beyond passive recruitment via job posts, the hiring staff also looked for qualified candidates via LinkedIN, social media, and industry events. This was done to ensure some applications from potential candidates who were not actively searching for new jobs but who may have been perfect for the role were received. The main focus was on applicants' experience, skills, work history, and most important on the personal fit for the project. This project demands high flexibility and adaptability as it is much like a Startup. Moreover, the operations are happening on-ground in rural India – some might say innovating in disastrous and highly difficult conditions. This especially demands extreme adaptability from people outside rural India, as well as a great passion to sustain in such conditions.

Before, during, and after interviews, applicants were tested on their understanding of the project, communication skills, presentation skills, and various other soft skills. Certain topics were assigned to evaluate their knowledge for the applied position. Ultimately, the core team got finalized based on their fit to the required criteria. However, two core team members came into the project in a very unconventional way – Werner Fischer and Arun Sharma.

"When I was attending Professor Darwin's lecture in Berkeley learning about Smart Villages I was immediately fascinated by his vision. As he eventually reached out to me saying, Werner, you should join this project in India, my recruitment was almost finalized. Four weeks later I was sitting on a plane to India and my great journey began. It is all about channelizing someone's passion and interests in the right manner, which I clearly could do with that project!"

Werner Fischer, Former Research Director SVM
and Research Scholar at UC Berkeley

"Getting accepted to the 42 Silicon Valley coding school program at the Paris campus determined my promising career in the field of computer science for the upcoming years – my plane tickets were booked and apartment in Paris was arranged. I was about to leave India for this relevant opportunity when a good friend of my family told me about the Smart Village project, I immediately got the gut

feeling to explore this further. Instead of complaining about things which are going wrongly in my country, I now faced the unique and wonderful chance to apply my gained knowledge to change the future of my country with an approach, which was never done before. It happened that I cancelled all my Paris plans, revolted against my parents, who were really happy with my Paris plans and took upon the endeavour of living and working in the remote rural areas of Andhra Pradesh, which seemed to me like a foreign country compared to New Delhi. It was all worth it seeing the impact we are creating.

— Arun Sharma, Former Lead Architect of SVM platform,
Data Analyst and Business Model Expert

After finalizing the core team, Professor Darwin trained the team on important concepts like Open Innovation, ecosystem approach, triple helix, and lean startup methodology. Team building measurements had been conducted and the team was prepared to hire the remaining people needed in this phase 2, operating in 472 villages. Overall, all core team members gained unique tactic knowledge and expertise for rural development in emerging economies through business model innovation.

Hiring of the Mandal Directors

In order to manage operations in all given provinces (in the following: Mandals) from five districts, Mandal Directors needed to be hired, which followed the same approach as hiring the core team. Therefore, the hiring was handed over to the new core team to ensure compatibility in the organization. Being that the Mandal Directors were managers for interns from villages belonging to respective Mandals, the emphasis was given on communication and management skills. Requirements deviated slightly, as the job role was focused on on-ground operations. Therefore, high acceptance to stay on-ground was required as well as understanding the local situation and culture. Persons coming from Andhra Pradesh were preferred as the cultural match was a key success factor when operating in rural Andhra Pradesh. Again, training by the core team for the 34 recruited Mandal Directors and guidance throughout the hiring process for village interns were given. Mandal Directors were mainly managing respective interns regarding data collection, technology implementation or awareness campaigns, but were also to explore solutions for experienced pain points, reaching out to companies and proposing their concept to the core team. This was great support for the project.

Hiring of the Village Interns

The organization was designed in a way that one intern per village is present to understand the ground realities, to realize research through surveys, and to communicate to local communities. Village interns have therefore been the backbone of the project and were hired from the respective villages, taking responsibility for their villages and acting as a bridge between the village and the Smart Village organization. Moreover, a good and trusting relationship ensured robust and authentic data collection. Mandal Directors along with consultation from the District Directors hired village interns for the villages under their respective mandals. Being the on-ground force, the efficient flow of knowledge to the core team played an instrumental role in the success of the project. The requirements for village interns covered passion, basic technological knowledge, proficiency in local language and communication, and lastly, assistance in the implementation of technology according to the Open Innovation Framework. Over 500 interns were hired.

"Our responses to recruitment really showed the willingness of this generation to step out of city life, sacrifice comforts and move to villages to serve rural communities. They understand the vision and believe that this is the time to break certain barriers through disruptive technologies."

– Shreya Evani, Former Project Director Smart Village Movement

CHAPTER 9
HOW TO DEVELOP THE DATABASE FOR UNLOCKING NEW VALUE

Collecting reliable data from the ground is critical for understanding precisely the village dynamics and occurring pain points to eventually extract this information for multiple purposes effectively. Succeeding here requires an adequate process to collect data, which is explained along with emphasizing the value of data for innovating in rural emerging economies in the following.

Data is one of the most important and vital aspects of any research study. Moreover, it provides eventually the evidence-based foundation for decision making regarding political, economic ecological, and social aspects. From understanding the pain points to laying the foundation of the project plan to defining the scope of work to consulting corporates on viable business models, data has been essential everywhere in this project. Operating in rural Andhra Pradesh stressed the need for collecting authentic data as there wasn't enough detailed and specific information available regarding the village situation in terms of needs and areas to be improved within the smart village scope. The Smart Village project relied extensively on primary data; 38 surveys were conducted in Andhra Pradesh for various tasks like pain point evaluation, business model validation, and exploring new economic opportunities.

The project initiated its research based on secondary data available from government departments, agencies, and other sources. SLAP data was also integrated for setting up the foundation for further research. Lack of secondary and untrustworthy available data, however, emphasized again the importance of collecting primary data.

Door-to-door surveys on the before mentioned sectors were conducted to assess and evaluate the status quo. The surveyed audience under the data collection process comprised of various age groups, occupations, caste, religion, geographical regions, and mixed backgrounds. Randomization took place. A village footprint has been created (see exhibit 14) when leveraging relevant collected data.

Exhibit 14 – Examples for the Village Footprint – Compared to District Level and Prospective Growth

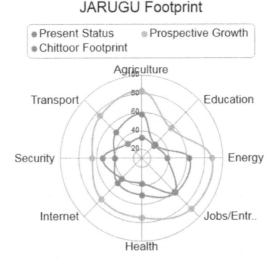

JARUGU Footprint

Moreover, existing assets in each village have been geo-tagged and made available online to everyone. The detailed village footprint design can be requested and is not being further described in this book since being beyond the scope of this book.[1] A high-level overview of the collected data is as the following:

- Demographic Data
    - Age, Sex, Education Level, Marital Status, Occupation etc.
    - Complementing consensus data with updated data/ missing data
- Sector-wise Data
    - To form the basis for the definition of the scope of work (sector-wise) initially
    - To understand the status-quo, e.g. in Agriculture
    - To validate the acceptance level and adoption levels of digital technologies
    - To conduct in-depth research through scientific theoretical models, e.g. How digital transformation in small family business in rural Andhra Pradesh effects entrepreneurship
- Business Model Specific Data
    - Primary & Secondary data to formulate business models
    - Feedback collection from the ground on proposed business models to validate the feasibility
    - To discover the scope of businesses in the villages
- Satisfaction Level
    - On-ground feedback on existing policies and the status of various sectors/policies
    - To analyze the public perception on various issues & challenges

- Awareness Level
  - o Acquaintance of villagers with various existing policies/schemes/technologies
  - o To specifically target subject for the awareness drives & campaigns
- Socio-Economic Data
- Village Asset Data

The overall quantitative data collection was facilitated by the 500 village interns on-ground using digital tools for collecting and uploading the data. The Smart Village team at the village level visited door to door conducting surveys and collecting data. Randomization took place within the pool of people being asked for their relevant feedback. The survey design was mainly done for providing descriptive and normative outcomes, however, empirical, cause-and-effect research design, was applied when needed, e.g. for academic purposes. Therefore, based on the developed theoretical research model, variables have been derived from existing research, providing robust data and being able to generalize and compare results within the research set and beyond. In all research appliances, mixed methods have been applied to design surveys in the most effective way. Therefore, quantitative data has been completed with qualitative data. Initially, focus groups have been thus defined and through interviews via open-ended questions, the context was ensured. If needed, this was repeated throughout the whole innovation process. For example, government departments and companies have been leveraged for stakeholder validation. Moreover, this approach made it easier to understand the given context and research outcomes, although not being statistically representative. Pretesting of the surveys in a small sample was critical for the overall feasibility of the objected survey design.

After the validation, the survey was pushed to the village interns and door-to-door surveys were conducted. The data was collected through the web application created by the in-house software development team. Once the village interns completed the survey, it was securely submitted on the server. Measures were taken to prevent the loss of the data due to technical glitches, thus multiple copies of the collected data were made in multiple local machines. After successful submission and storage, the data was further analyzed by the Data Analysts and was made available to all given stakeholders.

Data Collection Process

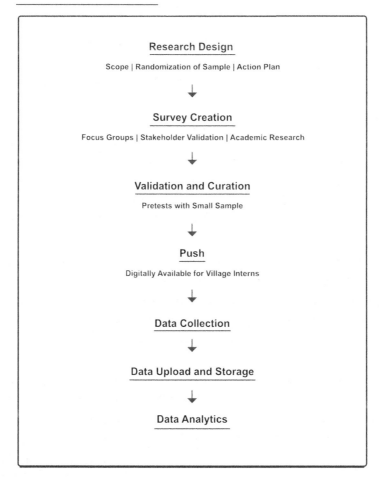

Research Design

Scope | Randomization of Sample | Action Plan

↓

Survey Creation

Focus Groups | Stakeholder Validation | Academic Research

↓

Validation and Curation

Pretests with Small Sample

↓

Push

Digitally Available for Village Interns

↓

Data Collection

↓

Data Upload and Storage

↓

Data Analytics

The Smart Village team conducted 38 surveys on-ground to that date, taking into consideration the responses from more than 100,000 respondents/rural population.

Moreover, village profile reports have been created to consolidate the collected data from the ground with existing demographic data from local authorities. Ultimately, existing infrastructure, a financial and social balance sheet, basic demographics and village specific dynamics in terms of key influential people, brand & cultural heritage and existing barriers to innovation have been elaborated.

Extending the project to another state in India – Arunachal Pradesh in the mid of 2018 came with new challenges for the objected data collection respectively. One of the major flaws was reliance on internet connectivity for it to operate. The new platform leverages mobile technologies to operate in areas with zero connectivity and captures data efficiently. The data collection module will now be available on the web as well as mobile application user interface. Major enhancements have been made also to the data collection process as migrating the survey design (questionnaire curation) from an offline to an online process, improving collaborative work between the stakeholders.

The analysis and the representation of the data have also been automated, the platform is equipped with functionalities to perform certain statistical tests leveraging statistical packages. Using data visualization libraries like D3.JS, capabilities to turn raw data into informative visuals have also been added.

With the start of the Smart Village program in Meghalaya in 2019, villages were selected with a random factor in the first place. Compared to previous initiatives where mostly political motives determined the selection of villages, the Meghalaya Government created a pool of 500 villages that qualify for the Smart Village program, e.g. have basic internet connectivity. Among this pool, randomization took place by UC Berkeley ensuring a non-biased selection of villages. It is this aspect that vastly improved the academic research approach. Since the pool was large enough and selection without any political bias, a treatment group and control group could be realized. 50 villages that got selected as the treatment group would be used to implement pilots. In contrast, 50 villages that got selected as the control group would be used to control the generated impact of initiatives from the treatment group.

CHAPTER 10

HOW TO EXECUTE THE SMART VILLAGE IDEA WITH AN OPEN INNOVATION FRAMEWORK

A central part of the philosophy to pursue the idea of creating Smart Villages is letting the private sector tap into emerging markets in a village setting. In this chapter, the framework and manual on how innovation can effectively happen in rural markets is explained.

A recent study from Price Water Corporations (2017)[1] emphasizes that in general, corporates need to enhance several critical capabilities to win in emerging markets. First, aiming for operational efficiency is crucial, which comes with flexible business strategies and efficient supply chains through technology and local partnerships. Second, Innovation capability is required to find new ways to reach untapped markets and to design localized products for consumers of emerging markets. Therefore, the respective innovation process needs to be executed in a stepwise and continuous way. Third, having go-to-market excellence is required to let companies adapt to evolving consumer trends and maturing business environments. This enables a significant presence across multiple channels and price points. Furthermore, this requires new technologies or sales channels, as part of an eco-system of partners that "includes crosssector players, public sector entities, and social sector units"[2]. In fact, it is necessary to develop a strong organization and ecosystem with local entrepreneurship and companies. Fourth and last, the needs of people are complex, are rapidly changing and differ from region to region or village to village. Thus, companies have to be on the ground to tap fully into diverse, unpredictable markets. In the end, best practices should be cross-shared globally.[3]

The following Open Innovation Framework for Rural Emerging Markets, executed since mid-2016, addresses all these factors and beyond. It builds on several research-based methodologies, such as *Open Innovation, lean startup,* and *business model canvas* as well as on continuous learnings and research from ongoing practice.

Introduction to the Healthcare Case Example

One example of applying the Open Innovation Framework for Emerging Rural Markets comes from the healthcare sector in rural south India. It is commonly known that there are serious problems in Indian healthcare. Reports show that the density of all doctors (allopathic, ayurvedic, homeopathic and Unani) at the national level was only 80 doctors per 100,000 population com-pared to e.g. 130 in China in 2016. In fact, the doctor-patient ratio in India is at a shocking ratio of 1: 1,700. Moreover, 80% of Indian doctors are located in urban areas serving only 28% of the populace.[4] This endangers the rural areas in India drastically. An innovative way to address such disastrous conditions needs to be approached to provide adequate healthcare in the village setting. The following case shows how the Smart Village initiative success-fully developed a model to overcome this situation when applying the Open Innovation Framework for Emerging Rural Markets. It refers to the different respective phases and stages from the framework.

To better understand the rural healthcare scenario, several forms of health workers are explained who emerged in the village setting over time to compensate for the scarcity of doctors. The following are the most prominent types.

ANM (Auxiliary Nursing Midwifery): Grassroots workers in the health organization pyramid. ANMs run health Sub-centers, which are village level healthcare facilities for the community working under a Primary Health Center (PHC). Based on the population, each PHC will have 5 to 10 sub-centers. One ANM looks after 5,000 people through a sub-center. ANMs are expected to be multi-purpose health workers. ANM-related work includes maternal and child health along with family planning services, health and nutrition education, efforts for maintaining environmental sanitation, immunization for the control of communicable diseases, treatment of minor injuries, and first aid in emergencies and disasters. The provided services are cost-free as part of Primary Healthcare, which is run by the Government in India.

ASHA (Accredited Social Health Activist): Community health workers who visit each household to advocate preventative healthcare in general and to deliver basic medicines (mostly preventive measures). ASHA workers serve mainly as a proxy for the ANMs since it is difficult for an ANM to reach 5,000 residents every day. Moreover, they ensure that patients go to the Primary Health Center (PHC) when necessary. They are mostly focused on childcare and maternal health. ASHA workers are less qualified than ANMs. Their offered service is cost-free.

RMP (Rural Medical Practitioner): People, who are practicing without a medical qualification and charging for their services. It is a violation of law as it is illegal to practice healthcare without having a license. Moreover, the abbreviation RMP actually means

Registered Medical Practitioner. To hold such a title, a Bachelor of Medicine and Bachelor of Surgery (MBBS) degree is required. This term evolved due to the high presence in villages in the form of Rural Medical Practitioner. To this date, the government has no clear strategy to address this issue.

"As we started interacting with villagers and local politicians we noticed the seriousness of the bad situation in the Indian health sector. The idea of this healthcare model started with the question, is it possible for the remaining 20% of the doctors to address the needs of 72% of the Indian population that lives in rural settings?

We came to an understanding that this can only be achieved by strengthening the existing system by equipping the rural healthcare workers with advanced technologies and imparting knowledge and skills needed to leverage on technological advancements from the healthcare Industry. Our journey began and it showed me what innovative ways along with technology can achieve to benefit society."

– Venkat Krishna Kagga, Former Smart Village Fellow

Exhibit 15 – Applied Open Innovation Framework

Open Innovation Framework for Rural Emerging Markets

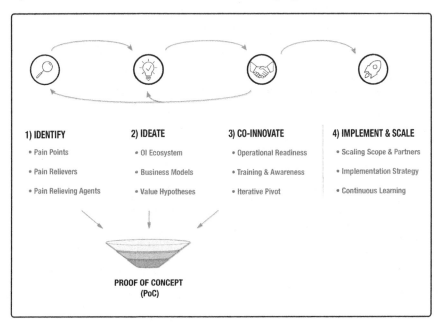

The Open Innovation Framework for Rural Emerging Markets provides a dynamic process to innovate in rural emerging markets, considering the unique setting and various prevalent challenges. The framework was developed by Werner Fischer and Solomon Darwin with advice from Henry Chesbrough and is being applied since 2017.

Phase 1: IDENTIFY

The first phase in the Open Innovation Framework for Emerging Rural Markets comprises identifying relevant local pain points, identifying solutions to these pain points, and identifying corporations or other agents which offer specialized solutions. Within this phase, a clear sequence is not required nor recommended, as the micro and macro environment keeps changing in an utmost dynamic way and all three pillars are mutually depending on each other. An iterative and dynamic process is therefore recommended.

1.1 Identify Pain Points

In order to identify prevalent pain points on the village level, it takes multiple efforts to obtain an objective analysis. First, incorporation of existing demographic data from e.g. the public sector helps to assess the general situation of a specific country, state, and specific area. For Andhra Pradesh, the annual socio-economic survey, provided by the government of Andhra Pradesh, presented relevant insights about the general situation of the state. Second, local government authorities are a great source of information. Merging existing research and insights with its database is crucial to prevent redundant work. However, collected data from local bureaucrats need to be evaluated in terms of objectiveness and correctness. Research methodologies from local sources might not fulfill quality standards or might be biased. Third, evaluating and incorporating existing national and international research on rural people's pain points addresses research gaps and helps to better understand the given situation. In fact, different countries often face similar problems, and therefore, it is important to accumulate information and knowledge from a broad spectrum. Fourth, conducting general surveys on prevalent pain points builds the in-depth foundation of the overall research. Covering needs in different relevant sectors provides a broad spectrum where innovation can improve the respective economic and social situation. A general footprint survey, which covers 9 defined verticals, was conducted throughout the assigned five districts of Andhra Pradesh. Over 40,000 households were asked to provide their valuable feedback about their perception regarding prevailing pain points.

Fifth and last, on-ground community interaction gives a voice to the people to express their needs and sorrows. Continuous events in various sectors (e.g. agriculture) via focus group interviews can novel insights but and an understanding of the priority of specific needs concerning to other pain points. Community interaction is a prominent part of the Smart Village research to get valid and straightforward feedback.

Identifying pain points is an ongoing and essential process. It lays the foundation for all further innovation-related activities. Moreover, it serves as a database for companies to ensure that their solutions meet specific pain points. The provision of in-depth research about people's needs guarantees a customer-centered innovation design. However, this research requires to be routine enhancement with new information to address changing behavior, evolving consumer trends, and shifting complex consumer needs.

Finally, the identified pain points should relate to valid business opportunities for offering scale and relevance to solution providers, such as startups and corporations. When having identified that millet farmers in Arunachal Pradesh are exploited by middlemen and not having the option to add value to their raw materials, such as producing healthy millet bars, reaching out to Nestle confirmed that millet farmers' challenges also translate to a huge business opportunity. Nestle stated that healthy nutrition is a core business to them and organic, healthy millet bars would be a huge market within their scope. Therefore, connecting pain points to business opportunities ensures relevance to the private sector and accelerates participation and market readiness.

Establishing such a knowledge database ultimately serves beyond enabling successful innovations in the rural sector. It can support the public sector to better frame policies and create an indepth understanding of the urgent rural needs by deriving novel research findings when applied academically.

Healthcare Case Example

Identify/Stage 1: Pain Points

1. Limited Access to Healthcare

a) Village setting is characterized by 1 doctor for around 1,700 people (optimal: one per 400 people)
b) Low presence of private hospitals; are located far away
c) Inefficient process itself is time-consuming (no proper system for appointments)

2. Unaffordable HQ Treatment

a) Rural people cannot afford treatment from private hospitals
b) Need to rely on cost-free treatment from government hospitals, which lack quality, and unqualified rural healthcare workers

3. Lack of Accountability. Risky & Dangerous Treatment

a) Rural Medical Practitioners (RMPs) are primary source for villagers and are not certified healthcare workers (illegal)
b) High acceptance through easy access and large availability; treatment at door step (90% presence in villages)
c) Risky Treatment due to missing qualification and incentive to earn more money (e.g. wrong diagnosis)
d) Missing accountability leads to repetitive or wrong treatment

4. Missing Quality and Efficiency in rural Healthcare Sector

Sources:

- Derived from experiences working in the healthcare sector since 2016 and from a survey conducted in Andhra Pradesh in 2017, where over 6,000 villagers were asked regarding healthcare. Outcomes include:
  1) 25% go to Government Hospitals, 55% to RMPs, 20% to Private Hospitals
  2) People choosing RMPs are mainly satisfied with this service (15% rather satisfied, 44% neutral satisfied)
  3) However, 76% of people using RMPs want to use suggested Cloud Physician Model
  4) 8% have low satisfaction, 40% rather low satisfaction, 44% neutral satisfaction, 16% rather high satisfaciton and 2% high satisfaction with existing medical system.

- 2016 report from KMPG and the Organization of Pharmaceutical Producers in India (OPPI)

1.2 Identify Pain Relievers

Ultimately, there is no defined path for identifying needed pain relievers. New thinking of horizontal innovation, where various expertise or resources from different domains can converge, new business methodologies like the Open Innovation paradigm and lastly, new dynamic capabilities can ultimately foster identifying the right solutions.

Knowing specific pain points provides detailed insights into various sectors (e.g. healthcare). It reveals gaps to be addressed. Therefore, analyzed pain relievers need to be identified with respect to innovative processes, technologies, and approaches for combining several human and capital resources from multiple parties. Considering that innovation needs to come from a perspective of vertical innovation rather than from horizontal innovation is hereby significant. This comprises creating something new, learning from many sources and having no particular formula for innovation. By contrast, repeating what was done before and copying best practices (vertical innovation) ultimately does not lead to transformational or disruptive innovation which are required to provide high value and low-cost solutions for rural markets.

When identifying the right technologies, processes and resources, new thinking needs to be considered. In fact, this process lays the foundation for creating an Open Innovation ecosystem to combine and consolidate identified pain relievers for end-to-end solutions. It is critical to developing dynamic capabilities for adequately reacting to external changes and changing environments when integrating, building, and reconfiguring internal and external competencies[5]. Moreover, such abilities help to orchestrate deployment and redeployment of resources to successfully execute the innovation process

Healthcare Case Example
Identify/Stage 2: Pain Relievers

In order to address the gap of qualified doctors in the rural setting (Primary Healthcare), new methods needed to be explored. However, rural healthcare workers are already there, but qualification and experience to provide needed quality treatment is missing. Moreover, many rural health workers are illegal. The classical telemedicine approach, where patients talk to doctors online, needs to be enhanced with technology and innovative processes to integrate rural health workers. High quality medical services for rural patients must to be offered with a holistic approach to address given pain points; **Access, Affordability, Accountability and Quality.** The following technologies, resources and processes were identified when considering the horizontal innovation thinking, the open innovation ecosystem methodology and the dynamic capability approach.

_____

1. Needed Innovative Technology

Digital platform to connect available doctors with patients; Technology to equip rural healthcare workers:
a) Cloud platform to efficiently connect doctors with patients
b) Cloud platform to anchor rural healthcare workers with verified cloud physicians to provide high quality treatment at doorsteps
c) Cloud platform to connect medical equipment to capture data and to ensure transparency
d) Cloud platform to capture diagnosis data from the lab
e) Portable medical equipment to do basic diagnosis and capture basic vitals

2. Needed Resources

a) Medical Service Provider: Lab to perform tests to provide diagnosis (with connectivity to the cloud)
b) Human Resources: Rural healthcare workers (legal status) with decent knowledge to perform tests and execute and communicate given advice; certified doctors to act as cloud physicians; platform owner and manager
c) Equipment: Portable equipment (ECG, Glucometer, Blood pressure), Smartphone or Computer with decent network connectivity to ensure Audio/Video consultation with the cloud physician

---

3. Needed Processes

a) Peer-to-peer process to bring together supply and demand (appointment system or call center)
b) Rural health workers need to be fully anchored in the system to ensure absence of mistreatments and to guarantee quality and accountability
c) Technology equipped and anchored rural healthcare workers to provide high quality and transparent medical services at patient's doorstep (at low costs)
d) Medical equipment to connect to the cloud platform through an application
e) Data capturing and electronic medical records (EMRs) created
f) Data sharing throughout the whole process with relevant stakeholders (secondary and tertiary healthcare)
g) Consultation, diagnosis and getting the right treatment and medicine need to be transparent and reliable

---

1.3 Identify Pain Relieving Agents

When aiming to identify suitable partner companies, both approaches like proactive search and leveraging the existing network can be applied. When acquiring new partner companies, certain partner criteria need to be considered to assess the suitability of collaboration within the targeted ecosystem. The Smart Village project acts as the facilitator and consultant for innovation activities and organizations in such positions are acting as knowledge brokers for establishing co-innovation efforts.

For an effective collaboration process, Emden et al. (2006) identify three factors to address when aiming to collaborate for innovation: relational, technological, and strategic alignment. Within compatible cultures, relational alignment ensures better conflict management and mutual alignment towards common goals (partner compatibility). Secondly, technological alignment requires unique expertise from each partner including complementary skills, resources, and assets (partner expertise and partner complementary). Lastly, strategic alignment requires correspondent motivations for collaborative activities. This refers to reliability based on a commitment to developing collaborative partnerships (partner reliability).[6]

Ultimately, partner criteria are critical for establishing Open Innovation ecosystems to tap into rural markets. Extreme conditions in the village setting require special alignment and commitment from participating companies as the overall prevalent situation is very likely to change. E.g. shifting consumer needs and consumer behavior or external alterations like policy changes. Consequently, the knowledge broker (Smart Village team) needs to ensure that strategic alignment is high among collaborating partners. Moreover, to guarantee the successful and efficient execution of the Open Innovation approach, and technological alignment with respect to unique partner expertise and partner complementarity as well as relational alignment in terms of compatible partner culture are needed. Therefore, the knowledge partner has to screen potential partners with these criteria in relation to other partners among the targeted ecosystem.

Healthcare Case Example
Identify/Stage 3: Solution Providers

After identifying the solutions to address given pain points, several solution providers were identified. Leveraging suitable companies from the existing corporate partner network enabled bringing in latest, innovative Silicon Valley technologies (Cosine Labs and Coherent Med). However, a proactive approach to acquire missing solution providers was needed. Therefore, several eligible companies were identified and negotiations were started. Based on the above-mentioned criteria, Cosine Labs, MedTel and cloudphysician.net were selected.

1. Cosine Labs

- US-based startup to provide the cloud platform (SaaS)
- Catalyst for Indian Partners (investment and consultancy)

2. MedTel

- IT Development to deliver all services seamlessly
- Equipment and needed resources (strips etc.) provider

3. Cloudphysician.net, KIMS & MedTel

- Cloud Physician Communites of certified doctors

4. Academia

- UC Berkeley
- Students from KIMS Hospital to consult project

Phase 2: IDEATE

Identifying pain points, pain relievers and fitting solution providers lays the foundation for ideating innovative ways to merge and consolidate given pain-relieving agents. Therefore, an Open Innovation ecosystem approach is applied. Moreover, the concept of shared value is implemented, where all participating actors and stakeholders benefit when companies optimize financial and social goals. Also, the concept of triple helix is part of this ideation philosophy. The concept of triple helix concept is also part of this ideation philosophy – it refers to the essential inclusion of the public and private sectors along with academia to provide the most efficient solution as these sectors are depending on each other.

Moreover, the process of ideating is dynamic and iterative. This framework builds on the lean startup approach, which continuously ensures customer-centricity and concept evaluation.

2.1 Ideate an Open Innovation Ecosystem

Creating and delivering new products, services or technologies requires business model innovation via co-development to significantly reduce R&D expenses, to expand the outputs from innovation, and to tap into new markets that have otherwise been inaccessible. Possible objectives can be 1. increase profitability (by lowering costs), 2. shorten time to market (by incorporating already-developed components or subsystems), 3. enhance innovation capability (by increasing the number and variety of front-end technologies), 4. create greater flexibility in R&D (by risk-sharing with partners) and 5. expand market access (by broadening pathways to market for products and services). Chesbrough and Schwartz (2007) state in that context that defining such business objectives for partnering is critical for designing an Open Innovation business model that leverages co-development partnerships.[7] When acting as a knowledge broker, organizations (like the Smart Village project), which orchestrate Open Innovation ecosystems, need to hence clearly define the business objectives along with the participating companies from the beginning of this ideation phase. The applied Minimum Viable Ecosystem (MVE) builds on the participation of key actors, who complement each other to bring ideas to the testing ground and eventually to markets in a lean and effective way.

In general, ecosystems tend to prevent cost aggregation and timeinefficiency for the customers since end-to-end solutions are delivered to the customer instead of having isolated and sometimes redundant solutions. In fact, end-to-end solutions not only reduce costs and time inefficiency but also diminish the complexity of operating when offering a central interface to the customer instead of multiple needed products and services. Competing companies and complementary industry sectors therefore converge to provide unique customer solutions. Such ecosystems are difficult to imitate, which leads to competitive advantages and a diversified product and service portfolio from individual companies when combining their expertise, knowledge and, resources.[8]

Having identified solutions for given pain points and defined business objectives, it is then about ideating the aimed ecosystem by consolidating given technology, processes, and resources from different actors. Despite having a crucial orchestrator and knowledge broker, participating companies need to start building relationships with each other, ideating the ecosystem design, and discussing the way forward. It is crucial to design the processes collaboratively in detail for all participating actors (see case example). It is recommended that all parties co-ideate the ecosystem mutually and simultaneously. First attempts for prototypes (Minimal Viable Products[9]) and negotiations for revenue, risk, and IP sharing can emerge among this early ideation phase. Such efforts can spur commitment and alignment among all participating actors to guarantee a successful project.

To ensure overall acceptance and feasibility, feedback from all stakeholders needs to be collected. Especially when innovating in the rural settings of emerging economies, it is recommended to integrate the government in this ideation stage to assess the practicality of the ecosystem design with respect to legal and regulatory aspects as well as potential collaboration opportunities. Moreover, feedback from directly affected actors, e.g. service providers using co-developed solutions, needs to be collected. This can be done by product tests (in case there is a prototype available, e.g. MVP) or by feedback surveys. Ultimately, the response from the end consumers is critical for the overall traction and success (through e.g. surveys). In fact, applying build-measure-learn iterations as a part of the dynamic character of this Open Innovation framework is significant to create first ideation results. It facilitates and guarantees a process where ideas are turned into products, where consumer response is collected. It also ensures a step-wise evaluation, whether changes are needed or if continuing one's strategy seems promising.[10]

Ideating an Open Innovation ecosystem (or MVE) is a process that takes many iterations and feedback collection efforts. It builds the foundation for the value creation for all participating actors as well as for the end-consumers. Therefore, knowledge and information gained in this stage prepare participating companies for developing their proprietary business models and for deriving the shared value creation. Ultimately, this design needs to be turned into working prototypes to extensively test and ultimately achieve a Proof of Concept (PoC) for further implementation and scaling.

Healthcare Case Example

IDEATE/Stage 1: Open Innovation Ecosystem

To address given multiple pain points from primary healthcare in the rural set-ting, a digital platform is needed, which links all required resources (medical equipment and labs) and actors (cloud physicians, rural healthcare workers and patients) to provide a holistic solution. When equipping rural healthcare workers with portable medical equipment and anchoring them with verified cloud physicians, high quality and affordable treatment can be delivered at a patients' doorstep. Data collection and sharing throughout the whole process ensures transparency and improves the overall efficiency. Electronic Medical Records are available for relevant actors beyond primary healthcare (with patient's consent).

Providing a holistic solution for given pain points requires an Open Innovation Ecosystem approach. All identified pain relievers and respective agents, such as detected technologies, needed resources and necessary processes from different stakeholders are therefore consolidated. The ecosystem design itself is capable to create unique value beyond the isolated solution's value. Moreover, it accelerates the innovation process extremely when converging complementary expertise, resources and technologies.

Patient's Journey within the Healthcare Ecosystem

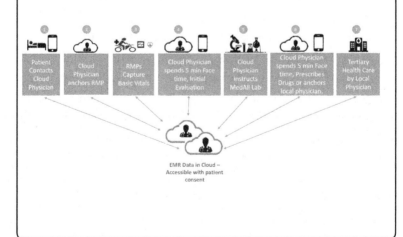

Open Innovation Ecosystem Design

1. **Customer Participation.** All needed services (consultation, diagnosis, treatment and medicine) are offered under one umbrella.
2. **Health Worker Participation.** Equipped with digital, advanced technologies to deliver services with required quality and accountability at patient's doorstep
3. **Cloud Physician Participation.** Connected with the cloud platform to best utilize their time and to advise and anchor health workers with support of data.
4. **Corporate Participation.**
   a. Cosine Labs and MedTel collaborate to develop cloud platform
   b. MedTel to provide healthcare equipment, translate analyzed data into common language (e.g. ECG) and provide diagnosis via given equipment
5. **Smart Village Participation.** Central Orchestrator and Knowledge Broker. Organizing and identifying participating health workers on ground; driving public awareness
   a. Conducting Training
   b. Facilitating bureaucracy clearance
   c. Facilitating overall innovation process

Design Process

The ecosystem design was co-developed and co-designed with the participating corporate partners. Their expertise and broad experience in their respective domains and fields helped to ideate this ecosystem in a lean and fast way. The smart village team acted mainly as the orchestrator within these efforts. To enable a hassle-free development process, all partners agreed on general terms and conditions regarding the needed IT infrastructure. A rough draft about economics was agreed on that all parties fully committed to move the initiative forward.

Direct feedback regarding this design was collected from rural health workers and potential patients to assure first hand acceptance and demand for the model. Moreover, a general survey was conducted to validate the ecosystem design among the population of 472 villages in Andhra Pradesh. Over 6,000 data points were collected. The response was overall positive and emphasized the need and relevance for this solution.

First talks with Government helped to understand their perspective on how to complement the existing system and to develop the ecosystem in a way which aligns with the legal framework and objectives from the government.

2.2 Ideate Business Models

After designing the Open Innovation ecosystem, every participating actor is required to develop an individual business model, which aligns with the ecosystem. However, there are critical aspects to follow. Every party needs a guarantee to sustain its overall business model, and it needs to have incentives to apply Open Innovation. An orchestrater is crucial for achieving consensus, alignment, and commitment among the actors. Therefore, the following steps are recommended.

Classifying R&D Capabilities

The decision to partner externally has different implications and requires strategic (or various) management approaches. Therefore, R&D capabilities need to be classified to formulate effective codevelopment structures.

Exhibit 16 – Co-Development Partnerships and Required Capabilities (Chesbrough and Schwartz 2007)[11]

Partnership Attributes	Core Capabilities	Critical Capabilities	Contextual Capabilities
Partner Role	Vital; utilize in-house R&D or very select strategic partners	Important, but not core to overall business	Necessary but not value-adding; develop multiple sources capability
Number of Partners	None or very few	Small number	Safety in numbers
Depth of relationship	Deep	Medium	Low

Contingency Plan	Best to develop yourself; recruit strategic R&D supplier if needed	Partner on win-win basis; align business models; go in-house only as last resort	Switch to another partner if one partner is not performing

Core capabilities refer to key sources for distinctive advantages and value creation of companies. When co-developing and leveraging these core capabilities, they need to be managed closely and shared carefully. In fact, only after an extensive strategic analysis, business enterprises should take on developing a business model which shares their core capabilities. Reducing risk can involve partnership arrangements with equity investment or even an acquisition.

Critical capabilities are not in reference to a company's core capabilities but are critical to the offered products and services. Value propositions of a company can be easily expanded when enhancing its own business with such capabilities. Business models leveraging critical capabilities therefore can create new value without investing drastically in R&D.

Contextual capabilities are able to complement a partner's core business and are not critical for its own business as these have little impact on its own value-added, albeit completing the offerings. Sharing of such capabilities are very likely.[12] Ultimately, participating companies need to assess their capabilities, which they aim to share, in terms of how critical these are for their overall success. Moreover, assessment of the other business models with respect to the different capabilities is required at the same time. Given the ecosystem design, the knowledge broker is then to orchestrate these efforts as the foundation for further business model development and the co-innovation management.

Individual Business Model Development & Optimizing the Resource Distribution

When designing the individual business models for all participating actors, the orchestrator and knowledge broker needs to ensure overall alignment & commitment from all parties for the Open Innovation ecosystem. Building upon the *Want, Find, Get, Manage Model* from Slowinski and Sagal (2010)[13] for executing Open Innovation systems, the knowledge broker along with assigned parties can optimize the distribution of resources and assets among all actors to achieve needed commitment and alignment. Therefore, from individual perspectives, the following approach is to be followed.

Questions to be answered for orchestrating individual corporate partner's resources:

"What are the resource needs?"
"Which ones should be developed internally?"
"Which should we find externally?"

In order to address these questions, identified pain points and resulting pain relievers serve as a reference point to determine clearly what resources are needed. The ecosystem design already gives an overall picture of how the value can be delivered to the customer. In order to derive the particular business models for all companies, the following equation helps the orchestrator and the individual businesses to effectively balance needed resources among the targeted ecosystem.

Exhibit 17 – Equation for Distribution Optimization: Make/Buy/ Collaborate

Fulfilled Customer Needs / Pain Points (C) =
Internal Asset Base (A) + Externally Available Resources (E)

In order to meet the overall determined objective of fulfilling given pain points (**C**), the individual equation of each actor is being freed from the constraints of its own existing capabilities through externally available resources (**E**). Due to the ecosystem design, organizational openness is required when integrating externally available resources (**E**) and sharing internal assets (**A**). The classification of resources in terms of core, critical, and contextual characteristics (see above) is crucial for this process. This equation is then to be applied to each individual case and marks the start of the detailed planning process for the particular business model.

However, distributing the needed resources among the given actors requires a methodology to ensure overall efficiency and feasibility and lastly, alignment, and commitment. Therefore, from each of the companies' perspectives, a Make/Buy/Collaborate decision for determined resources must be taken. This choice refers to developing particular assets in-house ("Make"), procuring them through traditional channels ("Buy"), or partnering Open Innovation ("Collaborate"). To effectively make a decision, it is crucial to take into account the full cost of internal development, Net Present Value (NPV) effects of collaborating (shorter time to market or reaching the objected innovation goal more easily) and specific administrative efforts and execution challenges when collaborating. The pros and cons of sharing the particular resources need also to be integrated into this decision. In fact, implications of the specific resources in terms of core, critical, or contextual characteristics should be assessed when resources are being shared (as explained above). Chesbrough et al. (2018) state that for actors deciding to participate in an Open Innovation project, a realistic opportunity for value partaking such as getting benefits from later value creation or capturing needs to exist. Since many uncertainties occur in an Open Innovation system, trust between all actors is important to ensure commitment and establish a substitute for control and eventually motivate its participants. Moreover, when the value is realized meaning the process of application and utilization of resources in later stages, it is not only necessary to be able to eventually realize the value from exchanged resources but also fairly distribute the created value between contributors. Actors tend to compare their outcome with one another in the same system forming the basis for fairness perceptions, which can result in behavioral consequences, such as exiting the innovation ecosystem when feeling treated unfairly. Transparency among all actors in an Open Innovation system and building trust from the beginning is therefore supremely important.[14]

Taking these factors into consideration, each case can be individually defined. However, specific criteria and decision-making protocols need to be developed and applied individually, e.g. minimum requirements, assets to be complementary, transaction costs etc., which differ among various domains. Ultimately, the derived scenario needs to ensure that expected outcomes overweigh the direct and indirect costs of the collaboration.[15] Negotiations among the participating actors regarding revenue and IP sharing need to therefore continue and emerge into first drafts to ensure early commitments and furthering trust among the Open Innovation ecosystem.

The optimization of each company's business model needs to incorporate the shared value methodology from Porter and Kramer. Taking into consideration that financial and social goals need to be met to create shared value in the long term for all stakeholders, it is critical to align with the Smart Village vision. Because villagers typically have very low income, the products and services that can both improve their lives and fit within their budgets must come at a low price and provide high value. To meet both those criteria, companies must innovate rather than rely on a basic strategy of either product differentiation or cost leadership. They must take an uncommon approach to innovate. Rather than adding new features, they must remain focused on simplicity.

There are straightforward reasons why not only businesses are in need to develop a model that serves as an incentive to participate. Ideally, every participant would have a quantifiable incentive. If the government would determine the opportunity costs that can be saved if promised impact could be realized, this budget could be used as a success premium. The executing entity, e.g. the Smart Village Movement, would get additional budget when being successful and thus would have a major incentive to perform.[16]

In the end, the described process orchestrated by the knowledge broker is understood as an iterative process with all involved actors and should lead to an overall commitment and alignment for the developed business models. Moreover, evaluating the extent to which the individual business models are aligned with each other is significant to provide mutual benefits and not undercut each other.

Chesbrough and Schwartz emphasize this importance as "few companies in our experience take the time to articulate their own business model. Fewer have only a clear idea about the business model of their external relationships. By assessing others' business models, understanding one's own business needs, and the degree of their alignment with one's own business model, one can turn these relationships into more valuable co-development partnerships."[17]

Framing the Business Models

After classifying particular resources and optimizing their distribution among the Open Innovation ecosystem, the individual business models need to be framed. The *Business Model Canvas*, developed by Osterwalder and Pigneur (2010)[18], provides a simplified scheme for assessing how the business is formulated for value-added, creation process, customer relationships, and financial aspects. For the Smart Village initiative, Professor Darwin built upon this framework and changed it slightly for the context of emerging rural markets. It consists of eight building blocks: 1) customer segment and respective pain points, 2) value creation: what are the pain relievers?, 3) customer relationship with focus on digital relationships, 4) value distribution, 5) value capture with revenue sources and expenses, 6) needed resources which contribute to the value creation, 7) activities for value creation and which activities customers value, 8) partners to reduce risks & costs to create value. The main focus of this model lays in the characteristic of a pull business model (see exhibit 18), which combines all building blocks in the sense of Open Innovation when leveraging and sharing resources, expertise, and knowledge. Moreover, the demand comes directly from the customer (pain point).

The Mission, vision and, core values of the company or future startup need to be addressed. Goals and critical success factors define the way for succeeding with this model. In order to measure the progress, performance metrics need to be included. Timebound targets and the strategy then ultimately translate into an action plan for the business model execution.

Exhibit 18 – Push and Pull Business Models

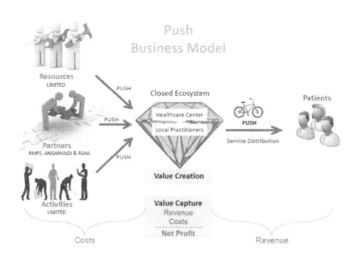

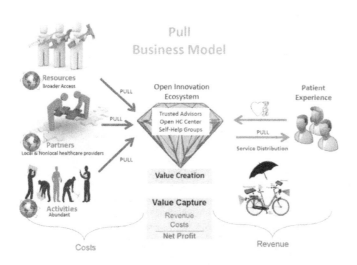

Lastly, developed business models need to be evaluated to ensure ongoing customer-centricity and acceptance. Therefore, feedback surveys and user tests can be conducted.

Healthcare Case Example
IDEATE/Stage 2: Business Models

After designing the ecosystem, the respective companies, the rural health workers as well as the cloud physicians needed to design their own business model within the given ecosystem. With the help of the Smart Village team and the UC Berkeley faculty as the central orchestrator, independent business models were developed. Optimal resource allocation was achieved through many iterations and negotiations (see above described methodology). The models align with the created ecosystem and with each other and give each actor monetary incentives to sustain and to further scale their participation. Critical parameters like the willingness to pay for such services or the acceptance from village population were tested in the survey with over 7,000 potential patients.

Note that the following descriptions of the individual business models focus on value creation and value capturing and are meant to give a brief overview.

1. Cosine Labs

Isolated Value Creation: Providing the digital infrastructure and connecting all actors and resources to enable a seamless and data rich process.
Isolated Value Capture: As a platform owner, Cosine Labs gets small transaction commission. Co-ownership of data and IP (of the platform) with Smart Village project. Monetizing data with consent of Smart Village and customers.

2. MedTel

Isolated Value Creation: Provision of healthcare equipment (SanketLife – Pocket ECG Monitor device and plugin device to measure blood pressure and blood saturation and oxygen) along with a customized mobile application. The application serves as the main User Interface for the rural health worker through which health workers can operate their services and patients are able access personal (historical) health data. Translation of analyzed data into common language that rural health workers can be easily processed. Provides cloud physicians by sourcing them from various hospitals.
Isolated Value Capture: Sales of equipment (along with cost free mobile application). Health workers can decide between CAPEX (investment and subscription) or OPEX (commission; pay per use) pricing model. Monetary compensation for development support is given by Cosine Labs. On average, the break-even point for an individual case is assessed to be 13 months.

---

3. Rural Heath Worker

Isolated Value Creation: Acts as the extended hand of the cloud physician to touch and feel the patient and to execute the instruction by the cloud physician. Acts as a communicator between the patient and the doctor at patient's home.
Isolated Value Capture: Commission for every guided treatment he/she performs.

4. Cloudphysician

Isolated Value Creation: Consultation service to provide high quality healthcare treatment remotely.
Isolated Value Capture: Commission for each consultation service.
The overall monetary distribution was negotiated multiple times throughout the whole process. Due to confidential disclosure agreements, details about revenue sharing etc. cannot be highlighted in this case example.

2.3 Ideate Value Hypotheses

Finalizing the individual business models among the ecosystem design leads to the necessity of having to formulate fundamental value hypotheses along with success KPIs before testing the model. Since the build-measure-learn approach was continuously applied within the ideate phase, it is now time to build the foundation for applying this holistically to the whole model. The arising complexity of having an overall ecosystem design comprised of several individual business models requires a clear understanding of which value is to be delivered to particular stakeholders, and which objectives are set and which other hypotheses need to be fulfilled, are required. Aligning with philanthropist philosophy, the pain-relieving value creation for the customers – the rural people in emerging economies, is to be derived in great detail along with specific KPIs.

For a successful pilot evaluation and results to be representative, methodologies to properly evaluate the impact of any interventions should be decided on. Ultimately, success depends on how innovative, replicable, strategically relevant, untested, and influential the pursued intervention or program is. Moreover, pilot size, budget, and requirements of stakeholders on how scientific the results are to be objected determine the depth of incorporating and applying impact evaluation methodologies. In the context of evaluating innovation projects, it might not be necessary to conduct a detailed effectiveness study with affiliated results to be generalized at a large scale. Rather, it's more about showing the efficacy of the innovative intervention in a small, specific setting to achieve a PoC. Producing evidence on the performance can be generally done by addressing descriptive, normative, and cause-and-effect questions in a prospective way, in other words, setting a baseline before the intervention starts and continuing to collect feedback throughout time. Complementary to that, monitoring for verifying activities, process evaluations for ensuring conformity with the original designs and validating operational processes and lastly, cost-benefit and cost-effectiveness analysis should be integrated. When it comes to ethical considerations, interventions shouldn't be denied or delayed for the purpose of the evaluation and randomization among participants/beneficiaries is to be applied to provide an equal chance of participation to avoid bias and to increase the overall credibility.[19]

When applying impact evaluation methodologies and in order to derive the value creation for the stakeholders, overall fundamental value hypotheses along with success KPIs are required. All participating companies, actors, and organizations as well as stakeholders, like the government, should be consulted to formulate them. In this case, it is recommended to form focus groups to conduct qualitative research. These outcomes among available general information and research then can be consolidated in order to formulate central hypotheses.

The derived value hypotheses are critical for further testing and implementation efforts when deriving the baseline to assess the model on. In fact, detailed success KPIs need to be determined to quantify the measurement. Such results make the concept accountable and reveal weaknesses or failures immediately. For every testing phase, an evaluation based on hypotheses ensures the broad application of the build-measure-learn methodology for fast and effective adaptation of feedback (pivoting) and effective improvements. It is recommended to incorporate digital tools for data collection and data analytics that provide data accessibility for multiple actors, which can be turned into useful information to better plan, assess, and improve the progress. Notwithstanding the importance of businesses, people, and other entities revolving around humans, value hypotheses should be also formulated for another relevant entity – our planet. It is this aspect that puts equally, ecological impact alongside social and economic impact. Please see the following exhibit to illustrate KPIs that measure and control the determined impact in various fields.

Exhibit 19 – Impact Measurement KPIs (Example)

Phase # 1: Evaluation of Value Creation - Impact measurement Dec 31, 2020
1. Traction for value propostion or solution? (% of customers interested)
2. Adoption of the solution (% of village customers adoptiong the solution)
3. Pricing acceptabiltly (% of cutomers find the solution affordable)
4. Product market fit?
5. Size of targeted market?
6. Competitiv advantages ?
7. What would be the potential economic impact to your firm if it is deployed statewide? ($ Revenue/year)
8. What would be the potential social impact if the solution is deployed statewide? (# of Jobs - Year 1-5)
9. What would be the potential environmental impact if the solution is deployed statewide? (equivalent CO2 emissions/eco labels)

Phase # 2: Evaluation of Ecosystem - Impact measurement Mar 31, 2021
1. Cost elimination leveraging ecosystem partners (% of costs that could be eliminated)
2. New revenue sources generated thought partnerships (% of new revenue sources)
3. Risk sharing opporuntities through resource sharing opportunitis (% of risk reduced)
4. How much will you be saving in expenses by leveraging the ecosystem resources? (% of costs saved)
5. Did you needed to refine your business model to work with the ecosystem? Yes/NO
6. Are refinements needed to make your solution or technology more user-friendly? Yes/NO
7. Is your ecoystem sustainable? Yes/NO

Phase # 3: Evaluation of Business Model - Impact measurement June 30, 2021
1. Is your business model scalable and sustainable?
2. What percentage of growth can you expect over the next 5 years? (% growth)

Healthcare Case Example
IDEATE/Stage 3: Value Hypotheses

The given Ecosystem design is capable to provide value creation beyond the value from the isolated solutions. When targeting the needs from the rural population in terms of primary healthcare, all given pain points **Access, Affordability, Accountability and Quality** can be addressed. Ultimately, the ecosystem is able to create value for all participating companies, actors and organizations.

Value Creation for Stakeholders

The following value creation for each stakeholder is based on initial surveys and assumptions, derived by the participating corporate partners, the government of Andhra Pradesh and the Smart Village team along with academia. Success KPIs are hereby integrated to quantify the measurements.

1. Value Creation for the Villager

a) Timely delivery of critical healthcare services
   i) Reduction of travel time (alternative to PHC since door step delivery)
   ii) Reduction of waiting time compared to the situation at the PHC when having a proper appointment
   iii) Accelerate the service delivery time throughout the whole ecosystem (patient data sharing: electronic medical records (EMRs) now available for every relevant actor), no repetitive diagnosis from different actors in the short term

b) Increased transparency
   i) Access to personal health history
   ii) Provision of information and knowledge to enable preventive healthcare

c) Increased quality of treatment
   i) Certified doctors ensure reliable and accountable diagnosis with the help of the health worker
   ii) Prevents wrong diagnosis because of EMR data and cloud physician
   iii) Transparency through data sharing across stakeholders (with patient consent)

d) Cost reduction
   i) Prevents repetitive diagnosis to save costs (and time)
   ii) Reduced travel costs
   iii) Open Data increases efficiency and therefore lowers costs (every dot is connected and has access)

2. Value Creation for the Cloud Physician

a) Increased time utilization
  i) Saving more lives
  ii) Increasing income
  iii) No need for medical infrastructure to consult remotely
b) Expanding knowledge base when practicing in rural areas remotely

3. Value Creation for the Rural Health Workers

a) Improves work efficiency and accuracy
  i) System provides information to better execute
  ii) Advice from cloud physician is a continuous skill training
b) Licensing enables social reputation and improved credibility among village communities
c) Increased monetary income

4. Value Creation for the Businesses

a) Improved time-to-market (open innovation)
b) Access to new markets when having local partners
c) Improving objective to save lives
d) Access to data from same and outside domains to improve prevalent solutions
e) New revenue source with this business model

5. Value Creation for the Public Sector

a) Digital Footprint for health records in rural setting
  i) Preventive Healthcare
  ii) Data provision supports policy making
  iii) Transparency
b) Improved Healthcare in rural areas
  i) Social and economic value increases
  ii) Optimizing healthcare supply chain via data driven forecasts

6. Value Creation for Academia

a) Data from rural healthcare provide new insights
b) International publications
c) KIMS college to better frame rural healthcare policies and programs when having data and research

Fundamental Value Hypotheses

The overall fundamental hypotheses for the conceptualized healthcare eco-system represents the ideated concept in terms of ecosystem design, business models and provided value creation. The following hypotheses were used to test and assess the model among other parameters. This served to derive the baseline for the pivot (iterative test with stakeholders) to continuously improve the model.

———

Hypothesis 1) A scalable healthcare delivery model for rural areas is created by leveraging world-class industrial medical devices and connected care cloud infrastructure. *KPI:* overall long-term success based on all KPIs

Hypothesis 2) The model is able to create collaboration among rural healthcare facilities, qualified labs and clinicians to create a self-sustaining ecosystem. *KPI:* overall long-term success based on stakeholder KPIs and qualitative feedback

Hypothesis 3) All medical records are captured electronically including demographic and clinical information that can be available on demand to authorized clinicians, or government institutions. *KPI:* rate of digitization

Hypothesis 4) Rural health workers are fully monitored and anchored into the system to ensure full transparency and accountability. *KPI:* rate of monitoring

Hypothesis 5) The model can provide the assumed value creation for all stakeholders. *KPI:* see overall value creation KPIs

Hypothesis 6) The model is adapted by patients, health workers and cloud physicians. *KPI:* Adaptation Rate

Hypothesis 7) Healthcare entrepreneurship is fostered as more people start the occupation of healthcare. *KPI:* long term rate derived from the number of healthcare workers

Phase 3: CO-INNOVATE

"Co-innovation with villagers promotes a sustainable future by eliminating waste – it produces a better mouse trap."

– Emma Brunat, Visiting Scholar, UC Berkeley

Ideation in collaboration with all stakeholders in the sense of Open Innovation merges eventually into the extensive customer-centered phase of co-innovation. It is about testing and changing the designed models and defined value hypotheses with the help of villagers to eventually co-innovate self-contained and scalable solutions for existing needs. Therefore, all participating parties are required to reach their operational readiness and to develop a prototype to test the model in a broad manner on the ground. Additionally, people who are part of the solution need to be trained and awareness among the rural population is to be spread. Then, the iterative testing, to evaluate whether change is needed (pivoting) can happen, to ultimately accomplish a Proof of Concept (PoC). The dynamic characteristic within this framework is dominant in this phase, to ensure adaptation in an effective manner.

3.1 Operational Readiness and Prototype

After designing the ecosystem along with individual business models and formulating success KPIs for measuring the model, operational readiness and a running prototype need to be accomplished.

All actors are required to validate the ecosystem model in the form of legal agreements, commitment, and alignment. Creating a detailed action plan for the iterative test phases is hereby critical when allocating resources, IP, and expertise among the ecosystem partners. Clear scope for the pivot needs to be agreed upon. Therefore, legal agreements in the form of MoUs and other formats need to be signed. The focus hereby lays clearly on the phase of iterative tests and feedback adaptation (pivot), but also should include contingency agreements to renegotiate terms and conditions after successfully achieving a Proof of Concept. Legal agreements must contain IP sharing, revenue sharing, resource sharing, and overall cost-sharing aspects to ensure utmost alignment and commitment for the ecosystem from all corporate partners and other parties. It depends on each individual case, which agreement is to be signed from which actors. Moreover, in some cases, legal clearance from the government is required. Therefore, agreements with local and even state-level bureaucrats are to be facilitated. Ultimately, the knowledge broker, which is providing on-ground support and stakeholder facilitation (e.g. government) can be part of these legal agreements. This can particularly reduce the risk for participating companies when the orchestrator gives legal commitment to determined efforts.

Accomplishing overall validation and legal agreements, the hands-on co-innovation effort for developing a working prototype is likely to begin. In an optimal case, the co-development already started within the Ideate phase in form of MVPs (Minimal Viable Product) with first-time collected feedback, on which the companies can build on. The knowledge broker is required to support the co-innovation process for the prototype in terms of providing advice and knowledge and orchestrating the overall co-development. It is recommended to continuously monitor the progress in terms of compliance with the determined ecosystem design, individual business models, and agreed value creation (captured in the legal agreements). Lastly, before rolling out the prototype for testing in the broad scenario, feasibility tests need to be conducted to assure that no logical or technical complications will arise during the testing phase.

Healthcare Case Example

Co-Innovate/Stage 1: Readiness & Prototype

After the ideation phase, the actors started co-innovating and co-developing a working prototype in depth to test the model. At the same time, the operational readiness was achieved to ensure the feasibility of the upcoming pivot

---

Operational Readiness

In order to start the pivoting process, all stakeholders needed to finally validate the ecosystem model. First, a detailed scope for the pivot iterations was defined. Eventually, commitment and alignment with the co-innovation project from all participating actors was achieved in this stage of operational readiness. Therefore, MoUs, agreements and legal clearance agreements were signed.

1. Scope

Due to the illegal status, Rural Medical Practitioners (RMPs) are not the main focus in the pivot to represent rural health worker. However, three RMPs participated under strong surveillance from the Smart Village team to derive the potential of shifting their situation to a legal status with technology empowerment. The group of health workers are covered by ANMs, as they are experienced, educated and have a legal status.

An appointment system was not part of the first pivot iteration since mobile phones are not available within the target audience. Instead, a call center was established to connect patients to the doctor (manually). Additionally, the call center verifies the submitted data and the overall experience of the patient and collects feedback from the patient. Moreover, the experience of former telemedicine efforts (without diagnostics) within the Smart Village project showed, that rural residents are not familiar with an appointment system. In order to ensure firsthand acceptance from the patients, this system will then be implemented in the second pivot phase. Step by step adaptation is therefore ensured.

There is a clear schedule for offering the medical services. The ANM's medical center is open to public in a designated timeframe from 9am – 3pm, where patients can come to get needed treatment. After that, a defined patient audience will be visited from the ANMs on a daily basis. This given pattern will not be changed again to ensure easy acceptance for the novel, advanced medical services from the patients.

Overall, it was planned to offer medical services to approximately 1,000 patients in 9 villages by 6 ANM health workers and 3 RMPs in two iterations (each one month long). The advanced healthcare services were offered for no cost. The corporate partners agreed to invest in this pivot to test the design and improve the solution until it reaches high acceptance, adoption and assumed value creation.

2. Corporate Partner's Commitment

After designing the ecosystem approach and the individual business model in consultation with the Smart Village project, the general value as well as the individual value creation and capturing convinced all participating companies. Results from the conducted survey validated the ecosystem model in general with data from over 7,000 potential customers. However, detailed negotiations regarding financial KPIs and sharing of intellectual property among the corporate partners were needed to agree on the required MoUs (Memorandum of Understanding) before testing the solution. A final validation from all participating companies was achieved in individual terms and conditions.

3. Rural Health Worker's Commitment

The Smart Village team briefed the participating Auxiliary Nursing Midwifes (ANMs) on the ecosystem model and explained the value it will bring for themselves and rural healthcare in general. An agreement, which ensures no financial liability and expenses for the ANMs during the pilot was signed.

4. Patient's Commitment

In order to validate the overall acceptance and willingness to use such services, over 6,000 potential patients have been asked through a survey. Over 75% stated that they want to use the proposed healthcare model and getting certified treatment. This trend continues regarding getting ECG done at their doorsteps (83.5%) and RMPs being the health workers to execute the treatment under supervision of cloud physicians (82%).

5. Government's Commitment

In order to get approval for doing the pilot, a clear understanding about medical policies and legal terms was developed by the Smart Village team. Therefore, the elected member of a constituency (MLA) and bureaucrats (Indian Administrative Services (IAS) Officers and District Medical Health Officer) consulted the team and the corporate partners on how to move forward in terms of logistics and on how to get the required legal clearance. Given the constraint that rural medical practitioners (RMPs) have illegal status, RMPs were excluded from the pilot (besides three to test case for evaluating possible solutions to verify them). Eventually, regular clearance was achieved from high bureaucrats on the district level.

Prototype

A prototype was developed collaboratively among all corporate partners. Cosine Labs took the lead and pooled in all given partners in to the development process. The Smart Village team consulted for the development in terms of addressing derived value hypotheses and ensured that the prototype can address the identified pain points. A first dry run was conducted with the Smart Village team to guarantee the functionality of all given features and the seamless process. There were multiple iterations to achieve the overall feasibility.

3.2 Training & Awareness

Training for participants and spreading awareness among the public is essential before broadly testing the ecosystem. Integrating novel processes, technologies, and resources, and thus forming a completely new approach requires specific training. This can comprise in-depth seminars, workshops, and online/video training. Educating rural people, who might lack education, literacy, and technology exposure to certain extents demands sensitive and patient social interaction. In fact, miscommunication, misperception, and wrong expectations can arise quickly among the participating actors. Therefore, a local team, which understands the prevalent situation and speaks the local language is recommended to support training efforts from the experts (e.g. from corporate partners).

In order to tackle the challenges of acceptance and adaptation of the novel solution among rural populations, awareness needs to be widely spread. Having determined the detailed scope of the upcoming test iterations (pivot), the affected villages can be individually addressed. Door-to-door awareness spreading, public gatherings with presentations, involving local media and government as well as conducting workshops are a few ways to create broad awareness. Such programs must be offered for no cost to gain traction.

Ultimately, an orchestrator helps organize and executes training and awareness programs. Having a clear understanding of the rural setting and therefore being able to guide a local team or even having a local team is a major success factor for those efforts. Moreover, the orchestrator can consult the participating companies or government in detail to effectively train rural people and to effectively spread awareness among them.

Healthcare Case Example
Co-Innovate/Stage 2: Training & Awareness

After achieving the operational readiness, required steps in terms of conducting training for the rural health workers and creating awareness among village population were executed.

_____

Training

Equipping rural health workers with the latest technology required basic training. In this case, the one-week long training on provided equipment and digital tools complemented the existing medical skillset. In detail, participating health workers were trained on how to operate the given solution in different scenarios. Question and Answers sessions were repeatedly provided. In the end, it ensured that the health workers were fully understanding the process and were able to perform all needed activities to execute the designed solution.

Awareness

When introducing new innovative processes, technologies or models, the executing actors like the health workers need to be trained and beyond; awareness among the impacted population needs to be created. Acceptance and adaptation can emerge. Therefore, door-to-door presentations were being conducted to educate about the new solution, which is being tested. Additionally, awareness about preventive healthcare in general was spread to educate on the long-term impact of preventive and high-quality healthcare. Linking this to the presented solution, it strongly emphasized the individual value for potential patients.

3.3 Iterative Pivot

Upon completing a first prototype, an ecosystem design, individual business models and receiving initial feedback from multiple stakeholders, it is finally time to assess if the original strategy (and hypotheses) can be persevered or whether changes are required to test new fundamental hypotheses about the model – which is called *pivoting*. Only when testing the model with real customers, with real actors executing it and finally discovering to which extent the defined and pivoted value hypotheses are true, a successful model can emerge. Building on the *Lean Startup* method from Eric Ries (2011) to let companies recognize the need to pivot a designed model and therefore save time and costs, a pivoting process for rural emerging markets was designed. Upon figuring out what model to test (Open Innovation ecosystem along with individual business models), how to measure its overall success (value hypotheses) and to figure out what product is needed (prototype), the final step is "to run that experiment and get that measurement." [20] A baseline with real data can be derived and it can show whether the model is effectively on the right track or not. Moreover, feedback collection from real customers and participating actors is then likely to highlight whether serious changes are needed. In case of required changes, existing hypotheses need to be altered and the baseline reestablished – pivoting is happening. A structured course correction is hence to be designed to test new fundamental hypotheses about the model, the product, the service, the strategy, and the engine of growth. The process starts all over again. Phase 1, 2 and 3 are likely to be redone dynamically to eventually change the fundamental hypotheses and to reiterate the testing. Such dynamic co-innovation efforts are of utmost importance to tap into rural markets that have very dynamic and niche characteristics.

Ultimately, the derived results from the pivoting should show in the end that the tests are running more productively and successfully than before. Finally, a Proof of Concept (PoC) can be achieved when showing that a determined extent of the defined and pivoted hypotheses is true – validated by real customers using it.

Exhibit 20 – Iterative Pivoting Process

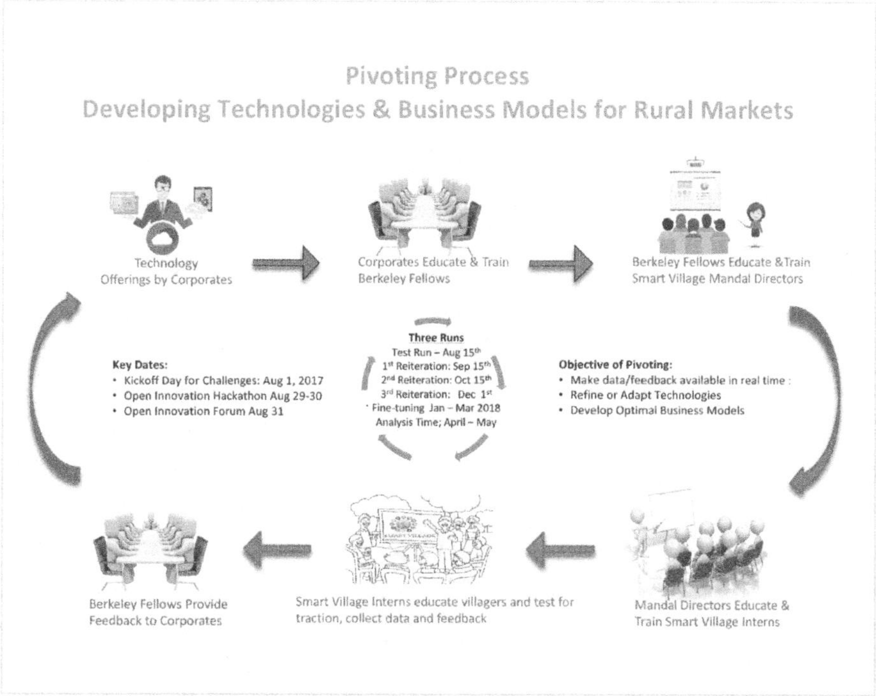

Pivoting Process
Developing Technologies & Business Models for Rural Markets

Technology Offerings by Corporates

Corporates Educate & Train Berkeley Fellows

Berkeley Fellows Educate & Train Smart Village Mandal Directors

Key Dates:
- Kickoff Day for Challenges: Aug 1, 2017
- Open Innovation Hackathon Aug 29-30
- Open Innovation Forum Aug 31

Three Runs
Test Run – Aug 15th
1st Reiteration: Sep 15th
2nd Reiteration: Oct 15th
3rd Reiteration: Dec 1st
Fine-tuning Jan – Mar 2018
Analysis Time; April – May

Objective of Pivoting:
- Make data/feedback available in real time :
- Refine or Adapt Technologies
- Develop Optimal Business Models

Berkeley Fellows Provide Feedback to Corporates

Smart Village Interns educate villagers and test for traction, collect data and feedback

Mandal Directors Educate & Train Smart Village Interns

The pivoting process (see Exhibit 20) itself is designed to emphasize the co-innovation between companies and villagers to analyze and adapt profound learnings to effectively tap into rural emerging markets. Central to this process is the knowledge flow within the smart village organization (orchestrator) to ensure high-quality standards and overall success. From corporates to Berkeley fellows to Mandal Directors and lastly, to Smart Village interns, everyone is required to have in-depth knowledge about the designed model and its deployed technology. In order to execute the testing of the model and to decide whether to change fundamental hypotheses (pivot), on-ground support with in-depth knowledge is consequently needed. Although actors, using the novel technology e.g. rural health workers, were already trained (see stage 2), profound assistance is needed to help for the overall operations. These include inter alia logistics, technology and knowledge support, continuous training and guidance, overall orchestration, and eventually the feedback collection. It is recommended that representatives from participating companies are on the ground to better understand the customer base. However, a workforce from (or lead by) an orchestrator is able to cover all tasks since being experienced in the rural setting and well-educated on the model and technologies. Moreover, following the collection and analysis of the feedback after each iteration, companies are provided with recommendations on whether to persevere or change the ecosystem design, business model, and implemented technologies.

The duration of a test iteration and the number of needed iterations depend on the individual requirements and the overall progress. Also, when pivoting is happening extensively, it is recommended to iterate the overall framework. Reflecting the identified pain relievers, the participating companies, the designed Open Innovation ecosystem along with the individual business models and lastly changing the fundamental value hypotheses along with a new test is ensuring a demanded and ready to scale solution. The orchestrator hereby plays a crucial role to be a guide and consultant for all actors. Having broad experience with such iterative processes in various domains in village settings, stakeholders can effectively and efficiently be mentored to win in rural emerging markets.

Excursus: Co-Innovation Process Phase 1 in Mori

In the first stage of the smart village prototyping process in Mori, every village household was interviewed to identify the pain points shown in Exhibit 1. Interested companies then joined the project to create potential solutions.

Because people from outside the village were organizing the coinnovation process, it was important to build trust with villagers before pursuing the project further. Students from Andhra University visited each household to introduce the next stages of the project and explain how it would benefit villagers. And, because connectivity is essential for the project to work, the state government provided fiber-optic Internet access to the village and an incentive for each household to fully participate in the prototyping process: a box that, in conjunction with a small keyboard, converts a television set into a basic personal computer.[21]

Next, a co-innovation space was built. It is a two-acre site with buildings that look similar to those already in Mori, to make the prototyping space feel like a representation of the village's future. It is at this site that the proposed technologies are displayed for villagers to view, interact with, and evaluate. All village households were invited to participate in the program, and those that participate in all three evaluation rounds received the connectivity box.

In the first round, villagers listen to a presentation about the concept of a smart village and how the evaluation process works. Then, they visit each station in the co-innovation space to learn about each proposed solution and provide feedback on the proposed features and price. They do not have to answer complicated surveys; rather, they vote using simple icons: one of a smiling face, one of a frowning face, and one of a neutral face.

Using the data collected in the first round, companies will revise their proposed solutions, which villagers will evaluate in the second round. In their third visit to the co-innovation space, villagers learn about the final solutions they will be able to purchase.

One proposed solution from IBM intended to help farmers increase yields and decrease expenses. Sensors placed in the soil will measure the levels of water, nitrogen, and other crucial factors contributing to yields. With this information, farmers can optimize both water usage and fertilizer purchases. Another proposed solution comes from Ericsson and is intended to monitor the gates and canals used to distribute water in the village. Sensors will be installed to measure real-time water flows. A display showing these flows will sit in Naidu's office, and farmers can provide feedback on their access to water using just their cell phones.[22]

After the third round of the prototyping evaluation in Mori, leaders from 40 nearby villages will visit Mori to learn about the proposed innovations. They will also offer feedback on how well they believe the proposed solutions will meet the needs of their communities.

The entire prototyping process is intended to facilitate the development of a self-contained sustainable business model that is scalable. To succeed, firms will have to create products and services that meet villagers' needs – as defined by villagers – at affordable prices. Those successful offerings will therefore be more likely to offer value to villagers elsewhere in the state of Andhra Pradesh, in India, and in other developing countries (excerpt from the 2016 HBR Case *"Prototyping a Scalable Smart Village to Simultaneously Create Sustainable Development and Enterprise Growth Opportunities" by Henry Chesbrough and Solomon Darwin*).

Healthcare Case Example
Co-Innovate/Stage 3: Iterative Pivot

During the ongoing ideation process, the scope for the upcoming pivot was finalized and the iterative test was ready to start.

———————

First Iteration

The first pilot started with 9 pilot sites, out of which 6 pilots were being carried out by ANMs whereas the other 3 were carried out by 3 RMPs. While the RMPs can charge the patients a nominal fee (50 rupees for expert consultation), the ANMs were not to collect any fee from the patients due to their legal situation being under a government body.

We observed the number of patients taking consultations through the RMPs were constantly increasing when compared to the number of patients getting consultations through the ANMs. In absolute numbers, this was surprisingly the case although the number of ANMs was more than twice. Feedback from patients was collected reflecting an overall satisfaction with this model. However, the question why the ANMs were not giving as many consultations as any RMP remained unclear since the service from ANMs is free for patients in general. From our experience as an observer, ANMs were having some extra time to treat patients via the cloud physician model beyond their normal duty.

Second Iteration

In order to increase the number of consultations from the ANMs compared to the potential seen by the RMPs, the idea of a monetary benefit for ANMs evolved. Providing a monetary incentive for ANMs to increase their consultations via a cloud physician model for rural patients was seen as an obvious and effective change for the model. This pivot of the model was then to be tested in the second iteration to further the model and to evaluate its overall effectiveness.

We informed all participating ANMs about the change in the revenue model and that they would get paid for every consultation. In order to comply with their legality, they would get exclusively paid by the Smart Village initiative - not from any of their patients.

Therefore, we started paying them on a weekly basis beginning in late April based on the number of their given consultations. Immediately after the first week doing so, it could be seen that ANM's behavior changed dramatically (see upcoming exhibit). Earlier ANMs used to claim that consulting via the cloud physician model was almost impossible due to missing additional time since being fully occupied with work given from Primary Health Centers. It is astonishing how a small monetary compensation changed their willingness to spend time on this pilot. ANMs now felt really happy to do these consultations as they were earning additional income. It can be concluded that in this case a behavioral change required the ANMs to receive an immediate benefit without any affiliated risk.

Number of consultations during the first and second pivot:

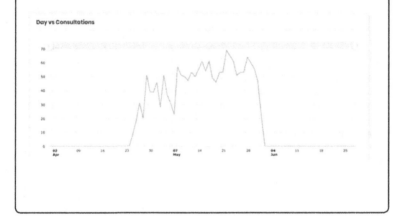

Milestone: PROOF OF CONCEPT (PoC)

The Proof of Concept (PoC) can be reached after proving the fundamental hypotheses (to a defined extent) with feedback collected by all stakeholders before, throughout, and after the pivot process. Therefore, a quantified methodology needs to be followed to achieve robust results. Final quantified results with respect to the defined KPIs are compared to the baseline (and changed baseline when being pivoted) and to the desired results. An overall evaluation of the achieved result needs to be discussed with all stakeholders to evaluate the achieved impact. The given results are then decided to be sufficient for a Proof of Concept (PoC). Otherwise, a reiteration of the 3 phases namely identify, ideate, and co-innovate of the framework are to be considered.

Healthcare Case Example

Milestone: Proof of Concept (PoC)

In the Healthcare case, basic short term KPIs have been fulfilled during the two pivot iterations as the following:

Value Creation for Stakeholders

1. Value Creation for the Villager

a) Timely delivery of critical healthcare services
 i) Reduction of travel time (alternative to PHC since door step delivery)
  -> 45% of the patients strongly agree; 52% of the patients agree

 ii) Reduction of waiting time compared to the situation at the PHC when having a proper appointment
  -> 45% of the patients strongly agree; 52% of the patients agree

 iii) Accelerate the service delivery time throughout the whole ecosystem (patient data sharing: electronic medical records (EMRs) now available for every relevant actor), no repetitive diagnosis from different actors in the short term
  -> EMRs are now accesible for all relevant parties

b) Increased transparency
 i) Access to personal health history
 ii) Provision of information and knowledge to enable preventive healthcare

  Applicable for i) and ii):

   -> EMRs are accessible for patient and provide rich data analysis.
   -> 59% of the patients strongly agree & 36% agree that this type of consultation helped them to understand the diagnosis and applied medicine and tests.
   -> 78% of the patients received a printed valid prescription.

c) Increased quality of treatment
  i)   Certified doctors ensure reliable and accountable diagnosis with the help of the health worker
  ii) Prevents wrong diagnosis because of EMR data and cloud physician
  iii) Transparency through data sharing across stakeholders (with patient consent)

  Applicable for i), ii) and iii):

  -> *67% of the patients feel very confident and 27% find it confident about the diagnosis given by a reliable doctor.*
  -> *70% of the patients find that the time given for the tele-consultation was very desirable and 25% find it desirable.*
  -> *59% of the patient had a very desirable experience with the tele-medicine doctor, 28% a desirable experience.*

d) Cost reduction
  i)   Prevents repetitive diagnosis to save costs (and time)

  -> *67% of the patients feel very confident and 27% find it confident about the diagnosis given by a reliable doctor, which leads to prevention of repetitive diagnosis*

  ii) Reduced travel costs

  -> *45% of the patients strongly agree; 52% of the patients agree that travel/waiting time decreased, which can be interpreted that also travel costs decreased*

Overall, 97% of the patients think that this service should be continued, which reflects the strong customer satisfaction and refers to the strong acceptance level.

2. Value Creation for the Rural Health Workers

a) Improves work efficiency and accuracy
  -> System provides information to better execute
  -> Advice from cloud physician is a continuous skill training
b) Licensing enabled social reputation and improved credibility among village communities
c) Increased monetary income

Collected feedback from ANMs and RMPs confirmed all of these points. However, due to the small sample size, more research needs to be done when increasing the scale.

Defined KPIs for corporate partners, public sector and cloud physicians target long term effects, which are to be researched in next phases. Preliminary overall positive feedback was collected from all these parties, in depth data collection regarding given KPIs is ongoing.

Fundamental Value Hypotheses

Despite given long-term success KPIs, the following fundamental value hypotheses could be fulfilled as the following:

Hypothesis 1) A scalable healthcare delivery model for rural areas is created by leveraging world-class industrial medical devices and connected care cloud infrastructure.
KPI: overall long-term success based on all KPIs: *Ongoing tracking.*

Hypothesis 2) The model is able to create collaboration among rural healthcare facilities, qualified labs and clinicians to create a self-sustaining ecosystem.
KPI: overall long-term success based on stakeholder KPIs and qualitative feedback: *Ongoing tracking.*

Hypothesis 3) All medical records are captured electronically including demographic and clinical information that can be available on demand to authorized clinicians, or government institutions.
KPI: rate of digitization: *The rate of digitization is 100% since every parameter is captured electronically (see exhibit at the end).*

Hypothesis 4) Rural health workers are fully monitored and anchored into the system to ensure full transparency and accountability.
KPI: rate of monitoring:
Since the process was designed in a way that in order to prescribe medicine and to charge fees for consultation, an interaction with a real cloud physician was needed, accountability and monitoring of rural health workers was therefore fulfilled. However, due to the restrictive design of the pilot, the decision what patient to approach is not fully transparent since the ANMs are randomly reaching out to villagers to consult them regarding health issues. A system to complement the call center and improve the match of supply and demand (appointment system) is planned to ensure full transparency.

Hypothesis 5) The model can provide the assumed value creation for all stakeholders. *KPIs: see value creation KPIs from villagers, other stakeholders have long term KPIs, which are being tracked continuously.*

Hypothesis 6) The model is adapted by patients, health workers and cloud physicians. *KPI:* Adaptation Rate: *Within the pilot phase, patients, health workers and cloud physicians adapted the model in a great way and appreciated its affiliated value. This could be derived from their application itself and collected qualitative feedback:*

Feedback Participating Cloud Physician:
"Providing high-quality health consultation to rural population in India is utmost needed and crucial. Being able to reach directly to rural people in needs via digital technology makes it very easy and flexible for me to spent a significant amount of time for underserved people. Due to the transparent process and the health workers being anchored in to the whole system, I can 100% rely on this platform that there is no fraud and the patients get communicated the right diagnosis from myself along with relevant prescribed medicines to improve their situation, eventually."

Feedback Participating ANM Health Worker:
"I see great value when a physician can diagnose a patient through a video call along with my help on ground. I could learn a lot from these professionals and it gave me a good feeling that I can provide extra quality to the patients when using this system. It was very easy to apply, however, poor internet connectivity from time to time delayed the process a little bit."

Feedback Patient:
"When the ANM came to my place and told me that today, a doctor would be joining us via video call I was a little bit concerned. When I could speak with him directly, I immediately appreciated his presence since he gave me the right diagnosis and described me the correct medicine."

Hypothesis 7) Healthcare entrepreneurship is fostered as more people start the occupation of healthcare. *KPI:* long term rate derived from the number of healthcare workers: *Ongoing tracking.*

The Smart Village team and the participating corporate partners, cosine labs and MedTel, mutually agreed on the accomplishment of a first successful Proof of Concept (PoC) that has been achieved collaboratively since the crucial value proposition for the rural patients could be delivered. Also, the feedback showed that patients, rural health workers and cloud physicians were adapting the model overall. However, the revenue model was not finalized to that point, since the equipment was sponsored by the corporate partners and the willingness to pay remained low by patients since the model was competing with free healthcare offered at Primary Healthcare Centers. Therefore, it was agreed on to integrate additional partners and work closely with the public sector to rather complement than compete with the prevalent system. There was also great potential to integrate an appointment system to increase overall transparency and efficiency of the platform. Also, connecting labs to this platform was on the agenda as it would mark the next big step to provide a more holistic solution when having lab results in real time.

———

To that date, promising conversations between relevant partners have been happening to scale this effort based on the achieved Proof of Concept. The following Phase 4 is therefore based on first outcomes from these discussions and to be understand as mainly conceptional.

Electronical Medical Records (EMR) from the pilot phase

MedTel Healthcare Pvt. Ltd.
304, KIIT-TBI, Campus 11, Bhubaneswar 751024
www.medtel.in | contact@medtel.in
Call us @ 8010508822

Teleconsultation Case No. ▓▓▓▓▓▓▓▓▓▓
Name: ▓▓▓▓▓▓▓▓▓▓
Ap
Mobile ▓▓▓▓▓▓▓▓▓▓

Date: 01/06/2018 13:17 PM
Age: 45 Year
Weight: 52 Kg.
Gender: Male

General Information

Cough (More than 10 days) - No
H/O Diabetes - No
H/O Smoking - No
H/O Alcoholism - No
H/O Allergy - No

General Examination

Blood Pressure - 125/80 mmHg
Pulse Rate - 82 /min
Temperature -
FBS - 99 mg/dl
PPBS - 132 mg/dl

Chief Complaint: Acidity with vomiting sensation with loss of appetite.

Provisional Diagnosis: Acute gastroenteritis ?

Rx

1	Themikool(20 MG) (Rabeprazole (20mg))	1 Tablet	Once Daily	X 20 Days	Before Breakfast
2	Gastica-Fiz (Alpha amylase 20 MG+Papain 60 MG+Simethicone 25 MG)	Take 1 Tablet with 150 ML with water when acidity starts.	SOS		After Food
3	Aristozyme (Syrup) (Fungal diastase 50 MG+Pepsin 10 MG /5ML)	10 ML	Thrice Daily	X 30 Days	After Food

Advice | Consult after 5 days.

Dr. ▓▓▓▓▓▓▓▓ (General Practitioner)
Tele Consultant (MedTel)
Regn. No. ▓▓▓▓▓▓▓▓

Dr. ▓▓▓▓▓▓▓▓
Inhouse Physician (MedTel)
Regn. No. ▓▓▓▓▓▓▓▓

THP Name - F. Dhanalakshmi, Mobile - 99XXXXXXXX28, Mogallu

Phase 4: IMPLEMENT & SCALE

Finally, after reaching the level of the Proof of Concept (PoC), scaling and implementation can follow. However, determining the detailed scope to which extent the model is being implemented marks the start of this phase. Based on that evaluation, it can be assessed if additional partners are required. Moreover, a strategy with specified objectives and activities linked to a compelling business scenario is to be derived in a collaborative manner. Lastly, only continuous learning and improvements are spurring long term impact on society and the economy.

4.1 Scaling Scope & Open Innovation Scaling Partners

Having proofed the overall model in the form of a Proof of Concept (PoC) provides huge scaling potential. Therefore, a clear scope for the desired scaling initiative along with its implementation (e.g. how many villages to deploy the model) needs to be determined. However, market research about the targeted areas is critical to assure that the model is working comprehensively. When deriving that similar applicable micro and macro conditions are prevalent, respectively, relevant and needed traction can be forecasted. Consequently, when setting the scope for scaling, these factors need to be considered. If different conditions are to be found within the scaling scope, it needs to be assessed if a direct implementation can be executed or another pivot iteration is to be done.

Upon setting the scope for scaling, it is necessary to assess whether existing partners within the Open Innovation ecosystem are sufficient for the aimed scale. A critical factor hereby is the availability of the orchestrator for the desired scope. Not only is this orchestrator a major success factor for the overall project execution, but it is also required to provide or lead on-ground resources for training and awareness programs as well as for implementation support.

In the end, the orchestrator plays a major role within all operations since having broad expertise, experience, and knowledge to let companies tap into emerging markets. This is crucial to take into consideration, especially when lacking an orchestrator for the aimed scaling scope. Therefore, an assessment about the potential in terms of resources, technology readiness, capabilities, and strategic commitment from participating companies needs to be taken on. In many cases, participating actors didn't have the resources and capacities to scale their products and services. Moreover, valuable collaborations with the government should be evaluated since those collaborations are intended to complement and enhance efforts from both – private and public sectors mutually to certain extents.

Ultimately, when deciding to enhance or change the existing constellation of companies and organizations, further Open Innovation scaling partners are to be recruited in the same way as the process of identifying pain-relieving agents. Since the network has significantly increased through the Open Innovation ecosystem, an extended corporate network can be leveraged for recruitment. Moreover, a proactive search for fitting companies can be conducted. Technological, relational, and strategical alignment are hereby to be assessed to derive a successful and promising match (see Phase 2). Dialogue needs to move forward for build relationships and discussing the upcoming efforts to eventually derive a scaling strategy.

Healthcare Case Example

IMPLEMENT & SCALE/Stage 1: Scope & Partners

Scope

After successfully achieving a Proof of Concept (PoC) for the Healthcare Eco-system, an assessment regarding the potential scope was initiated. There-fore, the smart village team and the participating corporate partners started evaluating the given micro and macro situation in detail, considering the prevailing particular healthcare ecosystem. In the end, the scope for scaling to approximately 12,000 villages of Andhra Pradesh (to aim at covering the majority of villages) within the next four years is being aimed at.

Scaling Partners

Potentially needed scaling partners are being determined in this phase, especially when considering that the smart village team is only present in 472 villages. Therefore, when scaling into other villages, resources for conducting training and awareness efforts and for generally supporting the model need to be ensured.

Moreover, the Government of Andhra Pradesh acts as a partner within this assessment and beyond, is seen as a strategic partner for the program to complement rather than compete with the highly regulated prevalent health-care system. There are multiple options for such a Public Private Partnership, which need to be discussed and finalized. Moreover, it is assumed that participating companies are not sufficient to provide needed resources for the aimed scale since being in a more early-stage startup phase and con-sequently, the following partners could address given requirements and are being researched on currently among the focus group:

Assumed Scaling Partners:

1) *Additional:* Government of Andhra Pradesh
    a) Health, Medical and Family Welfare Department
    b) Support and resource provider to be able to make the ecosystem sustainable
2) Cosine labs
3) *Additional:* Cloud Physicians (cloudphysicians.net)
4) MedTel
5) *Additional:* KIMS as investment partner to scale the solution
6) *Addtional:* Insurance Companies
7) *Additional:* Medall (Laboratories present in whole Andhra Pradesh)

4.2 Scaling & Implementation Strategy

Having determined the scope of scaling along with corporate partners and organizations, strategic programs need to be co-developed among all partners as preparation for successful strategy execution. Objectives, strategic activities, organizational structure, budgeting, resource allocation, and lastly, a detailed action plan are to be determined (see also phase 2 ideate) and linked to a well-founded business case. Channels to reach the customer, pricing strategies, and overall operations are to be addressed in this context.

Value creation, IP, and revenue sharing are again to be defined to reach overall alignment and commitment from participating actors. Research from the World Economic Forum (2015) on collaborative innovation indicates that being open about the likelihood of failure and respective risk is crucial when defining objectives and assessing the business case for collaborative innovation projects. Incorporating these factors into broader corporate risk assessments within the business case is therefore significant.[23] Due to the dynamic characteristics of the previous pivoting phase where changes are expected and appreciated for developing suitable models, the scaling phase should be executed in a linear way and with less risk since having achieved a Proof of Concept (PoC). Hence, a broad risk assessment is consequently to be executed.

Moreover, the scope of future business activities is meant to be vastly increasing compared to the pivoting phase, and therefore, renegotiations and new negotiations with respect to legal agreements, objectives, activities, and the overall business case are required (see also phase 3). An orchestrator in this context is crucial to ensure compliance with the overall vision about the value creation for all stakeholders in the sense of the shared value philosophy. Moreover, acting as an intermediate fosters timely negotiations and the finalization of the scaling strategy anchored to a business case. Ultimately, total consensus – on personal and legal levels is to be achieved.

In case of changing constellations within the Open Innovation ecosystem, it is recommended to reassess and, if necessary, change the ecosystem design along with individual business prior to developing the scaling strategy. When changing too many variables or aiming for markets with different situations (compared to the pivoted area), it is up to the risk assessment if new pivot iterations are needed or not.

After finishing the strategy, execution follows. Building solutions for the aimed scale in collaboration and in the agreed setting is to be done.

Healthcare Case Example
IMPLEMENT & SCALE/Stage 2: Strategy

After finalizing the Proof of Concept (PoC) and determining the needed scaling partners, a scaling and implementation strategy among the corporate companies, the smart village team and the Government of Andhra Pradesh needs to be developed. The aimed objective hereby is a sustainable approach. In order to ensure overall success for implementing the healthcare ecosystem in large scale, clear objectives for the whole ecosystem which require specific activities need to be derived. Important issues with respect to the design of the organizational structure, budgeting and resource allocation among all partners need to be included. Eventually, a well-founded business case with risk assessment is required to which all scaling partners legally agree to.

Assumed clear objectives from all actors

1) Complementing the existing healthcare ecosystem to fill the existing gaps
2) Equipping and educating rural healthcare workers with advanced technology and innovative processes
3) Increase the quality of the rural healthcare
4) Maximizing the reach of quality healthcare services to decrease the mortality rate
5) Each actor benefits from the ecosystem

Assumed strategic activities for further scaling

1) Government to provide needed resources that ANM services remain cost free
   a) Schemes are released to cover the costs of the healthcare service
   b) Develop a new healthcare policy
2) Cosine Labs to ensure training for all participating health workers
3) ANMs and Asha workers to provide awareness for respective villages where the services are offered
4) Government to build on the developed healthcare ecosystem for legalizing RMPs
5) Data sharing between Government and participating private companies
6) Smart Village team to consult and orchestrate

While the pilot covers 10 villages, scaling the consultative service model to 13,000 villages will require 1,200+ doctors, based on 6 appointments/village/day (see exhibit below). To support a gradual build up, the targeted pace is to involve one district every quarter. The organization is planning to bring 300 doctors by itself in the system by the end of 2018 to support onboarding of 2 districts (roughly 2,000 villages). In addition, an automation of appointment scheduling and call center support are planned to enable the aimed scaling.

Potential Business Case Healthcare Model

Scalable Healthcare Model
"Support Entire Rural Segment of Andhra Pradesh"

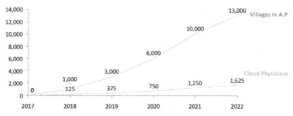

* Estimate based on 6 appointments/day/ RMP
* Team is planning to scale to 300+ doctors by end of 2018

Alignment and Commitment

Every actor needs to commit and align with the planned execution in the large scale of the healthcare ecosystem. Therefore, a MoU between the main actors needs to be signed. A possible approach would be a MoU between government and Cosine Labs, whereas the remaining actors (Medall, Med-Tel, cloudphysicians.net) have individual MoUs/contracts with Cosine Labs.

4.3 Continuous Learning and Improvement

Throughout scaling and implementation activities, continuous learning and improvement are a significant part of delivering value to society, the economy, and business enterprises. Incorporating the build measure learn cycle from the Lean Startup approach doesn't end after achieving a Proof of Concept (PoC). Due to ever-changing micro and macro factors like consumer behavior, markets, pain points, and regular frameworks, pivoting can never halt. Consequently, the ecosystem is required to evaluate regularly the prevalent situation in terms of adaptation needs. Continuous research efforts with respect to given micro and macro situations are required. Regular feedback collection from customers is especially crucial. Following the pivoting methodology, existing value hypotheses are then to be questioned and changed and eventually to be tested in the form of an (iterative) pivot. The framework cycle is to be executed again and the existing product and service need to be adapted to these changes. Continuous learning and improvement are fostered. This ensures not only the satisfaction of the customers when responsively addressing their pain points but also works as a growth engine for the ecosystem, when able to spread the solution to new areas.

It is recommended to establish such needed processes within the organization of the ecosystem model or executing these via knowledge broker/orchestrator. Measurement leads to learning and adapted learning eventually leads to improvement with extended value creation. Following the shared value and the Open Innovation methodology along with the triple helix concept, the private sector, academia, and public sector need to be continuously involved in a collaborative way to provide the best possible outcome for society and economy.

Healthcare Case Example
IMPLEMENT & SCALE/Stage 2: Strategy

Following activities need to be ensured to accomplish continuous learning and improvement for the healthcare ecosystem.

1) Continuous Monitoring from Government as well as from Cosine Labs
2) Feedback collection from health workers and patients
3) Regular strategy meetings to discuss feedback and the way forward
4) Providing data to Academia for research to get additional results and new ideas

---

PART IV.

Successes and Challenges

CHAPTER 11
WHAT ARE THE SUCCESS STORIES

"Transforming a village through technology starts with empowering the people at the grassroots level in the rural areas. The Smart Villages initiative driven through the Berkeley team, setup locally in Andhra, was a great partnership for the KETOS team to join forces and channel the best of people, talent, technology and resources to result with the right fit for every village and every individual in the new world."

– Meena Sankaran, Founder & CEO, Ketos Inc.

Three particular validations emerged from whole the project: villagers are ready and eager to embrace digital technology, (2) global technology firms like Google, Cisco, IBM, and Ericsson are willing to be investment partners in business model experiments in India, and (3) the scaling of the Smart Villages initiative can indeed be led by private sector funding. The government has provided less than 20% of the funds expended in the second phase of the project, which was similar to its level of support in the first phase of the project.

Thirty-seven examples of Open Innovation and co-innovation were realized during the prototype phase. Affiliated achievements led directly to the extension phase in 472 villages with 95-plus companies participating. Not all solutions met the corporate objectives of all firms but no firm withdrew completely. Smart Villages has teamed with corporations to identify an agreeable fix wherever possible. Several new solutions were added during the second phase. As companies departed or halted due to roadblocks, new companies joined, with new sources and innovations that potentially solved problems to mutual satisfaction by plugging into the Smart Villages ecosystem. Over 80 corporations aligned themselves with the Smart Villages vision of sustainable scaling and development. In the following, some of the many success stories are highlighted.

Google – Free Space Optics Internet

One prime example is Google, which began the large-scale endeavor to deliver Internet to every resident of every village via its Free Space Optics technology – a technology that has no need for cables. India's residents have embraced the new technology with pure delight, thanking their politicians and praising them for facilitating implementation. This grew directly out of the initial phase of the project. Google helped connect Mori village in the first phase, and then helped connect the 472 villages in the second phase. At the end of 2017, Andhra Pradesh signed an agreement with Alphabet X (formerly Google X) for a Fiber Grid (a breakthrough Free Space Optical Communication technology) installation to provide 38,000 villages statewide with internet access.

Google has been successful for three reasons: Significant scaling potential is present. Nearly a billion people live in India's villages. Even at a very low subscription price-point, there is a clear path for Google to achieve increased revenue and profit. Virtually no new physical infrastructure is needed for the product to be delivered and put into operation. The Free Space Optics is an appropriate technology for rural settings.

In rural India, Google is entering the market with no competition; no existing industry felt that their income was threatened. Also, there was no free government service present to cannibalize Google's sales. "Technology is disrupting the current system and cutting down political and bureaucratic barriers," notes Suresh Yadav, Officer on Duty for the former President of India and Advisor to the World Bank. "High-speed fiber optic networks are connecting the villages, so the village ecosystems will develop in such a way as to spur tremendous growth of eCommerce and the digital economy at the village level."

BigHaat – Agriculture eCommerce Platform

Another success story tackled the situation of farmers. They are susceptible to debt and then suffer tremendously with the struggle to pay high interest rates on the debt. Farmers can suffer from poor yields, poor crop quality, and lost crops due to a variety of factors. As a result, farmers in Andhra Pradesh suffer from one of the highest suicide rates of any demographic in India.

Among the many reasons that farmers are prime for financial distress is poor-quality agricultural inputs and improper advice on how to use the inputs. Most of the agriculture input merchants were located in towns away from the villages, so farmers needed to travel, on average, 10 to 15 km to reach them. This journey took at least a day and kept them away from farming tasks. Marginal farmers who own less than 1 hectare of land could not afford to hire a helper to procure the needed inputs, and so had to make the journey themselves. Farmers lost precious time the ability to efficiently maintain farm operations.

The challenges facing the farmers led to a very useful innovation. An Indian startup called BigHaat launched an eCommerce platform where farm inputs could be directly sourced from the companies' warehouses and shipped to the farmer's address. This solution offered high-quality supply, saved the laborious journey to town, and cost savings through the elimination of middlemen. This single innovation has the potential to help farmers avoid going into debt while employing more agricultural best practices. Moreover, BigHaat co-innovated when combining forces with an AI-based crop doctor from Plantix as well as connecting their services with C-Fog, the technology provider to increase the productivity for shrimp farmers via IoT sensor technology.

The milestones that contributed to increasing socio-economic prosperity for rural farmers via BigHaat were:

- 554 people in the villages during the period of the pilot used the BigHaat platform with a 2g mobile phone and made calls to BigHaat to get to know the products and services BigHaat offers
- The Bighaat Android application was installed in more than 1,000 mobile phones
- Farmers who ordered inputs from the platform saved up to 10% on the cost of each directly sourced product, compared with local shop prices
- Travel time was avoided by farmers who ordered through the platform
- The cost and time savings led to a sharp increase in self-reported happiness

- In the process of establishing this disruptive system, many entrepreneurs were created, including delivery boys and technical experts to teach and train farmers.

Infrastructure Planning

One major issue facing the AP government was the difficulty in planning in rural areas. Water supply, roads, canals, and several other high dollar construction projects required a high level of involvement and supervision of every aspect of the project. For example, maps have in the past been too large to process and store on any computer, required power processors, and absorbed large amounts of storage. A company called Dronamaps built upon existing technology to 3D-map the interior and exterior terrain for digital management of construction sites. Dronamaps developed an algorithm at Johns Hopkins University that allowed the company to process an interactive map and display it through a platform that allows remote access, bypassing the need for an inhouse server to store the data.

Removing the Middleman

An established national eCommerce company, Storeking[1], was able to expand its reach while simultaneously offering improved business opportunities to shopkeepers in even the most remote villages. Using an app on a smartphone, local shopkeepers can tap into the eCommerce company's inventory and restock their stores at lower prices and with greater variety. Importantly, ordering through the app eliminated the need for the shopkeeper to travel on poor roads for days at a time to the location of the nearest wholesale supplier. Like the farmers in the example above, some store owners previously had to close their shops during periods of restocking. With the app, they could remain open and avoid the loss of sales.

Surveillance via Security Cameras

Installing security cameras in Mori with the help of Johnson & Johnson / Tyco illustrates another successful initiative to enhance a village community with digital technology. As soon as cameras had been installed and connected with the local village authority (Mori Gram Panchayat) and police, many improvements were apparent. Traffic violence, theft, and other kinds of bad behavior were reduced. A murder was captured on a recording, and the police were able to resolve the case. Even littering declined. Ultimately, many positive behavioral changes were noticed.

> *"Johnson Controls is excited to be a part of the UC Berkeley Smart Villages initiative that brings together the best of today's digital technologies, platforms and partnerships with other businesses and the government to solve societal challenges to build more safe, sustainable and smarter villages in India. This initiative sets the standard on how businesses, government and knowledge centers like UC Berkeley can work together to solve everyday problems in a self-sustaining manner."*

> *– Robert Locke, SVP, Corporate Development,*
> *Johnson Controls / Tyco*

Access to Global Markets –
Village Digital Mall

The weavers' community is all but dead, both in Mori and in other villages in India. Many artisans throughout rural India are finding an increasingly interesting market difficult to access. In many cases, Indian produce is not available outside India but highly demanded. There is a lack of a market linkage between the supplier and the potential demand outside the village confines. In local markets, artisans also find it difficult to make a profit even when they are able to secure a buyer. Middlemen, retailers, and deliverymen eat up the profits at every step of the way. The Smart Village team designed an ecosystem type approach applying the before elaborated innovation process to disrupt the cycle that is keeping Mori weavers and beyond entangled in poverty. The Village Digital Mall is a platform that was developed with PayPal and streamlines the procurement process from the artisan to the buyer in both national and international markets. This process benefits the artisan without affecting the price for the buyer. Through this process, the buyer can order a local handloom product from any Internetenabled device through the Village Digital Mall (maintained and marketed by a separate player: Edvenswa) platform and using the PayPal payment gateway. The weaver can use his PayPal account to buy the necessary materials, and then creates a beautiful product to be shipped. The shipment is picked up by platform player Lal10 and is inspected for quality. The shipment is then sent directly from Mori to the buyer. No middlemen eat at the profits. This eCommerce process targets a lucrative niche market in the West, generally Indian immigrants and their families. This provides an experienced and more authentic Indian experience buying Indian goods from local Indian merchants. Previously, the weaver would retain only 10% of the revenue. In this model, he retains 70% (see Exhibit 21).

Exhibit 21 – Village Digital Mall Process to Empower rural Artisans

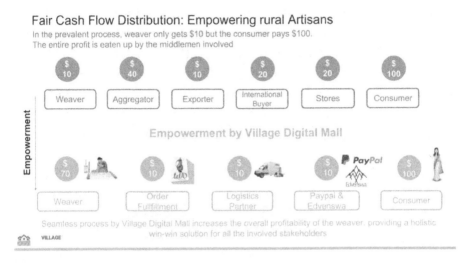

Fair Cash Flow Distribution: Empowering rural Artisans

In the prevalent process, weaver only gets $10 but the consumer pays $100.
The entire profit is eaten up by the middlemen involved

Existing government programs leave obstacles in the path of the transition to this new process. The government is currently buying products at the break-even point regardless of quality. This incentivizes weavers to produce low-quality goods for a small amount of money, which at least allows them to procure basic necessities. Weavers and other artisans, an aging community, are not motivated to position themselves more aggressively despite being offered a new platform opportunity to sell their goods (excerpt from the 2018 HBR Case *"Prototyping a Scalable Smart Village (B)"*).

Village Accelerator Program – Rural Entrepreneurs

Seeing the enormous need for rural entrepreneurship in India leading to mass emigration to e.g. the golf region and large cities in India due to lack of adequate jobs in villages, the idea of a village accelerator program was born. A general high unemployment rate in rural India clearly demonstrates the need for employment generation. However, although many aspiring Entrepreneurs are emerging, a viable ecosystem is missing to effectively accelerate business ideas in a rural setting. The village accelerator program called "Prahrambam" (Telugu language for "startup") addresses these needs and provides a comprehensive framework to validate business ideas with the Smart Village team through business model consulting and real customer interaction. Moreover, Entrepreneurs are getting trained and guided for a formal loan application to ensure funding for their promising business models. Launching this program in 2016 during the prototype phase in Mori, within a period of three months, 10 Entrepreneurs have emerged with growing businesses. Building upon this success, the program was rolled out in all of the 472 villages during the extension phase. Ultimately, 370 Entrepreneurs were selected among more than 2,500 applications to be trained on business models and loan facilitation for successfully accessing sources of funding. Now, 170 Entrepreneurs received their sanction letters from respective banks and to that date, around 100 Entrepreneurs successfully achieved adequate funding and started their businesses. This is a huge success given the challenging ecosystem in regards to an inefficient bank sector being characterized by insufficient coordination and a general lack of bank officers to be available in villages. Many times, banks already achieved their targets and were therefore unfortunately highly reticent to hand out additional funds. Another challenge comprises Entrepreneurs applying for loans without repaying previous loans. Also, participants were somehow reluctant for formal loan application when being scared of repaying loans in the future, wanting to avoid tax payments when being formal and, in some cases, were to fake bills to be handed out to respective banks. The prevailing situation is hence very tough when facing these challenges. However, the achieved successes show the possibility of overcoming given hurdles from multiple sides and rewards with promising traction resulting in overwhelming business successes from the many passionate emerging Entrepreneurs.

Story 3 – Satish's Participation in the Village Accelerator to Establish a Water Plant for his Community

"My name is Satish Kumar, 45 years old, and I used to do logistics work for a local company. Fortunately, I could afford a truck from my savings and therefore offer such driver services. When all the local companies needed to drastically cut costs, I couldn't maintain my own expenditures. I was forced to sell my truck and give up my work. I used to be a driver for over 20 years. The overall economic situation in my village didn't allow me to find a new job. After several months, I lost my faith – even small day-to-day jobs were not available.

One day I visited my good friend Visal and his family. After driving for almost 45 minutes on dusty roads and in intense heat with my bicycle, I was so happy to see him and his family. I also was craving for water, since I forgot my water bottle. I couldn't believe that Visal and his family are missing drinking water for the last three days.

It turned out that drinking warter scarcity is a major problem. The supplied water by the municipality is not sufficient for the population. In this area, we didn't have any private water plant. I couldn't think about anything else on my way back to my villages. The panchayat of my village luckily didn't facew these problems and I was really glad to be back. But what if Visal's family wouldn't get water the next days?

I was convinced to establish a water business to helpt with that but I facxed three big problems: Financial support. Finding the rightful technology. Technical support.

As I was facing the above problems and in search of some external support, I heard that a person named Chandu from the Smart Village Movement could help me and I approached him seeking some help. They explained me about different type of support which they can give me and I have explained them about my idea and I requested their help. As per their suggestions we sorted out the best company for buying the equipment for my water plant. With the help of the smart village team, we have prepared a complete financial documentation that shows that my business idea fulfills all given requirements to apply for loan. They also coached and mentored me to validate and perfect may business model.

I then proudly received the principal sanction letter and I was granted for the establishment of my water plant – my first own business. The whole panchayat in Satish's area has now ongoing water supply. It reduces water scarcity and makes all people happier – including Visal's family."

Satish Kumar, East Godavari District,
Andhra Pradesh, India

Professional Development Center – Hella

Student dropouts, missing relevant skills, and lack of adequate vocational training to succeed in job placements worsens the situation where income generation is very much constrained. Complementing the solution of creating rural entrepreneurs through the village accelerator program, professional development centers across the five districts in Andhra Pradesh have been established. Bringing in Open Innovation practitioners from the private sector to provide close to industry curricula is the core of that program. Therefore, an aspiring rural population can be equipped, developed, and empowered in their professional endeavors through training and access to tools and resources directly from industry partners. Certification programs eventually validate skills and capabilities and therefore, the program works closely with multiple third-party organizations to ensure quality standards. The government of Andhra Pradesh greatly supported this effort by providing facilities across given districts. Almost 20 company partners are working on this program to that date.

One of them is Hella, a German automotive supplier providing a 3 months program for creating certified mechanics. Having started this in late 2016, to that time, 8 batches have been successfully completed across 4 centers in the districts of East Godavari, West Godavari, Krishna, and Chittoor. Almost 100 graduated as certified mechanics so far and besides few going for higher studies, everyone else was able to get placed in an adequate job. The fees for that course are at a very low price point and the relevance for the rural population outstanding. This attracted a vast number of students, which required thus an entrance test to be implemented by Hella in cooperation with the Smart Village team. Ultimately, this program is able to create job placement and to reduce unemployment in rural areas. Concurrently, it benefits Hella in terms of innovative new programs to strengthen its corporate identity for addressing the many pain points of rural India as well as having access to a network of certified mechanics on the ground to provide repair services at quality levels. This in turn then improves Hella's spare part distribution and sales when customers are more satisfied with repair services through Hella-certified mechanics using Hella parts.

CHAPTER 12
WHAT ARE THE ROADBLOCKS AND THEIR LEARNINGS

The following describes different roadblocks from previous smart village activities. These are mainly derived from our experience of working in Andhra Pradesh since 2016. Therefore, it needs to be understood that these roadblocks can be only generalized to a certain extent – especially the experience regarding working with the government. A high-level summary of these learnings has been published as a Harvard Business Review Case Study "Prototyping a Scalable Smart Village (B)" by Solomon Darwin and Henry Chesbrough in September 2018.[1]

Barriers which Block the Project Flow (No more Flow)

Innovation barriers in rural markets are described as likely to block the entire flow of the ongoing activities. Understanding and anticipating these barriers and learning how to deal with them prevents blocking the project flow and ensures an ongoing execution when innovating with novel technologies, business models, and ecosystems in the rural setting.

Market Regulation: Entry Barriers (Outside-In)

When businesses conquer new foreign markets, there are country-specific rules and regulations in order to balance between the protection of domestic markets and to attract foreign investment. Foreign businesses hence are dependent on these policies, which in India tend to be more restrictive for outside companies. A good example can be found in the field of renewable energy. The Jawaharlal Nehru National Solar Mission (JNNSM), initiated in 2010, is a program to bring 100,000 megawatts (MW) of solar-based power generation by 2020 to India and to excel solar manufacturing domestically. However, this program imposes local content requirements (LCRs). In general, LCRs require goods to have a certain percentage of the production process sourced from local manufacturers. In order to participate in the JNNSM program, solar power developers must use solar cells and modules made in India for getting long-term contracts and to receive benefits from the Indian Government. In this case, inconsistencies with the WTO (World Trade Organization) non-discrimination obligations were found and not resolved yet. Outside solar technology providers, which could offer better and more efficient technology than available in India were systematically refused. Restrictive policies hence tend to limit foreign companies to address India's needs – even if providing a better solution than found domestically. Another example can be found in the case of Tesla bringing electric vehicles to the Indian market. Unless manufacturing locally in India, Tesla would face import penalties and import restrictions which hinders entering the market. Elon Musk is therefore requesting a temporary reprieve on local content requirements until Tesla can build a so-called giga factory.[2] In addition to local content requirements, exporters and investors to India face often unpredictable and non-transparent regulatory and tariff regimes.

Due to decentralized power and decision-making, state-level differences arise heavily in regards to political leadership, governance, regulations, taxation, labor relations, and education levels.[3] Elaborated policies and programs and lack of transparency can consequently prevent foreign companies from entering the Indian market on a larger scale. Moreover, difficult and non-transparent formal regulations and requirements can make it complex, time-consuming, costly, and to some extent risky for outside companies to enter.

In the case of deploying high-quality solar panels along with business model innovation to the rural sector, the government exclusively offered subsidies for solar panels, manufactured in India. To compete with Indian companies in a very price-sensitive market, subsidies from the government for offered products are therefore crucial for success. Kaneka, a Japanese Solar Company which focuses on high-quality solar products, was interested in working in India. Through the Smart Village project, Kaneka wanted to tap into the rural Indian market to provide solutions for prevalent pain points. However, they intended to test the market first and thus, were not committed to a huge investment for manufacturing locally in Andhra Pradesh (even when partnering with a local manufacturer) prior to that. The risk was too high without testing the market and without having full assurance that they would receive subsidies for offered products, even if manufacturing in India. As a result, Kaneka eventually backed out. Entering the market without manufacturing was consequently not possible.

This example emphasizes that local content requirements, which eventually can support the Indian private sector to succeed in its domestic market, also prevent (to some extent) foreign companies from entering India effectively. When corporates like Kaneka are not able to commit to what the government is asking for in order to enter the Indian market (due to high risks and other reasons), the inflow of new technologies, business models, and knowledge from outside slows down. This stifles innovation – in any market – be it rural or not since innovation comes from all over the world independent of national borders. However, India managed to increase the overall ease of doing business for the whole republic heavily. According to the World Bank, India ranked 130 in 2016 for its ease of doing business; many improvements in the fields of starting a business, dealing with construction permits, or trading across borders pushed India to rank 100 in 2017 and even 77 in 2018.[4] The Make in India initiative to attract foreign direct investments (FDI), which is bound with manufacturing in India to more efficiently fulfill LCRs, contributed to the better ranking.

Tapping into the Indian market, especially the rural setting, is a complex journey. 91% of interviewed companies and startups participating stated that they perceived the risk for tapping into the rural market in India as very high and high. Following the developed innovation methodology gives foreign companies the needed viable framework to successfully accomplish matching supply and demand. Yet the public sector is required to communicate regulations transparently and to commit to providing benefits as agreed on if the model is successful, e.g. subsidies for solar panels in the case of Kaneka. There needs to be a transparent process where companies can prove their models with low capital deployment to the government in order to receive relevant benefits (to eventually compete in the price-sensitive markets) when ramping up e.g. manufacturing. However, when it comes to scaling, it is highly recommended that partnering up with a local partner is crucial. Leveraging a contract manufacturer (CMOs), so-called *co-packers*, who can manufacture in collaboration for both Indian and global corporates to global standards with low-cost local labor is likely excelling the market entry. With this approach import duties and shipping costs need to be paid only on a small portion of raw materials from abroad or on proprietary intermediates for protecting intellectual property. Eventually, manufacturing can be rapidly facilitated with minimal capital deployment.

Govindarajan and Bagla (2016) state in this context in the Harvard Business Review that "once sales reach levels that impress the C-Suite, justifying an investment in factories is no longer risky or difficult; for example, Amway[5] relied on third party manufacturing for its initial entry and once volumes reached sufficient scale, it invested in a 50-acre facility in India's southern state of Tamil Nadu."[6] Since starting operations for the smart village movement in 2016 many outside India company partners successfully partnered with local manufacturing contractors.

Market Regulation: Entry Barriers (Domestic)

Having regulations for domestic market protection is a common practice among economies. However, it occurs that especially in India there are restrictive domestic entry barriers. When private companies related to the drone industry emerged in India, the Andhra Pradesh government initiated efforts to bring together the best drone companies to excel in this technology in multiple fields of application for the state. Therefore, Andhra Pradesh Drone corporations (a state-owned corporation) was founded, which offers drones made in Andhra Pradesh with the help of startups from the private sector as technology provider.[7] Since there were no overall formal regulations for drone usage and commercial appliance in that state yet[8] (which made this market highly risky), this was a big opportunity for drone companies to effectively enter the market via the government and in the end, gain a first-mover advantage in Andhra Pradesh and beyond. However, in that case, the government was selecting among existing, domestic corporates to determine which companies might be the best fit for scaling this technology in a state-owned way. We experienced this approach not only in the drone industry but in many more verticals when the government granted Memorandum of Understandings to selected companies for scaling purposes. Andhra Pradesh government plans to converge all governance services into a holistic e-governance platform to develop a government ecosystem. It is supposed to enhance efficiency, transparency, and convenience. However, this case emphasizes again the role as a gatekeeper in several cases, e.g. licensing dealers of seeds/fertilizers/ pesticides for agriculture and post-harvest management for horticulture.[9] Another example can be found when the AP Government issued tenders to private companies for implementing a state-own internet service.[10]

Ultimately, these cases draw the scaling potential away from the market into the hands of the government. Thus, it seems that to some extent a government-driven innovation approach is followed, where the government can act as a gatekeeper. This example could be a domestic market entry barrier for national companies operating in an industry where government is already facilitating technology adoption. However, additionally considering the given entry barrier for foreign firms, it is probable that this centralized, non-market driven approach might miss even more advanced or better fitting technologies, business models, and knowledge. Contrary to the market-driven approach, prevalent in western economies, the current framework for handling innovation in Andhra Pradesh seems to be therefore rather closed and seems to follow a market push methodology. However, it needs to be clearly considered that startups looking for government funding are mostly affected by the existing framework and many private sector companies are prospering without such public-sector support in an independent way.

Moreover, when the public sector is pushing for innovation to its markets (e.g. the 'Make in AP drones'), competition between private and public sectors can emerge. Competition is one of the dominant drivers for innovation in order to sustain its own market share. However, introducing new innovations e.g. in form of physical assets can come with high costs in the beginning as the scale is low and the level of maturity of the product and its production is in an early stage. When the public sector massively pushes early-stage products by covering the heavy costs and subsidizing the market price, innovation can slow down. A prominent example is the struggle of government-owned airline Air India finding buyers while being bankrupted. Being protected by Indian government for many years, modernizing structures has been delayed and costs cannot compete with competitors. Additionally, a huge debt prevents private investors from taking over and restructuring Air India.[11]

Throughout the past operations, we encountered challenges while dealing with the public sector. Particularly, we dealt with solutions that directly competed with the public sector, thus making the projects more complex. However, many opportunities for complementing each other arises then.

When facing such situations where market access is impeded, it is recommended to collaborate with and learn from given situations. In cases where government support is needed for scaling (e.g. legal clearance or financial support), it is crucial to strictly stick to the applied smart village innovation methodology where the choice for scaling comes exclusively from the end consumer in form of demand – regardless of any other criteria. Consequently, although deployment is executed partly through the public sector, a marketdriven approach is being followed. Ultimately, both partners, the Smart Village project and the government are required to align with the Smart Village vision that the right and proven solution from the private sector integrated into the triple helix system can transform the lives in rural areas in a self-sustainable way.

"It is difficult to enter into the rural India market specially if your product is dependent on availability of basics. Most corporations are dependent on some form of technology to help them scale their

solutions successfully, lack of which can come out as the biggest bottleneck to requisite growth. Also, without the government connects, it becomes extremely difficult to find the right stakeholder to sell your product. With UC Berkeley facilitating the connect for both the technology solution and government connects, entering the market becomes fairly easier.

– *Ronak Khandelwal, President DronaMaps (Indian Startup)*

Excursus: Government competing with the private sector

When the AP government launched the Andhra Pradesh State FiberNet (state public sector unit) to provide internet, TV, and telephone at nominal rates, it directly competed with private internet providers. Although its implementation is done through private bodies, e.g. local cable operators, the public argued that such government-controlled service was likely to control media and internet services but also that the government itself pushed its citizen to use AP FiberNet. This ultimately implies that the private sector internet providers are likely to be eliminated from the market.[12] If additionally considered that subsidized prices increase market power, competition vanishes eventually. Of course, this is not prevalent in every vertical but clearly emphasizes the power of the government on its citizen and on private sector companies and therefore affecting innovation. In this example, it is argued that insiders got preferred to get the contract for providing the hardware and software to roll out the State FiberNet. Despite having an existing e-tender process implemented by the government of Andhra Pradesh, some companies seem to struggle to succeed since the approval process was not immediately transparent to newcomers. Winning companies tend to be insiders.

Limited and Not-Timely Delivered Funding

In the case of the Smart Village project, which happened in collaboration with the government of Andhra Pradesh, funding came exclusively from the public sector. During negotiations for the Memorandum of Understanding, a budget had been determined to cover necessary expenses for the project, e.g. salaries, office expenses etc. However, the project couldn't start on time and as a matter of fact needed to stop due to delayed funding from the government. Necessary expenditures for salaries had been approved from the government but came with delay – both in the beginning and throughout the project when the second half of the funding was needed to be released. Moreover, the necessary funds corresponded not to the 472 villages but less, which tightened the budget noticeably. Establishing the smart village organization required hiring people at different levels with different expertise according to government standards without setting the wrong expectation of offering a public sector job. Moreover, it was difficult to hire passionate, young, English speaking, and tech-savvy persons in a village for the predetermined salary.

Ultimately, establishing the smart village organization with over 500 people within the given two months due to the delay of funding was difficult. There was the immediate need to start operations. The work pace from the Smart Village project and the government thus didn't align since the bureaucracy lagged behind. It was critical to have transparent communication to execute needed adjustments for the project. However, the government promised to deliver needed funds but were hindered by their different layers of bureaucracy, which made it very hard and almost impossible to assess when the project could start or continue. The on-ground team couldn't rely on the timely dispersal of funds, which created a tense relationship. The same situation repeated towards the end of the project. The second half of the accredited funds were not given on time (as committed) due to various political and economic circumstances in the state of Andhra Pradesh. Again, communication from the government wasn't transparent so that interns and Mandal Directors, which accounted for 95% of the workforce, couldn't be adjusted to either sustain operations with fewer people for the given time frame or to lay them off with enough time buffer. This not only stopped the project and its operations but also caused disappointment and even incomprehension among the employees on-ground. Dangerous riots and even lawsuits were averted through conflict practices. Core to these had been sensitive and transparent communication in small team meetings to address concerns and anger about the conflictual situation. Ultimately, out of passion and aspiration, the whole core team sustained the project for 6 more weeks for proper closure without any salary.

All partners (the Smart Village project and the government) need to fulfill the agreed deliverables on time. However, organizations need to consider unstable conditions, especially in developing countries. Therefore, research about how the respective government is operating should be conducted in advance. Risk management for such eventualities needs to be integrated to prevent financial and political barriers to stop the project. Moreover, conflict management should be required training for all managers to avoid riots and lawsuits.

Limited Resources for Piloting and Scaling

Many national and international companies and Startups were participating in the Smart Village initiative to solve prevalent pain points by providing technologies along with innovative business models. However, when it comes to testing the developed models by rolling out pilots, many companies, especially startups, faced severe problems for that, and in some cases, projects completely stopped. Five limits mainly due to financial resources were hereby main barriers.

First, many startups simply couldn't dedicate budget to such pilots in the first place. It happened that many of them became part of this project in a very dynamic way and thus, their overall budget had been already fixed. Funded startups tend to require a clear account of their financial activities to their shareholders and lastly, strictly stick to their determined budget allocation. It seems the issue was not only about the funds but also about being able to dedicate capital to projects like the Smart Village initiative. Healthcubed for example, an innovative startup that provides basic vital diagnosis with a small, portable device, could only provide a certain number of devices – significantly less than needed to successfully test the model since not enough budget could be allocated to the smart village pilots. 43% of asked participants within the smart village project used a dedicated budget whereas 20% were raising funds, respectively. Only very few used CSR funds or own private funds.

Second, companies, especially startups don't always have the financial means for piloting at times, even if they can and are willing to dedicate a budget for those. Early-stage startups were open to change their business model and were aspiring to test and pivot the developed model on-ground. However, missing capital often stopped or delayed executing pilots. Statwig, recently titled as one of the 15 Indian blockchain startups to watch out for 2018[13] was very much into piloting the created model on-ground (in the field of rural aquaculture supply chains) but needed to delay an extensive pilot due to the lack of a suitable budget (among other reasons like delayed hardware development). Eventually, the young and innovative firm raised a noticeable amount of money from UNICEF and dedicated their budget to roll out pilots in rural India as planned. Through a lack of appropriate funds, projects are likely to be delayed or even to be stopped, which was named as a major challenge by 53% of surveyed participating companies and startups.

Third, misperception about the Smart Village project being the channel to access the government to eventually obtain public sector funds occurred from time to time among participating companies, and Startups. However, financial support from the government for projects within the Smart Village scope only merely happened. In the end, this misperception attracted few companies without having the needed capital (for conducting pilots), which eventually delayed or even stopped their participation since effectively and efficiently accessing the government is complex, even when having support from the Smart Village project. It is ironic to some extent that both parties, startups and the government, had wrong expectations from each other (in some cases). Some startups to get financial support from the government while the latter one was expecting them to bring innovation and to create valuable impact for the state government independently without requiring financial support.

Fourth, when initiating a collaboration between private and public sectors, bypassing of the smart village team occurred. Google X offers a Free Space Optical Communication (FSOC) technology to provide internet in rural areas. When meeting CM Naidu on the December 29th event in Mori, the AP government was very much interested in that technology and spent most of their time allotted for corporate interaction with Google X. This very moment initiated the collaboration between Google X and AP government, and was facilitated by the Smart Village initiative to address the pain point of poor internet connectivity. Ultimately, the smart village project was excluded in further discussions between Silicon Valley businesses and the state government of Andhra Pradesh. Moreover, AP government claimed to have brought Google to Andhra Pradesh by themselves. Bypassing was a serious issue when startups and companies objecting to access the government via organizations like the Smart Village initiative.

There are two sides to every story. Governments usually try to get the best and most prestigious companies from abroad to invest in their state. (CM Naidu, for example, brought Microsoft to Andhra Pradesh in the late 1990s, which fueled Hyderabad to be a center of IT in India[14]). Leveraging this approach, middlemen are prevalent, getting a commission for bringing deals with foreign companies. Professor Darwin was prevented from attending meetings between AP government officials and Silicon Valley companies in California. The brokers in the middle simply feared that their efforts are not valued (and not monetized) when in fact Professor Darwin brought these companies for free along with the Smart Village project. Thus, such gatekeepers can be a huge barrier to innovation when selecting companies on criteria to maximize their very own profits.

Fifth, after having a proofed model, scaling requires resources (e.g. an appropriate budget) which can be a big barrier, mainly for early-stage startups. This happens particularly when the speed and scope of scaling are dependent on many variables, which underlay not only internal shareholders but also external stakeholders. In the case of the Indian-based startup named Storeking, a mobile application and order management tool for small general street shopkeepers, scaling to hundreds of villages with a very restricted timeframe required extraordinary resources. The acceptance rate of their solution from rural shopkeepers was enormous since providing great benefits when increasing their product portfolio and getting their procured goods delivered. In order to keep up the pace, quality and timely delivery decreased, and additional resources were needed. This barrier could be partly avoided in the 472 villages where the Smart Village team supported their operations heavily with the on-ground workforce and relationships with the local governments to keep up the claimed pace.

Faced challenges limited the overall potential of piloting due to missing capital, missing allocation of capital, and misperception about access to capital, and lastly missing scaling potential requires a vibrant and transparent platform to connect all dots. To overcome these barriers, first, transparent communication from the beginning for participating companies is crucial to be able to dedicate capital to pilots or evaluating the financial feasibility of its participation in general (to also reduce misperception about smart village project as a gateway for public support). Second, access to multiple sources for funding from the government and from the private sector (Venture Capital, Business Angels) as well as mentoring is to be facilitated from the Smart Village project. In turn, public and private investors receive expert advisory from UC Berkeley in terms of funding the most promising projects.

Business Model Adoption Constraints

Large corporations were very much interested in tapping into the rural market in India, but it is less likely to accomplish this when there is no flexibility of pivoting their business model to the rural setting. Moreover, it takes a dedicated budget, internal commitment (especially from the c-level) among many other resources. Ultimately, it can be argued that the less open a company is in terms of complementing its existing business model with new business models or pivoting their prevalent model to the rural setting, tapping into new domains and aiming for transformational or disruptive innovation instead of incremental innovation is unlikely to happen. Coming from different markets to the rural setting requires many changes or extensions in the business model to address the identified needs and eventually merge into an ecosystem with other parties. In many cases, these requirements couldn't be fulfilled and projects halted or stopped. Needed adjustments and changes were too extensive, were not aligned with the overall strategy, affected the core business, or came with high risks. When SAP Ariba, the largest global b2b procurement platform, wanted to enter the rural market, the possible fit was narrow from the first place, since the platform usually addressed sophisticated businesses. In the Indian rural market processes, technology utilization and the general situation differ vastly. For SAP Ariba it was not possible to change whole processes and functionalities on their core platform in order to test the proposed business model, which was recommended from UC Berkeley and was derived from intensive research in this field. The scope from the core platform was too different for the rural setting and new resources couldn't be committed for completely developing a suitable solution. However, SAP continued their great efforts with different existing solutions (e.g. SAP Rural Sourcing) to address given pain points in rural India. Almost every third surveyed participating company and startup named the difficulty of adapting one's business model to the rural setting as a major challenge they have faced.

Having a clear objective and commitment to apply an independent, new business model that clearly can deviate from the existing one gives fewer constraints but can require many resources for implementation. Incorporating a lean startup philosophy and culture is a major requirement for all kinds of corporates participating in the smart village project. Processes to be simple and fast adaptable to the particular scenario should come along with the willingness to change or extend the existing business models or technologies for the necessary market fit. Being open and having the commitment and culture to do so is then a crucial factor for success. Therefore, prior to joining innovation activities in such projects, both sides (company and smart village orchestrator) are to evaluate the success of the potential collaboration. The presented Open Innovation framework for emerging rural markets provides a methodology to assess the match of collaboration and if the core business gets affected in any means. This prevents many barriers, which are likely to come when having not the right culture, alignment, and commitment for the smart village vision of co-developing models for the rural market.

IP and Data Sharing

Open Innovation is the core methodology and design philosophy of the Smart Village project. Every participating company should incarnate this philosophy for creating the aimed value in a collaborative way, especially via Open Innovation ecosystems. If a company is closed and not willing (to certain extents) to share resources, information (data), and expertise with other parties, it is consequently difficult to sustain the participation within the smart village project.

Prior to the above-described healthcare ecosystem, another healthcare platform design existed and was partly executed. The approach emphasized on capturing basic vitals in remote areas with portable devices and to connect this data with doctors (Primary, Secondary and Tertiary Healthcare) and the government to provide data-driven treatment. Therefore, sharing data with multiple actors was central to this idea since companies like Care Hospital, Apollo Hospital, Bodimetrics, and AP government were involved with complementing roles in this project. The technology wasn't the problem, even giving away the needed technology for low cost or even for free was committed by participating companies. When the government required the companies to share the captured health data, the companies refused to share the respective data. Data sharing turned out to be the major barrier, which eventually stopped this project. Moreover, even data sharing between the three companies was not possible since everyone wanted to keep their own data or wanted to get an excessive commission in case of sharing.

When a company's business model mainly banks on data, the willingness to share data is, of course, limited and comes along with sharing agreements, which in the end can increase the overall costs for the end consumer purchasing the provided solution. Sharing agreements tend hereby to be very complex and time and money consuming, which can slow down the overall innovation process or even halt it. However, through data, private companies can better develop products and services for the consumers and lastly address their needs and pain points. Nowadays, in the digital economy, data rather than physical assets tends to be the new capital and the overall basis for creating value for private companies. The trust in the government and private companies for data collection from the rural sector is therefore critical. Indian's openness to share data with private companies is high until the user experience is bad. Only 29% of consumers in India have concerns about the amount of personal data that companies have about them.[15]

Business model designs for the rural sector come with the exchange of data for outmost efficiency in any matter. Therefore, data capturing is an essential part of business operations. As described above, relevant data from the rural sector is perceived to be difficult to acquire. Closely collaborating with the government and spreading awareness about the benefits customers are getting when sharing data is consequently essential. However, privacy regulations are strictly to be followed and communicated to sustain long-term customer trust. Smart Village partner Storeking, which designed their model with a major success (shopkeeper procurement application) to address the pain point of missing supply in villages are continuously improving the customer experience and beyond through data richness. Founder Sridhar Gundaiah states that "the idea is to become a powerhouse of rural data and emphasize the usage of consumption data to power the supply, and be present in all 650,000 villages of rural India".[16]

SUMMARY:

Barriers which Block the Project Flow

Experienced Barriers	Possible Solutions

Market Regulations

• Foreign and domestic companies & startups are impeded to tap into the Indian market. • Pace of projects is slowed down.	Provide an ecosystem of local partner companies that outside businesses can leverage to enter the market. Bypass regulated market entry process when state government is in charge for scaling by operating purely market and customer driven.

Limited Resources for Piloting & Scaling

• Not-timely delivered government grants. • Missing dedicated budget (startups, corporations) • Lack of funds in general (startups, corporations) • Misperception from private sector of Smart Village being a channel to government funds. • Succesful pilots require powerful scaling partners to reach full scale.	• Don't start operations before government grants are wired. • Establish and provide a rich ecosystem consisting of accelerators, venture capital firms, private investors and corporate venture programs to let startups access funding for various lifecycle stages. • Educate participants about possibilities and frontiers of funding to prevent misperception.

Business Model Adoption Difficulties

• Changing its own business model to rural settings can be challenging.	Curate business enterprises that have the alignment, culture and commitment to pivot their business model to the rural market.

IP & Data Sharing Issues

• Open Innovation requires in- and outflow of knowledge, expertise or resources. • Willingness to open can be a barrier in cases.	Consult and advise partners for sharing agreements to accelerate data driven business models or IP intensive collaborations.

Weak Links within the Existing System (System itself Hinders Flow)

The fragile portion of a chain, where it is most likely to break is in this context referred to as weak links. These trigger inefficiency within the existing system that a project is operating in and hinder the overall project flow. Although many weak links have been obvious prior to starting the project, their extent was not clear in the first place, respectively, and new unforeseen issues emerged during the ongoing operations.

Impact vs. Innovation for Rural Populations

The political situation (as perceived in Andhra Pradesh) might be a significant factor to handicap innovation. On many sides of the political spectrum, there are candidates from competitive parties. Political parties in rural India seem to follow similar approaches for rural development, mainly providing subsidies and free benefits for people to gain attraction and to ultimately win votes among the rural population. This approach is of course not unique and prevalent in many countries and systems everywhere and emphasizes generally various efforts from politicians to be channelized to the people to eventually win their votes. Although rural Indian population is living their everyday life more simple than western rural populations (in some states like Andhra Pradesh or Arunachal Pradesh) where they don't have to put much effort in place to get benefits from the government to address their necessities. Thus, basic needs are being taken care of (in states like Andhra Pradesh) by the government, which is very valid and necessary in such conditions since many people face poor nutrition or insufficient health support.

However, this system, which provides relevant incentives for both sides (politicians and citizens), tends to sustain itself as a continuous cycle without providing room and the need for innovation.

Innovation particularly happens often from places of poverty, out of chaos or disorder where a clear need exists to overcome such situations – not in scenarios where the government is taking care of it. Moreover, the design of campaigns and voting behavior in the rural setting is special. In order to win elections in rural India, politicians are required to show results from the past period. People in rural areas tend not to vote for prospective visions and roadmaps like in western countries, where the future agenda holds the most weight. They heavily rate results from the past, e.g. throughout the last year, how much subsidies on rice were given to the people via fair price shops in each village to targeted cardholders (at quantum and rates fixed by the government)[17]. Consequently, politicians need to showcase their effected efforts and which impact they created on people.

Understanding this given scenario helps to further grasp the constraints given by the government in terms of innovation. As a government-funded research project and thus being accountable for all executed activities comes with the requirement to align with objectives (to a certain degree) from the respective local and state governments and their political parties. This was experienced initially when villages were partly selected based on political means not based on their feasibility for being a testing ground to deploy technologies. Additionally, in the situation where clear, obvious benefits help not only the population and are additionally able to influence the success of elections positively, merely have short to medium-term impacts on citizens and seem to be strongly favored.

However, the innovation process requires flexibility and therefore time, especially when providing novel technologies, business models, and processes to the rural sector, as the fit between offered products/services and the end consumer needs to be outstanding to ultimately reach the objected acceptance and traction. Facing the overall political situation, which steadily was getting tenser due to upcoming elections, expectations for the project from the government changed. The impact on rural citizens, proved by hard numbers was requested. Even if long term projects would pay off (in terms of e.g. impact), it was still not relevant or not important for politicians since the window for seeing cause and effect is very narrow.

It takes a long time to eventually succeed with projects and to create an impact for people. However, people tend to not attribute efforts to specific political actors being responsible for projects, which happened a long time ago and therefore forget about it. Politicians need therefore show quick wins – even if not sustainable and endurable. Winning elections therefore clearly correlates negatively with innovating in a perpetual and time taking pace. This constraint clearly restricted the innovation process in many means and comes with high risk when being indirectly associated with bureaucrats and politicians.

Public Sector Managing Innovation

The government of Andhra Pradesh is very progressive in implementing technology and bringing in innovation to their state to further develop its economy. Chief Minister Naidu sees that the government has given the priority to changing people's lives with the help of technologies.[18] However, as described above, governments can act as the gatekeeper for innovation from outside the countries as well as from inside the country. Innovation coming from private industry is somehow managed and controlled by the public sector (as experienced in Andhra Pradesh). This is reflected in a heavily regulated framework for the private sector. Based on the Indian National Innovation Survey, 2014, Pachouri and Sharma (2016) indicate, that nearly 68% of innovative small firms and about 75% of innovative medium firms have the perception that government policy and to meet government regulatory requirements are barriers to innovation in India. India's ranking in the ease of doing business index reflects a burdensome regulatory environment for businesses when high costs to meet a large number of regulatory requirements restrict innovation capacity.[19] In addition to that, India still ranks 80th (out of 190 countries) globally in the corruption index 2017 from Transparency International.[20]

Larry Downes (2019) emphasizes in his book *The Laws of Disruption: Harnessing the New Forces That Govern Life and Business in the Digital Age* that lawmaking in modern days of the information age is characterized by the law of disruption and that "technology changes exponentially, but social, economic, and legal systems change incrementally."[21] This emphasizes the conflict between social, economic, political and legal systems. Ultimately, innovation and prevailing public-sector frameworks have difficulties to align as implications from this pacing problem will affect the way the private sector, public sector, and culture evolve together in the future. It will be harder than ever to govern using traditional legal and regulatory mechanism when facing highly dynamic technological developments with the ongoing potential for disruption.

Generally, micromanaging and highly regulating innovation refer to a regulated framework, which can reduce the development of the full growth potential of innovation and even increase the pacing problem regarding technology vs. social, political, and legal systems. In the end, innovation happens often best when initially being unregulated like AirBnB or Uber, which immediately faced tremendous demand. Disruptive innovation can change prevalent industries and emphasizes the need for policymakers to adopt regulations according to new paradigms, as in the cases of AirBnB and Uber. Ultimately, demand-driven, customer-centric innovation will prosper which requires an ecosystem of policies that fosters the progress instead of overregulating it. Building social capital via new models and technologies can eventually become a leverage to let innovation thrive along with the public sector.

Public Sector Bureaucracy

As mentioned before, working in India and getting things done requires ultimately public-sector collaboration since interlinkages with the government throughout the whole ecosystem seem to be extremely high. Therefore, valuable advice and support were asked and then given from many government officials but ultimately having no single point of contact (from the government) given for the project created a rather inefficient collaboration in terms of accountability, delivering agreed objectives, and sharing the same expectations. Having had a dispute with the initially assigned owner of the project from the government in terms of the general approach for the project left a big gap. Eventually, this dispute couldn't be resolved by both sides, which led to unclear ownership. The needed criteria for a project owner from the government as aligning with the overall vision for innovation and being highly respected in the government are to be secured from the beginning. In the end, there were multiple points of contact during phase 2, which made it difficult to get the overall support from all government departments. Not reporting to a single person but to many persons slowed down the progress and restricted the project from being fully accountable to the government.

It is understandable that not being handheld by one government key person creates information asymmetries among the departments and different government levels. Thus, the lack of information about the project emerged into different acceptance-, expectations and support-levels regarding the smart village project. It happened quite often that individual officials on various levels had the wrong perception about the smart village project, having the scope for creating short term impacts or providing free goods/services to citizens since local government leaderships had the perception that the project is a government project as funds came from the state government. Consequently, the extent of support varied dramatically. To adjust such different perceptions, it was required to start all over again by explaining the project, establishing good relationships, and eventually starting the initiative to receive the necessary individual support from the public sector.

Moreover, there were issues in terms of alignment and support within the government structure per se when executing the required, committed (e.g. from state-level) support for the smart village project. Generally, it seems that the mindset of the governments relates to maximizing control within the respective sphere of action of its actors. This is not limited to India or any other country, it is obviously prevalent in any democracy. Orders for project execution diluted when coming down to the district or Mandal levels because of differing opinions which in the end refer to efforts of prevailing power in the first place. This made it tough to operate when commitment from a higher level for e.g. providing promised facilities for the *Professional Development Centers* vanished at the district level and eventually at the Mandal level. This very process of following up and reassuring the promised support was highly time-consuming and slowed down the overall progress significantly.

Ultimately, having government departments and government levels with different perceptions about the project due to asymmetric information (e.g. when missing a single point of contact for the project) and due to the overall driving force of sustaining power on multiple government levels also affects other stakeholders. At the ground level, this can influence people and determine their expectations about the project. If e.g. a member of the Legislative Assembly (local politician) has insufficient information about the project, a misperception can arise which eventually is communicated to the panchayats (local government) and the respective citizens. We faced such difficulties many times when people were asking for and expecting infrastructure e.g. roads when talking about the smart village project.

Communication about the project starts initially from the top and it needs to be ensured that this knowledge is passed to all kinds of government levels. Since people tend to highly appreciate government efforts and value their opinions, it is crucial that along with the on-ground force the message is consistently communicated to the people – by both, government and the smart village project.

Moreover, following up with the government officials often requires personal attendance. Being located in Mori, far away from all district headquarters, additionally limited the capacity to meet in person as the travel was costly and time-consuming. The probability of eventually meeting the targeted person was small since the government officials tend to be very busy and not easily accessible. As higher government officials are fully scheduled, it occurs that appointments get spontaneously rescheduled or shortened. It might happen that a scheduled meeting happens on the walk to the office or car. This was especially so for the multiple nodal officers for the smart village team. The higher the nodal officer's position within the government, the busier he was and the less effective the communication and exchange with the smart village team was. Thus, many times, meetings were confirmed but lastly not possible. Access to the AP government for the smart village team was therefore limited and difficult (of course few exceptions such as the East Godavari Collector were prevalent).

Described weak links also affected indirectly participating corporates. Since the Smart Village team having the role of an orchestrator in the innovation process, restricted access to the government along with inconsistent support from different departments and the bureaucracy itself slowed down innovation projects which were relying on government support. For example, getting needed clearance and formal agreements (MoUs), facilitated by the smart village team for the TechMahindra incubated Startup Hygge from California, proved to be a big challenge. Hygge provides a smart peer-to-peer energy trading platform along with energy buffer systems and renewable energy production infrastructure (e.g. solar power) and was willing to come to Mori to transform this village into an energy self-sustainable village with reliable power supply. Moreover, it raised 5 million US-Dollars from the Canadian government as a Foreign Direct Investment (FDI) for India. However, it took over one year until finally signing the deal with AP government to start operations in Mori. Every second participating company and startups named government bureaucracy slowing down or stopping one's project as a major challenge while requiring regular clearance at the same time. Eventually, resources for pilots, scaling efforts and needed regulated clearances, committed by the government clearly contribute to the success of projects but delays or halts really slow down or stop any progress.

In the end, all parties (the government as the provider of funds, smart village team as executing the project, corporates as innovators, universities as knowledge providers, and villagers as the stakeholders) need to stick to the overall agreement and the deliverables written in the MoU within the specified time frame. But from all sides including the Smart Village project, inconsistency emerged when new deliverables, changes in deliverables and, cutting of deliverables evolved. Government politics on all levels, corporate politics, team politics, and also consumer behavior on the ground caused such changes in expectations. Then, communication from all sides needs to be very efficient and transparent and an accountability structure that integrates the necessities of the government needs to be implemented. It is very important to closely work with the government to ensure these objectives. However, the work culture and way of execution differs vastly between government and lean organizations like the smart village project. One perception occurred that the project itself was mainly under the prevailing public-sector hierarchy e.g. Chief Minister among other high officials being the overall advocates to satisfy.

Prevailing Innovation Perception

According to a World Bank report (2012), poverty in rural areas still remains at 25% and 14% in urban areas. 1 in 5 Indians is poor.[22] (The international poverty line is $ 1.90 per day.[23]) With India being a very poor country a few generations back, the government had and still has the necessity to provide resources (e.g. via schemes and policies) to address the basic needs of its people. This shapes the overall prevailing perception that the introduction of technology on a large scale comes through the government which again implies the public sector taking care of the needs of its population and improving livelihood. Seeing this from the perspective of innovators, we experienced many business models having the government as the major client in mind. Value capturing is projected by coming under specific schemes or getting general funding for scaling. The cloud physician ecosystem model as described before is mainly dependent on the government as a funding partner since health workers in Andhra Pradesh are providing free services for people. Moreover, primary healthcare is free in India. The willingness of patients to pay extra for treatment is therefore very limited. In the end, the government can fund the private companies, which are providing the service for high-quality treatment, and which are able to build on public sector rural health workers at the same time. Such a technology introduction from the private sector consequently happens via the government on a big scale, which is again stirring up the perception level of government taking care of needs.

This existing framework building on the history of India heavily fostering such a mindset among its population and lastly, affects innovation approaches when primarily banking on the public sector as the main collaboration partner. Independent, private businesses are of course successfully existing, although this mindset seems to still be there to certain extents, e.g. in the case of WIPRO (major technology services corporation) co-developing business models with the Smart Village team. WIPRO proposed multiple solutions to tackle the lack of information among villagers or missing financial inclusion. Market research was conducted to evaluate the design and product-market fit. However, in the end, the value capturing design from WIPRO was banking on the government to pay for WIPROs services when it was implemented on-ground. In general, only one out of the 21 surveyed companies and startups participating in the Smart Village project stated that no resources from the public sector were needed during the project. Among the remaining ones 38% required funding from the public sector, 81% asked for Government being a scaling partner, 62% needed the government as a channel to promote their goods and services, and lastly, 38% leveraged the additional network through the government.

When addressing rural markets like Andhra Pradesh, it is very difficult to independently introduce and scale technology without government assistance. Since many needs are being taken care of from the government, the system is heavily interlinked with the public sector (as described above), which creates the need for government collaboration and gives in return rise to this mindset among the population. However, with new disruptive models, the cycle of rural poverty can break when both villagers and companies stop being dependent on government-led development assistance programs to eventually enter markets and thrive in a self-entrepreneurial driven way. Serving as a role model, such models can eventually change the existing mindset among citizens and Entrepreneurs to a more open way of innovating.

Internal Hurdles

Fully reproducing the Mori pilot to 472 villages was impossible due to the pain points, demographics, and culture differing vastly across the state. Implementing technologies in different areas always meant different outcomes and acceptance levels. As mentioned before, the complex ecosystem consisting of local governments differed in terms of commitment and execution power across constituencies and even villages. Companies couldn't provide investment for large pilots in all the 472 villages. Ultimately, the villages were used as laboratories for gaining research insights when implementing novel solutions, but somehow, technology implementation couldn't be ensured everywhere. Moreover, establishing an organization with a size of over 500 employees within two months for phase 2 was a big challenge. Organic growth couldn't happen and thus, internal organizational hurdles emerged from time to time. In general, adequate processes were to be implemented and adapted, leadership to be proven and project execution to be managed. A lean organization was set up but could never hold up to the fully aimed quality and extension level during a short period of time.

Differences among the team regarding work culture, innovation perception, and culture itself happened when different Indian, American, and European mindsets collaborated. Although many different perspectives can lead to innovative and outside-the-box thinking, the extent of variances caused inefficiencies at times. A very prevalent mindset in India is the close relation and dependency of the government.

Work quality sometimes became a major challenge when the available level of quality was not sufficient for the required tasks.

This happened for example when conducting more sophisticated surveys with the help of the on-ground team. In order to get the desired results, a detailed understanding of the survey and the respective field is required but was lacking in some cases. However, in-depth coaching and teaching the interns prior to each survey could prevent such issues. Ultimately, the quality level of the whole organization could improve during the operations, however, quality differences among teams along all hierarchical levels remained and slowed down progress. Moreover, it was perceived that the overall level of intrinsic motivation happened to be little. Beyond fulfilling orders, employees tend to not come up with own ideas or initiatives. This can also be referred to as the hierarchical structures in the rural culture and to the on-ground leadership within the organization. It is important to understand and respect such cultural tendencies to better operate with mutual benefits. Consequently, sensitive incentives and support to establish intrinsic motivation are to be implemented, e.g. with internal innovation competitions, which was a successful campaign during phase 2. Mandal directors along with their interns were to search for new innovative companies to address given pain points. Best models have been chosen and implemented. Additionally, best teams were appreciated with future promotion options and letters of appreciation.

Due to changes in the project scope caused by all participating parties, the utilization of the on-ground team couldn't be fully ensured to the determined level. Having had fewer pilots than expected in all of the 472 villages on-ground, in some villages, pilots and technology deployment was not happening from time to time. This caused miss-utilization in some instances and moreover, it couldn't fulfill the expectations from the interns deploying technologies, which affected their motivation. The scope needs to be reasonable and realistic in the first place when determining deliverables.

Opportunistic behavior within the smart village organization occurred when aiming to leverage the project to access the government for getting job placement. Andhra Pradesh is a state where government jobs are referred to as having a very high social reputation, the incentive for employees to shift to public sector jobs was big. Moreover, in phase 1, people from startups were closely working with or were a part of the smart village organization which leads to biased decisions, e.g. which company to choose for given pain points. Such behavior caused miss utilization of time and efforts from some employees which affected work quality and the overall progress.

A major weak link was non-transparent communication and the unavailability of information. Depending on individual work quality levels, documentation of information was not prevalent and created huge information gaps. Moreover, monitoring and reporting processes were at some points tough to implement, especially on Mandal and village level because internet connectivity and efficient local leadership were missing.

Ultimately, establishing a medium-size organization in the rural setting which needs to fulfill high-quality requirements and standards is a major challenge. Variances in culture, work approaches, work quality or innovation perceptions need to converge into a firm and efficient form of organization, with which every employee can identify and can operate positively. Of course, this takes time and effort; continuous learnings are to be implemented.

SUMMARY:
Weak Links Within the System

Experienced Weak Links	Possible Solutions
Public Sector Bureaucracy and Politics	
• Short term impact is preferred over sustainable models. • Misperception about Smart Village project (e.g. infrastructure implementation) on various government levels. • Challenges when working with public sector in terms of access, slow processes & different support levels.	Being aware of political constraints and deal with them effectively when sticking to fixed, reasonable deliverables. Continuously update and explain your mission and nature of your project towards all levels of government stakeholders. Determine a nodal officer as the main point of contact from the government.
Prevailling Innovation Perception	
• Startups, companies and citizen perceive government to be responsible for innovation and being a channel for its deployment. • Hinders disruptive innovation.	Educate stakeholders about government independent innovation strategies and be a role model among citizens and entrepreneurs when showing respective results.
Internal Project Hurdles	
• Scaling to 472 villages couldn't be fully achieved. • Establishing a 500+ people organization in a short time couldn't be done organically. • Changing project scope and lack of information on various levels.	Organically grow and develop comprehensive leadership to move along with a diverse organisation. Establish a strong strategy and stick to it consequently.

Bottlenecks to Slow Down the Progress (Bottlenecks Slow Down Flow)

Bottlenecks describe any point of congestion within an organization or ecosystem that hinders the workflow across the various processes that make up the system. This leads to a lot of work in progress, queues, and will increase the overall project life cycle time and eventually the project costs. Factors that may cause bottlenecks are e.g. resource inefficiency, lack of resources, and improper communication, which are described in the following.

Missing Internet Infrastructure

In December 2016 Andhra Pradesh Government launched AP FiberNet in Mori when CM Naidu went to see the Smart Village prototype (see also chapter 3.2). AP FiberNet provides internet along with telephone connection and 250 cable television channels at a low cost. Implementation is done through private bodies. The whole village of Mori with its 1,189 households and a population of 4,500 got access to AP FiberNet. CM Naidu stated that "Mori is the first Smart village in the country to achieve 100% digital literacy. The government would put its efforts to change all villages into Smart Villages in a phased manner." The government announced its plan to implement 1 million AP FiberNet boxes across the state.[24] Extending the Smart Village project to 472 villages in 2017, the government assured that all respective villages will have full connectivity via AP Fiber. In May 2018, only 214,000 households across Andhra Pradesh were connected and it was announced that by December 2018, 25,000 villages would be onboarded.[25] This caused serious issues when internet connectivity was missing or was poor among the 472 given villages, which slowed down the overall progress. In the rural context, the following problems give an interesting picture of what issues emerge in rural India, which would be not assumed viewing from a western perspective.

1. Local cable operators didn't have any training, technical expertise, or awareness about optical fiber. Therefore, deployment came with delay and many technical and maintenance problems emerged.[26]

2. Deployed cables had quality issues, e.g. easily breaking or damaged by trees and animals.
3. Voltage problems and missing stabilizers in villages lead to an interrupted connection. Boxes broke easily.
4. There is no proper billing mechanism established.
5. Inconsistent Internet speed.
6. Some people were financially suffering because they had to maintain 2 connections for some time when switching from normal cable to AP FiberNet.
7. No implementation of AP FiberNet and therefore no internet connectivity, especially in Srikakulum District.

The smart village idea banks mainly on digital connectivity that lets village communities uplift in a self-entrepreneurial way. The above bottlenecks and given that many assigned villages were not equipped with internet connectivity at all, made it very tough to operate and slowed down or stopped the process.

Especially data collection and introduction of mobile applications could not be executed properly, and in some cases stopped completely. Ultimately, it is to be ensured that villages participating in initiatives like the smart village project have basic connectivity. Fulfilling agreed deliverables needs to be reasonable and achievable. Therefore, required basic infrastructure such as internet infrastructure must be available in the determined areas of operations.

Villager's Consumer Behavior

In general, rural consumers in India are understood to be widely ignorant as well as unorganized. Village people face poor knowledge about individual rights and lack skills to execute rational decision-making based on information regarding the services or products. In several cases, rural consumers are therefore exploited in many ways, e.g. sub-standard products and services, adulterated foods, or defective seeds.[27] Operating in and targeting such markets is therefore complex and takes a sensitive approach, especially when introducing new technologies and business models. Consequently, it can be a huge bottleneck when not properly understanding the consumer behavior and prevailing conditions of the rural setting.

According to the report on the buying behavior of rural consumers in India, Department of Consumer Affairs (2016), "consumer behavior is the behavior exhibited by people in planning, purchasing and using of economic goods and services."[28] Consumer behavior in rural areas is influenced by various factors and is seen as complex and dynamic. Major general factors affecting the buying behavior are geographic influences, family (e.g. joint family influences), economic income (e.g. quantum of income & earning stream), places of purchase (e.g. open-air market or village shop) and cultural influences. The latter ones refer to the most basic element shaping one's wants and behavior and have thus the broadest and deepest influence on rural consumer behavior. Culture in India is reflected by traditional society influenced by multiple social practices and customs. A vast amount of different cultures exist. Moreover, India still can be seen as a patriarchal society, where the male is the main decision-maker, especially in rural areas. Ultimately, social norms, perceptions, traditions, and values differ among all states.[29]

However, a shift from the traditional joint family composition (like big families) to single households can be seen in urban areas, which shifts consumer behavior to more lifestyle consideration than functional needs. Ultimately, there are changing social norms as in expanding the role of women, increased individualism, shifting roles within families, and rising national pride which are affecting acceptance levels of consumers.[30] These structural changes will eventually shift to rural areas – although it will take some time. Moreover, changing lifestyle compared to a few decades ago has happened in the rural areas due to better education, better per capita income and therefore high growth rates as well as the advent of media and globalization. Especially food consumption, fashion trends, entertainment and use of technology shifted away from old habits and lifestyle. Expenditures on food articles have moved largely to non-food goods.[31]

Going further into detail regarding the decision-making process from villagers for purchasing a particular good or service, the following influential factors from existing research and our own experiences are highlighted. Examples from our journey as well as common ones emphasize these critical factors along with our learnings from them.

Price, Quality and Testing

Price, quality and testing are prime factors for buying a product. The lower the purchasing power, the more price-sensitive villagers become. Rural people look for value for money and are concerned with functionality and durability. Too many features tend to confuse rural consumers. Moreover, when purchasing expensive products, durability is ensured and heavy checking and counterchecking is done to seek the reassurance of the buying decision. See and touch is a major requirement for villagers to decide whether to buy or not.[32]

Example: Buying a phone is for many villagers mainly a necessity rather than a fashion-driven decision. Our experience showed that rural people are looking mostly to make calls, take pictures, and sometimes listen to music. Since most villagers are not able to read English, traditional cellphones serve their needs. Smartphone features are then likely not required and therefore, the higher price is not justified. For choosing the right phone, price is the main criterion right after quality and durability since the purchasing power is low. However, disregarding price and quality, testing in a local store is critical to touch and feel the product. Comparing available alternatives dependent on price and quality by playing with these different phones can lastly lead to the purchasing decision. Online retailers like eyewear retailer lenskart.com follow a multi-channel strategy when adapting to the rural setting by having physical stores that customers can test the products locally, which builds trust and brand awareness[33]. These are not out-and-out shopping hubs, but shops to exclusively test and then order the product, which is lastly being shipped to the customer's house.

Brand Loyalty and Adherence

Brand loyalty and adherence are significantly higher when compared to an urban setting in India. Limited access to alternatives and a lack of information about possible choices make rural customers stick to already experienced brands. Brand recognition in rural markets refers often to logos, symbols, and colors rather than brand names. Spurious and look-alikes products consequently are very widespread in village markets. Consumption of branded products is seen as a special treat and indulgence. However, a slight modification in communication and brand-building efforts from the urban market is not sufficient (Rural consumers tend to be distrustful and wary about urbanities). Brand identity needs to involve a relation to the rural lifestyle, behavior, and environment and with appropriate status symbols. Movies and celebrities are providing effective brand ambassadors.[34]

Example: Coca Cola first entered the Indian market but left in 1977 after refusing a government order which required to transfer 60% of its equity to an Indian company. When Coca

Cola was entering the Indian market the second time thanks to economic reforms in 1992, Coca Cola had three options. First, establishing plants in India to expand operations step by step. Second, entice bottlers and third, acquire a company having facilities already in place. Coca Cola decided to entice many franchise bottlers under Parle, which possessed brands like Thums Up, Limca, and Gold Spot and eventually bought Parle in 1993. Coca Cola made a successful deal since having the instant reach to all parts of India and getting a huge share of the competition since Parle was a leader in the soft drink domain. Originally, Coca Cola laid off Parle's brands to get rid of redundancies, although the founder of Thums Up, Limca, and Gold Spot, Ramesh Chauhan, tried to explain that Indian tastes are catered by known brands for a long time. Thums Up was hugely popular and most of its fans switched to Pepsi in its absence, while Pepsi marketed their product very aggressively with Indian sentiments. Realizing that laying off Thums Up costed a huge market share to Pepsi, Coca Cola revived Thums Up in 1997, which eventually let Coca Cola brands overtake the market share of Pepsi's brands. The Thums Up brand regained its place as the top cola brand in India.[35] Brand loyalty and adherence have been one of the major success factors for Thums Up to ultimately gaining the largest market share, even after being absent for two years.

Community Decision Making

Individuals in urban areas are freer to take upon their own, independent decisions regarding purchases. However, in villages, strong social structures (including caste consideration) are present, which leads to community decision-making being common. Since high interpersonal communication happens, word of mouth can effectively influence buying decisions. Existing customers, dealers, village influencers, family, or youth being part-time in urban locations are consulted before making the decision to buy a particular product or service.[36]

> *"People are asking every person in their community and beyond before purchasing. Having made a good deal in terms of price and quality, they share this among their community. New must-haves are spread fast. When a bike or phone has certain features available for a good price, it becomes soon the new standard as people trust each other very much and word of mouth is strong. Information thus comes mainly from communities rather than official channels and decision making for purchasing remains mainly community based."*
>
> *– Y. S. Michael, SVM Director AP; born and raised in greater Mori area.*

Social interlinkages are deeply rooted in Indian culture, which still emphasizes close family relationships and decision making to this date. This is reflected by the high rate of arranged marriages, which 74% of Indians still prefer over "love marriage" in 2012[37]. Family heads take the decision for the match of their sons and daughters. Arranged marriages in India are seen as a social and economic necessity that both families can continue to economically and socially thrive. In most cases, criteria like caste, economic status, education, location, astrology etc. play a decisive role in matchmaking. This highly dependent decision making often continues beyond marriage for many fields like choosing the type of education, college, career, and lastly, purchasing of goods or services. It is important to understand Indian culture, which itself differs among India, to fully be able to relate to the dynamics of local and national decision making.

General Restrictions

First, the availability of products and services is limited as 627,000 villages are scattered among 3.2 million square kilometers throughout India. Moreover, the poor state of roads in rural areas deteriorate reach and availability on a regular basis. Second, affordability is a challenge since low disposable incomes exist coming from mainly daily wages. Smaller packs and cost-effective products can address that. Third, gaining the acceptability of products and services is challenging. Products and services need to suit rural markets and address needs. Fourth, creating wide awareness is difficult when only 41 percent of rural households in India have access to TV[38] and internet penetration being only 20 percent (2017) in rural areas.[39]

Changing Consumer Behavior

Change in the consumer behavior can occur in a short period of time due to better reach of new technology, mass media, and internet to village households or general external factors (e.g. economical). Trends are being adopted more quickly than ever. However, it seems that this mostly affects the non-food articles and betterearning households, not the people living below the poverty line. The International Poverty Line has a value of US$1.90 PPP, the lower middle-Income class poverty line has a value of US$3.20 PPP, upper middle-income class poverty line has a value of US$5.50 PPP. In India, 10.9 % of its population lives with less than US$ 1.90 PPP per day.[40] The following testimonial reveals the quickly shifting consumer behavior, perceived from a rural Entrepreneur.

Story 4 – Changing Consumer Behavior and Sudheer's Struggle to Keep Up

"My name is Sudheer Kumar. I'm a resident of Doddanapudi village, Kalla Mandal. I started a firm named "Kumar Decorations" 10 years ago. My business deals with supply of music systems, setting up generators, arranging lights and decorations for festivals, parties, functions and celebrations purpose on rental basis. I was self-employed by this business and I used to run it very successfully by making INR 15k-20k per month. By passage of time, the equipment which I was offering outdated gradually. My monthly income decreased vastly due to the sudden increase of a more diverse customer demand. In fact, the DJ music stereo and rolling colorful disco lights became extremely popular. As a part of to compensate my losses, it was obvious to move accordingly to the prevalent trend. I thought of purchasing the DJ music stereo and rolling colorful disco lights which costs up to 3,00,000. As I lacked funds, I approached the SBI (State Bank of India) Juvvalapalem branch and applied for the loan to expand my business.

Despite of my desire to revitalize my ailing business, my loan application got rejected. This was a major step backwards for me. Not only happened this once, but many more times as I was unable to provide collateral for the loan. The bank didn't accept my business for repaying the loan amount. I lost faith in myself and wanted to sell my remaining assets and quit this business."

Sudheer Kumar, West Godavari, Andhra Pradesh, India

Striving for a Single End-to-End Solution.

Providing solutions for given pain points via technology comes with challenges. For each domain, there are many e.g. mobile applications helping rural people solving their needs and hurdles. Over 50% of Indian population is dependent on agriculture[41], which makes this domain a target market. However, to reach the average farmer and providing the proposed value to him is complex. The mindset is perceived as farmers are looking for very simple solutions for all queries and needed information. Farmers consequently tend to not use multiple applications. Often, relatives install and teach about the application and farmers then use one particular app. Many farmers think that the smartphone itself is the tool for solving his pain points. Thus, one application as a source for solving all his needs by linking all required features as an end-to-end and holistic solution is very likely to succeed when excellent and simple user experience is ensured.

> *"A farmer looks for a holistic solution for all his farm requirements, at a single and trustworthy source, rather than depending on several independent resources. Creating a single, trustworthy source for a farmer is a really challenging task in India."*
>
> *– Naveen Kumar, Founder & CEO of NaPanta*

Timely Availability and Delivery

In many cases, villagers are purchasing their goods and services in a 'just-in-time' manner. Moreover, due to volatile, limited income, lack of cash in ATMs, or dependency on crop cycles, monetary means are not available consistently. Consequently, customers are very sensitive to the timely delivery of their objected goods and services. When offering products online, timely delivery is a critical factor for customer satisfaction. Since decision making is interlinked with the community as described above, positive and negative word of mouth effects can easily arise and spread among the village population. This has significant effects on the acceptance level of electronic services, such as eCommerce, as the following example explains.

> *Example:* When a bulk of farmers ordered paddy cutter machines from an online platform (being part of smart village project) to ramp up their harvesting efficiency, delay in delivery affected not only the customer satisfaction but also the economic situation of the respective farmers. Harvesting could not be done on time and moreover, helpers for cutting the paddy manually hadn't been requested since the machine could have easily replaced them. In the end, losses of yield arose and customers were highly unsatisfied with the eCommerce platform. In this particular area, its credibility, reputation, and trust diminished vastly and fellow farmers generally didn't order online since they were afraid of facing similar issues.

Rising Appeal of Indian Goods

Appeal of Indian Goods is shifting Indian consumer behavior in general. In the past decades, Indians tended to value imported goods like chocolates, perfumes, and brand-name fashion from abroad. Today, almost two thirds (60%) according to a BCG (Boston Consulting Group) study (2017) are willing to pay extra for products made in India. In all product categories, Indian consumers like to explore local roots, e.g. natural products, local packaged food, and clothing, which emphasizes the rising national pride.[42]

Example: The Indian FMCG (frequent most consumed goods) company Patanjali has recently (2017) overtaken many long-standing, international consumer good rivals like Nestle within the last 10 years. Especially thanks to traditional Indian products like Ghee (milk product, a form of butter), where they are not facing any competition, Patanjali could rise so fast[43]. This reflects the appeal for Indian Goods among Indian population.

Consumer awareness is still very limited and exploitation happens. Education and enhancing awareness are therefore important to let villagers make rational decisions when making a purchase. In the end, the fulfillment of legitimate expectations is to be ensured for gaining high customer satisfaction and establishing a sustainable relationship with rural customers.[44] Understanding customer's needs and behavior as emphasized above is a critical success factor for entering rural markets. However, companies need to offer fair and cost-effective products and services with high durability and quality along with transparent awareness about the offerings.

Example Case emphasizing distinctive rural consumer behavior: Skill Development

Facing many challenges related to finding employment in rural India, the Smart Village team created a program for skill development in collaboration with Open Innovation practitioners such as IBM, Hella, and USHA international. Relevant skill development programs have been co-designed for the rural setting to give unemployed youth a unique opportunity for stepping out of their unfortunate situation. However, in some cases, there were unpredictable, unique learnings. Hella, an international automotive supplier, very successfully offered a course for educating certified mechanics, many other programs didn't get the equally anticipated demand. It turned out that the main incentives for participating in such courses are immediate benefits, which leads to careful considerations from interested parties whether to join the program or not based on purely economic factors.

Even if highly renowned corporations such as IBM offered relevant courses at low cost, the main decision driver remains the same. The smart village team got to know, that very often, unskilled job opportunities e.g. to surveillance a designated shrimp pond give enough money to neglect the more sustainable way of getting skill development and earning rising income in the midterm. This reflects first, the price-sensitive behavior in the rural setting and second, the mindset of low risk taking and expecting instant benefits. This very same situation is faced by the government-led skill development programs, where interested students are incentivized through free classes, accommodation, and catering in order to fill the classes.

Villager's Behavior for Adoption of Innovation

Our experience and existing research show that adoption of new technology, new models or new processes is only then likely to happen if users perceive an immediate benefit with low risk. Juma (2016) argues in that context that "loss aversion, and other psychological tendencies tend to encourage resistance to technological change" and that "society is most likely to oppose a new technology if it perceives that the risks are likely to occur in the short run and the benefits will only accrue in the long run."[45] Informing, educating, and spreading awareness for the public is hence essential. Learning about potential future benefits is likely to decrease distrust for new technologies or models. When Napanta introduced its mobile application to farmers providing information about market prices and efficient farming methods (among many other features), farmers could immediately see the great future benefit which comes with low risk as the application is free and transparent. Over 50,000 farmers signed up within a short period of time mainly because of positive word of mouth effects. Another example can be seen in the explained Cloud physician health care model. Rural health workers started only then to really execute the model as soon as they got a monetary incentive to do so. It is all about getting immediate benefits along with facing low risk. However, the decision-making to apply new technologies remains complex since many factors influence the consumer behavior (as described above) and thus, is not to be only restricted to the trad-eoff regarding benefit and risk. Still, we experienced that this is a major factor for innovation adoption in the rural setting in India.

This learning gives great insights on how to effectively imple-ment new models, technologies, or processes in the rural setting.

It is inspirational to see how fast rural people adopt technolo-gies when seeing a direct benefit. Especially younger generations are letting this development thrive. New digital technologies are quickly adopted driven by their willingness to share personal data with brands or government when having a good user experience and value.

However, we experienced in many cases that especially older generations are more ignorant to adopt novel technologies and models when being used to their traditional way of doing things. This exists even if they would get immediate benefits. When it comes to washing laundry, older ladies in Mori are still doing it the traditional way – washing everything manually and beating the clean laundry against a rock to dry it. Even if they have access to a washing machine with no cost, which would save them time and energy, these ladies are still doing it in the traditional way. Moreover, one of the greatest hurdles faced was the villagers' reluc-tance to pay for services or products since everything in Andhra Pradesh seems to be subsidized, leading most villagers to be con-tent with lower quality services and products. For example, the team was unable to persuade villagers to pay for clean drinking water despite the obvious health benefits because the government subsidizes water or gives it away for free.

It is important to understand that described behavior not only is prevalent on the consumer level but also can be found on the business level. When partnering up to expand businesses, the immediate benefits are often taken into consideration rather than long term profit. Patterns of consumer behavior therefore can be found on various levels and need to be taken into consideration.

Of course, generalizing cannot be done here, it is a reflection of our experience which opens an opportunity for in-depth research in the future.

For research on how digital transformation influences entrepreneurship of mid-size and family businesses in rural Andhra Pradesh (in collaboration with WHU, Otto Beisheim School for Management), over 1,000 rural businesses were surveyed. Around 46% of these entrepreneurs use digital tools for their businesses, e.g. tools for communication, payments, or accessing various information. Moreover, among this group, almost every second entrepreneur stated that if they see the great capability of digital tools for their businesses, they will implement these tools. 44% of the entrepreneurs not using digital tools so far expressed that it is likely to use such tools in their business in the future. These are great findings of the acceptance and adoption level of technology in rural India and show the readiness in the rural setting of emerging markets such as in Andhra Pradesh.

Ultimately, where there are beneficiaries, on the one hand, there are also disadvantaged on the other hand. In the setting of rural India, middlemen are fighting for their existence with every new technology introduction threatening their current business. The middleman industry will not just vanish quietly. Commercial intermediaries are part and parcel of business throughout India, especially in remote, poorly connected villages. However, the internet enables direct connectivity between the consumer and sources and makes business more accountable and transparent. Especially the advent of blockchain technology can really improve the situation when anchoring every participant of a supply chain. However, middlemen are an entrenched part of the culture and resist being dislodged.

SUMMARY:
Bottlenecks to Slow Down Progress

Experienced Bottlenecks	**Possible Solutions**
Inadequate Internet Connectivity	
• Insufficient and unreliable connectivity or missing internet connectivity hindered progress among the 472 villages.	Required basic infrastructure such as internet infrastructure must be available in the determined areas of operations.
Complex rural Consumer Behavior	
• Diverse and distinct behavior across various villages. • Decision making is complex and dependent on various factors, such as price, quality, testing, community, brand loyalty & adherence, general restrictions (e.g. income, missing reach) and unique demands.	Understanding rural customer's needs and behavior. Educating and enhancing consumer awareness to prevent exploitation.
Adoption of Innovation	
• Rural population adopts innovation only if an immediate benefit without risks can be offered. • Older generations tend to stick to traditions. • Existing ecosystem prevents change (e.g. middle man issue).	Understanding consumer's tradeoffs to tailor products and services to address the same. Overcome rigid ecosystem bottlenecks with innovation, e.g. blockchain technology.

CHAPTER 13
WHAT ARE THE RESPONSES FROM STAKEHOLDERS

The concept of Smart Village has successfully spread among India and has shown that despite many prevalent challenges and its unique setting in rural India, private sector companies are effectively providing Open Innovation solutions to villagers for their socio-economic empowerment. It continues its journey, having taken upon a third state in India – Meghalaya, in late-2019 for further scaling. Seeing the ability of villagers adopting digital technologies, incorporating these in their daily lives, and therefore empowering themselves is making the Smart Village vision come true – at an increasing, fast pace.

Having seen the theoretical and practical perspectives of the Smart Village idea, the developed underlaying processes, the respective successes and failures and the scaling strategy as a platform, it ultimately needs to be concluded that the Smart Village idea is characterized by its very own dynamic comprising continuous learnings from its execution and aims for steady improvement throughout its application. Moreover, the implementation of its idea is not a state of accomplishment of a certain level for improving a specific village or part of a population but rather an ongoing journey and dynamic development of the original idea itself in which each of the villages being worked on, are moving towards the best possible outcomes. There are no limitations for its application. Eventually, the idea can incrementally and individually evolve when scaled throughout time for individual success.

The rural market in India characterized by its distinctive entanglement with the public sector along with its many unique attributes proves to be a challenge to innovate in. However, it is urgently needed to improve the life conditions of its citizen through a globally shared prosperity and a sustainable socio-economical boost.

If the explained success factors and challenges are lessons learned, and if the Open Innovation process is being applied to its individual appropriate extent, the chances of commercially succeeding in and providing value for the rural markets of emerging economies can increase for business enterprises, organizations, and governments. This book can therefore serve as a manual and playbook for the many aspiring individuals and organizations taking up such endeavors in future growth markets such as rural India. Now, in 2020 the Smart Villages Movement digital platform eases, enhances, and accelerates the innovation process for all participants. In the following, responses from stakeholders are provided to comprehensively conclude the Smart Village idea in its entirety.

Businesses

Businesses are looking for new business models that provide solutions to villagers' needs while opening up new markets for their business growth. In summary, there has been great interest and traction among the private sector to participate in the Smart Village program. Over 60 startups and large business enterprises have already actively worked and innovated within this program (see smartvillagemovement.org). It is great to see their willingness to collaboratively innovate and combine forces for tapping into the rural market when applying the Open Innovation framework as advised and orchestrated by the Smart Village team. The extent of embracing Open Innovation was hereby assessed by 43% of the participating companies as high and 14% as very high. 1 out of 3 companies stated the extent as medium. This refers to businesses sharing resources, expertise, and knowledge with each other. Also, as emphasized before, heavily demanded end-to-end solutions for villagers can be much more easily created and implemented when businesses converge and thus, proprietary customer journeys are linked with each other.

In example, Plantix, providing a crop doctor solution based on artificial intelligence converged their solution into the agriculture platform from BigHaat. Farmers, identifying a crop disease are getting now forwarded to the BigHaat platform to directly purchase recommended inputs for tackling their crop disease. These models are successful since the customer is getting access to the many solutions relieving his needs within one comprehensive eco-system. Although many corporate partners didn't succeed yet due to missing product-market fit, had wrong perceptions, e.g. about access to the government or funding, or didn't align with the Open Innovation methodology, e.g. sharing data, the successes and the number of companies interested and working within the Smart Village Movement highlight the relevance and potential of its important vision.

Moreover, especially in Silicon Valley, business enterprises tend to more and more acknowledge the need to address global challenges while leveraging those as a business case, including the United Nations sustainability goals for 2030. In fact, achieving these sustainability goals could open up $12 trillion of market opportunities in food and agriculture, cities, energy, and materials, and health and well-being alone and create 380 million new jobs by 2030 according to the United Nations Development

Program.[46] It is this aspect that makes VCs call for technologies solving the needs of tomorrow while capturing enormous business opportunities as these solutions will be undoubtfully needed in the future.

A first-mover advantage is what drives such investments. A recent study of Morgan Stanley's Institute for Sustainable Investing and Bloomberg L.P. found out that sustainable investments have more than tripled since 2012 in the United States of America. Sustainable investing refers here as the practice of making an investment in companies or funds that aim to achieving market-rate financial returns alongside positive social and/or environmental impact. Also, 89% of the 300 surveyed U.S. asset management professionals state that their firms will devote additional resources to sustainable investing in the next 1-2 years.[47]

This shift, of course, aligns with the prevalent work-force, consisting more and more of the generation y and z that are very much attracted to companies with goals beyond financial objectives, such as creating a positive impact for the planet. Today, every third startup globally aims for social good, according to a 2016 report by Global Entrepreneurship Monitor (GEM)[48] And, according to the Edelman Trust Barometer 2018, 64% of the people globally expect that CEOs should lead to social change rather than waiting for government action.[49] This overall shift towards more consciousness for sustainability is noticeable and urgently demanded. We can see this evolution day by day when working with a diverse set of companies and startups.

"The invisible hand that guides markets starts to finally put a heart into its equation."

– Werner Fischer, Former SVM Research Director and Research Scholar, UC Berkeley

Villagers

Villagers in emerging economies are generally looking for empowerment and economic prosperity. The engagement and response for the Smart Village program from villagers in the areas of operations led in the end to a two-sided result. One the one hand, villagers directly involved are appreciating the efforts from the Smart Village initiative. Involved refers hereby to either being actively involved, e.g. in pilots and skill development programs, to having seen impact within their social community and also to knowing and understanding the program. The following two stories provide in-depth insights about impacted rural citizens from Andhra Pradesh, fully understanding what the program is all about while actively participating.

Story 5 – Empowerment for Mrs. Kanthamma's shop with digital technology.

"When life was getting too harsh, and things seemed like going out of control, a research team from Smart Villages program came to our rescue. They were conducting awareness drive on eCommerce, and that's when I got introduced to StoreKing, an application which lets you expand your business without increasing size of the shop. The Smart Village team educated us on the application and got us registered to the app.

Since I have become a StoreKing retailer, footfall has increased significantly. My business is not just limited to selling daily utilities, but I now recharge mobiles, DTH Connections, facilitate money transfers, etc. Integration of these services has increased profits.

The Smart Village Initiative is a blessing for us as it came in and understood the core of the problem and also acted wisely to solve the issues, with commitment in serving the society. I thank them from the bottom of my heart for Improving our living standards and helping us in understanding the digital world, and now we understand the inevitability of adopting the new trends to sustain & grow in the current world scenario. Without their support and effort, we would not have been able to send our son to a medical college."

Mrs. Kanthamma, West Godavari, Andhra Pradesh, India

Story 6 – IoT sensors to increase shrimp farmer's yield.

"For generations, my family has been in agricultural professions. Recently, there has been a shift from paddy cultivation to shrimp cultivation due to rising demand for seafood. No proper hatcheries were available in East Godavari until my family started the first practice of aquaculture in 1989. We began by cultivating Tiger prawns, a tedious process in which we hatched the seed from the Godavari River. Initially, the harvest was prosperous, and the revenue generation was growing. However, as the cultivation increased, new viruses compromised the crop. Tiger prawns become unviable, and the boom of the aquaculture bubble busted in the years 1996 and 1997. In those days, the international trade regulations forced us to sell to a small domestic market. It became difficult to make a living. What were we to do with our farms and investments? It was our livelihood.

The market boomed once again for many farmers and me because of the introduction of a new shrimp seed type called Vannamei. In the initial years from 2003 to 2005, the seed was able to adapt to our local conditions and the harvest prospered. Eventually, new viruses started attacking the crop due to lack of bio-security, effluent treatment, and unsustainable practices like excessive antibiotic usage. For farmers such as myself, shrimp mortality rate is the highest challenge. We only have limited period of 24-36 hours. Within these critical hours, we need to respond and take critical corrective actions. Otherwise, we will lose our shrimp and our livelihoods. Waiting for time-consuming lab test reports increases mortality rate due to a lack of information to make an educated decision.

To address these problems, the Smart Village Team assessed our pain points by doing research and came up with a solution for these challenges. They introduced technology from CFog which is based on IoT sensor principles. Solar powered IoT sensors were placed in my pond. It gives me mobile alert data about parameters such as pH, Temperature, Dissolved Oxygen (DO) and Ammonia which are very vital for shrimp harvesting.

Overall this reduced the harvest risk by reducing the shrimp mortality rate. Because of the technology's success, I arranged a meeting with all shrimp farmers to spread awareness. I conducted pond tours for fisheries department to check its functionality and reliability. The Government partnered with the CFog and provided subsidies to the farmers who wanted to employ the sensors. I would congratulate the Smart Village Initiative for the work that they have done in our village and thank them from the bottom of my heart."

Pipapla Sathyanarayana Raju, East Godavari,
Andhra Pradesh, India

On the other hand, people not knowing in detail about the program, can misperceive the efforts and even show resistance, respectively. It happened that the Smart Village project was often understood as another initiative by the government that might fail to address their pain points. This goes along with villager's expectations and demand for government policies and schemes to create sudden impact, irrespective of sustainability and longevity. Therefore, if villagers are not aware of the Smart Village program, villagers might perceive it as a government initiative creating no impact at worst. Of course, innovation projects, as well as public policies, take their time, however, villagers ignorantly are not seeing this. Enlightenment for the rural population is hereby critical.

Another aspect is the villager's resistance towards the program as they don't want to change or even improve their livelihood. There are good reasons for that, e.g. preserving indigenous culture by not exposing the community to the world through technology. Respecting this and consulting with the government on how to deal with this situation is to be done.

Most villagers are looking for empowerment and access to knowledge, education, and markets. The Smart Village Movement can respond and provide solutions to them when directly involving increasing numbers of villagers in emerging economies.

"Cities may offer a variety of exciting experiences to fulfill our desires but villages are a lifeline to humanity. Villages are a habitat where relationships with family and community can be nurtured to last till the grave."

– Prof. Solomon Darwin, Haas School of Business

State Governments

State governments want their people to be happy that goes in line with a significant chance of being reelected. However, providing a clear assertion whether state governments appreciate the Smart Village initiative since its start is outstandingly difficult as there are many, sometimes even contrary variables involved, which need to be considered, respectively; individual advocates and opponents from local to state government official levels, changing political scenarios and emerging, varying government schemes and policies among many others. However, there are tendencies in both of its extremes.

In Andhra Pradesh, the support and appreciation for the project were huge in the beginning and decreased over time due mainly to political reasons and wrong expectations about deliverables and outcomes, there have been always strong advocates and strong opponents throughout. It is interesting that the role of support of many government officials mainly remained the same. Officials, seeing the project or particular pilots as competition to their very own effective area, expressed often serious criticism. Political issues when elections were getting closer seriously affected the support from the side of the government. In its extreme, when the political situation was heated, the former opposition party, initiated TV spots, documenting claimed failures of the Smart Village project to weaken the ruling party, which granted the funds to the Smart Village project. Despite many organizational challenges or changing political situation as described before, many officials were convinced from the efforts done so far and were very supportive and strong advocates for the Smart Village project.

"UC Berkeley's approach of firms coming together as an ecosystem through an integrated process to deliver value to the farmer is something that has not been tried before. The efforts being made by the university in bringing together large and small firms as an ecosystem to:

  a) Eliminate costs,
  b) Facilitate speed to market,
  c) Increase transparency,
  d) Lower risk for all
  e) Increase efficiency in the supply chain
  f) Time save for all
  g) Increase yields and revenues

h) Enhance data richness

i) Promote Uberization of Assets

This approach is supported as endorsed personally by our Hon. Chief Minister Naidu and we are hoping for great results in the future. Our state government in the agricultural sector is committed to be the key facilitator in the whole supply chain process to remove obstacles, bottlenecks and tighten the weakest links in the systems to improve the happiness of the farmer."

– Rajsekhar Budithi, IAS, Principle Secretary,
Department of Agriculture

In 2019, CM Naidu lost the state election and a new government gained power. The Smart Village initiative in Andhra Pradesh was in need of being re-strategized according to the agenda of the new ruling government to ensure ongoing support. It remains unclear to what extent CM Y.S.Jaganmohan Reddy, YSR Congress Party, will support the Smart Village Movement in the future, initially accelerated by his predecessor Chandrababu Naidu.

In Arunachal Pradesh and Meghalaya, the government has been very supportive of the project so far and the level of participation is high as they appreciate the vision and are therefore willing to contribute resources. It will be interesting if their support resists political complexity as faced in Andhra Pradesh.

Universities

Universities want to create new knowledge through data collection for research. Sharing unique datasets and even collecting specific data for specific research purposes at no cost is unusual. Thus, universities and academics from all over the world are responding to the Smart Village Movement and its Open Innovation approach very positively and are engaging in broadly. Much interest has been shown by several universities. See examples from this non-exhaustive list.

Teaching Smart Villages

- Smart Village Communities, Summer Semester 2016, Stanford University, Terry Beaubois (inspired by his field visit to Mori prototype).
- Creating Smart Villages Leveraging Open Innovation, Summer Semester 2017, UC Berkeley. Professor Solomon Darwin.
- Innovation in Practice. Creating Smart Villages, Spring Semester 2018, University of Lancaster, UK. Professor Solomon Darwin and Werner Fischer.
- Challenges Lab: Smart Villages, Fall Semester 2019, UC Berkeley. Professor Solomon Darwin and Gert Christen.
- Creating Smart Villages. 8 Independent studies, Spring Semester 2020, UC Berkeley, Professor Solomon Darwin and Professor Henry Chesbrough in conjunction with three universities of Northeast India.
- Executive Education on Smart Villages, early Spring Semester 2020, from Norwegian Business School, Norway at UC Berkley. Professor Solomon Darwin.
- Executive Education for Polish and Russian executives, early Spring Semester 2020. Professor Solomon Darwin (virtually).

Researching Smart Villages

- Smart Village Impact Measurement – Prof Jan Pfister, University of Turku, Finland, 2019 to that date (including field visits in India).

- Smart Village Research Methodologies – Sarah Jack, Stockholm School of Economics, 2019 to the present.
- Smart Village Research on Education – Eivor Oborn, Warwick Business School, UK, 2019 to the present (including field visits).
- Smart Village Research on Healthcare – Michael Barret, University of Cambridge, 2019 to the present.
- Smart Village Analysis and Feasibility Studies – Dr. Jie Chen, Chengdu University, China, Current Garwood fellow conducting research in India for future applications in China.

Academic Talks

Prof. Darwin was invited by a plethora of universities to talk about Smart Villages. For example:

- University of Cambridge, UK
- Oxford University, UK
- Stockholm School of Economics, Sweden
- Maastricht School of Management, Netherlands
- Norwegian Business School, Norway
- RWTH Aachen, Germany
- Chulalongkorn University, Bangkok, Thailand
- IIM Ahmedabad, Shillong and Vizag, India

Excursus: Open Innovation in Rural India Differs

Assuming that implications and outcomes of a concept such that Open Innovation works universally across markets and cultures is of course unrealistically. Having researched in rural Andhra Pradesh, India, how openly small, rural businesses are working together revealed new, unknown insights regarding the application of Open Innovation. Strong family bonds and a tendency to keep family secrets limit the enterprise's ability to participate in Open Innovation processes with other enterprises or business partners. A siloed society, the caste system, and a high need for trust have a significant influence on how Open Innovation is handled. The willingness of local enterprises to be part of openness is dependent on their socio-cultural background. The classic approach of Open Innovation, in which firm value is realized through cooperation between enterprises, can only be accomplished to a limited extent in this context. The strong cohesion between community members enters by force at this point. Instead of private companies, the family and the community are important stakeholders. These groups make it possible to enter into cooperation and develop firm value.

PART V.

What is the Future of Smart Villages

CHAPTER 14

MOVING TO A SHARING ECONOMY

By Solomon Darwin

We are told that Heaven is consists of a "Sharing Economy". Jesus Christ taught his disciples that in Heaven is full of people who esteeming one another by serving and sharing. Is this possible on Earth? I believe it is through sharing the most valuable resource that we capitalize on our balance sheets. It is called IP, knowledge held captive for selfish gain or greed. Knowledge is useless unless it is shared to benefit the people of the world regardless and bring them together as one family. You may say that this is very idealistic but it is possible; sometimes it takes a crisis like Covid-19, an enemy external to the human race to create this awareness and unite us as a human family.

On earth, Open Innovation facilitates Shared Value. The benefits of acquired knowledge will need to flows to serve the needs of others without any delay. If knowledge is held hostage for selfish gains by those who acquired it, it is worthless and does not benefit humanity. The good thing about Open Innovation is that knowledge flows in all directions piggybacking and gathering more of it through stickiness to accelerate solutions. In a harmonious world, the center of knowledge is everywhere and its circumference is nowhere. The three musketeer's principles of "All for One & One for All" should be taken seriously if we were to create oneness through sharing and openness to benefit all people.

The need for Open Innovation is articulated in the movie "The Matrix" from the quote from William Gibson "the future is already here – it's just not evenly distributed". Another way to put is " We need to look no further to find solutions to our problems all pieces to the puzzle are already on the table – they just need to be orchestrated to flow in a frictionless environment together. The solutions to many of our human problems are already here residing in all of us from around the world and from the times past. Created in the image of God, our imagination to create things is not bound by time and space. We can move mountains with what we already have residing in all of us. Jesus did say, look no further "The Kingdom of God is within you" it is already here if we choose to recognize, acknowledge it and tap into it. We can solve many problems but the barrier has been our self-interest and our lack of desire to share with others on earth or more powerfully put "loving others as ourselves"the golden rule. This harmony in creation can only be achieved by sharing all that we have. We are like channels through which care and love for others can flow to create a sustainable and peaceful habitat around the world.

Did you know that the radio was unavailable to the public for 10 years after it was invented due to the greed of a firm that invented it? This is an example of closed innovation, whereupon innovative ideas are restricted into a sphere within a company, government, or country. When knowledge is acquired, it is safeguarded and protected as intellectual property. Sometimes companies or governments choose to suppress or delay the knowledge flow due to selfish reasons to serve their interests. We are held as pigeons in a cage by those who hoard it.

The many firms participating in the smart village movement may start by asking the question what is in it for me? But I hope that they will come to realize over time that sharing and being a blessing to people is more rewarding. It is more blessed to give than to receive. We need to start asking the question of what is in it for those who are undeserved?

CHAPTER 15

TAPPING INTO THE TREE OF KNOWLEDGE

By Solomon Darwin

Exhibit 22 – Tree of Knowledge

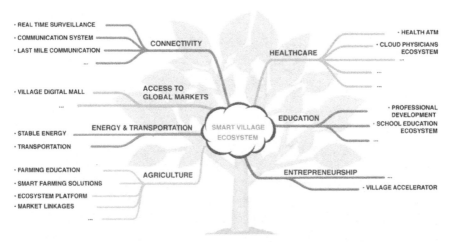

Tree of Knowledge · Minimum Viable Open Innovation Ecosystem

When I was in college, I was told by my accounting professor that revenue is generated by the utilization of assets on the corporate balance sheets. Back then, almost 90% of assets on corporate balance sheets were physical that can be seen, felt, and touched. Today, due to knowledge proliferation, 90% of assets on corporate balance sheets are invisible. These knowledge assets are tools created by the imagination in the human mind. They cannot be seen, touched, or felt – they consist of algorithms, formulas, ideas, processes, etc. They are often digital, portable, and accessible on-demand anywhere and anytime. However, unlike physical assets, the value of knowledge assets evaporates very quickly as new knowledge flows. As rivers of knowledge from diverse places flow into the ocean of the global brain, the world gets transformed very rapidly. This is the power of "Open Innovation" which taps into the global brain as we allow knowledge to be free. It is this power of openness that I am suggesting that we employ going forward to build a new civilization of Smart Villages around the world. I believe that sustainable and scalable business models are to be built on knowledge flows – rivers of useful information as opposed to knowledge lakes the swamps of stagnant information and data. This demands the creation of agile business models that need to constantly adapt to keep up with the flow of new knowledge. The smart village movement offers an opportunity to firms great and small to build new business models that are more flexible and enduring.

The Tree of Knowledge keeps growing exponentially providing fresh knowledge to repair, heal, and restore the old. From time immemorial, the Tree of Knowledge has been an attraction from the very beginning. It was first introduced according to the Judeo-Christian tradition in the Garden of Eden. However, the fruit of knowledge can be a blessing or a curse based on how we utilize it. The Tree of Knowledge can be good but it can also destroy us if our heart is not in the right place. Knowledge is both a resource and a tool that can be utilized to unite people, build a great community, heal the wounded, empower the underserved, and extend compassion, grace, and love toward one another. Knowledge can also be used to divide people, hurt others, destroy communities, or wipe out our whole civilization. The creation around us begs for the right use of knowledge – this is called "wisdom".

The Smart Village Movement will proposer when the right use of knowledge is employed in our individual and collective lives. I invite you to join the movement to create equity and bless the underserved people around the world. Heaven is a village.

ACKNOWLEDGEMENTS

This book and manual was made possible by the contribution and enthusiastic support of the following generous people who are passionate about the Smart Village Movement that got started here at UC Berkeley:

Arun Sharma for extensively contributing to this book with his research and inputs. He had been a tremendously valuable part of the Smart Village Movement in India progressing its corporate communication, digitalization, and operations functions. Many discussions with him greatly helped to correctly reflect the Smart Village journey and to draw the right conclusions in this book.

Shreya Evani for executing SVM as the founding director and making it a reality while working through many hurdles.

Dr. Murali, the founding SVM Chairman and retired academic who continues to contribute as senior advisor to Professor Darwin and SVM team.

Judah Darwin for providing great inputs on our learnings through the lens of political science. Raised in the US from an Indian father and American mother and spending one year in India for the Smart Village Movement, he perfectly understood both cultures and political systems which led to unique knowledge being reflected in this book.

Dr. Matilda Sea Bez for editing this book. Her great work vastly improved this book in terms of logical structure and reading flow. Her academic research perspective gave this book a very clean and crisp appeal making it intuitively understandable for a diverse array of readers. Her valuable time made this book comprehensively great.

Adriana Macias for proofreading this book multiple times and formidably improving its content. Also, her advisory on the book's cover design as well as her design work was pivotal to the great look it has now. Her fantastic sense of design gave this book the unique and stunning design character it needed.

Carly Hanson spent hours and hours in the office in Mori, Andhra Pradesh, proofreading and revising the book's chapters. It was great having her insightful inputs and discussions in the first phases of developing this book. We thank her for being so kind helping us for a good cause.

Y.S. Michael for input on real case scenarios discussed within this book, Director of AP SVM.

Tonya Lollen, our SVM Northeast Director for her dedication and sticking out in Arunachal during the most difficult transition and unrest in the state.

Emma Brunat, Visiting Scholar on Sustainability, UC Berkeley for proofreading and providing input and supporting the final editing process.

The Garwood team in Berkeley. Chris Bush, Dr. Chiara DeMarco, Anita Stephens, Tristan Gaspi, Jonathan Martinez and Gauthier Vasseur for providing always valuable feedback and engaging in multiple brainstorming sessions for this book. A real Open Innovation effort!

Ambassador Venkata Ashok, Consul General of India, San Francisco for providing valuable feedback to this book's content given his enormous knowledge and expertise about India. Also, he supports the Smart Village Movement since its beginnings with great efforts vastly contributing to our successes in India.

The founding SVM team in Andhra, for their hard work and passion, led to the astonishing successes and learnings in the field of sustainable development in rural India: K. Harshadeep, Venkat Krishna Kagga, YS Michael, Sravani Patnala, Prashant Nimmagadda, Rajasekhar Malireddy, Teja R P.

Mandal Directors for managing the on-ground teams. Interns to village ambassadors and field researchers for collecting data and supporting pilot projects. Without them, this movement would have not kickstarted. They were and are the backbone of this operation.

Dominik Strobel, digital media designer, for finalizing the book's formatting and cover design.

The Smart Village Movement only thrives through its powerful network of diverse, passionate, and aspiring people from the industry, academia, and public sectors serving as advocates to this movement. A few to name here but not limited to:

Terry Beaubois, Architect and Professor from Stanford University for his frequent visits to Mori and providing input.

Joseph Minafra, NASA Ames Research Center, Director of Innovation and Partnerships for visiting Mori to inspiring local school children to build the first satellite in a village.

Allan Walker, Kaneka, for his frequent visits to Mori and providing corporate support and input for this project.

Tushar Mangrola, CTO of SVM for further enhancement of the SVM platform and his loyalty toward the smart village movement

Harish Pindi, for taking time off from his Master's Program at Cal State Northridge and helping with our on-ground co-creation efforts in the Mori village.

Professor Jan Pfister, Professor, Stockholm School of Economics and Turku University for his significant contributions and research insights. His several field visits to Indian Villages helped document several research articles related to SVM.

Martha Nalli, the operations manager at Project India whose 24/7 efforts in making the Mori SVM project happen.

Others who provided support in special areas as and when needed: David Maracine, Pratima Narra, Jim Spohrer, Director Cognitive OpenTech at IBM, Professor Ganesh Iyver, Haas School of Business, Rajsekhar Budithi, IAS, Principle Secretary Andhra Pradesh Government, Former Chief Minister Chandrababu Naidu,

Andhra Pradesh, Conrad Sangma, Sampath Kumar, IAS, Chief Minister Pema Khandu, Arunachal Pradesh.

Lastly, a big thanks to Christa Fischer for always inspiring and supporting to follow one's dream. She is the mother of Werner Fischer, the co-author of this book. Danke Mama!

THE AUTHORS

The authors draw upon their previously published work on the subject: a) Prototyping a Scalable Smart Village to Simultaneously Create Sustainable Development and Enterprise Growth Opportunities Harvard Business Review, 2017; b) Prototyping a Scalable Smart Village (B)Harvard Business Review, 2018; c) Smart Villages of Tomorrow: The Road to Mori Peaceful Evolution Publishing, 2018; and d) Smart Village Ecosystems, An Open Innovation Approach, a white paper prepared for Bill Gates Foundation. This publication is greatly enriched by two prominent academics at UC Berkeley, who bring their diverse set of skills and insights from their many years of corporate and academic experience. Werner Fischer, a more recent scholar of Open Innovation, brings his passion and over a year of on-ground research skills from Indian villages to enrich the suggested solutions in the book.

Solomon Darwin

Solomon Darwin brings more than fourteen years of experience as a senior corporate finance officer at Bank of America, First Interstate Bank, GlenFed Inc. and Motorola. His experience in managing balance sheets and stewardship over assets and resources at these firms brings the accountability perspective to Open Innovation. Following his corporate career, Darwin served as an accounting professor at USC Marshall School of Business and later at UC Berkeley. As fate would have it, he ran into Henry Chesbrough who introduced him to Open Innovation. Darwin found much value in Open Innovation as an approach in optimizing asset utilization to achieve better stewardship of resources in corporate entities. Darwin finds that Open Innovation as the basis of creating value by optimizing resources – not just knowledge assets but also physical assets, financial assets as well as human talent. Darwin grew up in an Indian Village having first-hand experience about the pain-points and barriers that still exist. He was invited by the president of India and several chief ministers of individual states within in India to advise and orchestrate the smart village movement.

Darwin also brings over thirty years of extensive working relationship with the government of India through establishing several charitable educational and healthcare institutions in villages. Darwin is the Executive Director of Garwood Center for Corporate Innovation where Henry Chesbrough serves as the Founding Faculty Director.

He is the author of: The Road to Mori: Smart Villages of Tomorrow, The Untouchables: Three Generations of Triumph over Torment, and How to think like the CEO of the Planet: Restoring the Declining Balance Sheet of the Earth.

Werner Fischer

Werner Fischer is an expert in sustainable development managed through collaborative business and technology innovation. His research and professional focus is on creating shared value among businesses, governments, and civil society while providing models that generate impact alongside profit. He graduated in Business Studies and Economics (B.Sc.) from the University of Konstanz, Germany, and Technology Management (M.Sc.) from the Braunschweig University of Technology, Germany. Having a strong interest in Open Innovation and socio-economic sustainability, he studied at UC Berkeley in this field as part of his master program and spent one year in rural India as director of research for the Smart Village program, developed at UC Berkeley and piloted in the Indian states of Andhra Pradesh and Arunachal Pradesh. This role in India included consulting with state governments, technology firms interested in scaling, and local villagers to formulate solutions to prevalent pain points of rural India through business model and technology innovation. Fischer played a key role in further growing the SVM by establishing partnerships and consulting and managing businesses on tapping into emerging markets troughout his tenure. Leveraging this truly unique experience, Fischer consecutively conducted extensive research in this field at the Haas School of Business, as part of his UC Berkeley scholarship. Eventually, his research and experiences built the foundation of this book.

Henry Chesbrough

Henry Chesbrough is known as the Father of Open Innovation for coining the term based on extensive research. He is the most cited professor at the Haas School of Business. In addition to his academic acumen, he brings over 15 of years corporate experience as a senior executive officer in the technology industry in addition to academic acumen. He taught at the Harvard Business School as an assistant professor he is currently an adjunct professor and the faculty director of the Garwood Center for Corporate Innovation at the Haas School of Business at the University of California. Chesbrough was instrumental in working with Darwin in coming up with a definition for smart village which has become an Open Innovation approach to empower rural people in emerging markets. He co-authoring two Harvard Business Review cases and white paper for the Gates Foundation. He has been an active participant in smart village activities, given his interest to understand the receptivity of Open Innovation strategies in rural communities.

Chesbrough holds a BA in Economics from Yale University, an MBA from Stanford Graduate School of Business, and a PhD from the Haas School of Business at the University of California, Berkeley. He acts as the chairman of the Open Innovation Center

– Brazil and serves on several corporate and university boards. Chesbrough was acknowledged as a thought leader by firms across the world and was honored several times over by Thinkers 50 Global Ranking of Management Thinkers. He is an accomplished author of several bestsellers:

- Open Innovation: The New Imperative for Creating and Profiting from Technology. HBS Press.
- Open Business Models: How to Thrive in the New Innovation Landscape. HBS Press.
- Open Innovation: Researching a New Paradigm. Oxford. 2006.
- Open Services Innovation: Rethinking Your Business to Grow and Compete in a New Era. Jossey-Bass.
- New Frontiers in Open Innovation. Oxford. 2014.
- Open Innovation Results: Going Beyond the Hype and Getting Down to Business. Oxford 2019

APPENDIX

University of Lancaster Class Innovation in Practice:
Creating Smart Villages Leveraging Open Innovation

<u>Opening Statement Example – Exporting Fish Pate from India to Europe</u>

"What if farmers of Arunachal Pradesh were surrounded by gold without knowing it?

You have to know that there are many golden pieces, which are ignored by people. Farmers in the Lower Subansiri district are not aware of the growing potential of caviar and fish pate worldwide, especially in France. Indeed, France is the biggest consumer of both caviar and spreadable seafood in Europe, consuming approximately $48million of caviar (European Commission Report, 2018) and spending around $40million of spreadable seafood, (FranceAgriMer, 2016). That is why we will produce caviar and fish pate. We want to transform Arunachal Pradesh from being an importer to an exporter region.

After the implementation of the project, state farmers will be able to triple their incomes and overall wealth by taking a piece of the 'Golden Cake'. We have contacted Carrefour who confirmed to us that once we have the Safety and Quality certificates, they will be able to buy all our supplies (1,500,000 cans per year).

There will be $2,959,680 of revenue created from 160 tons of fish produced by 910 ponds in Lower Subansiri (District Census Handbook Lower Subansiri, 2011). And following this, our farmers will have $844,462 of total revenue, which will be redistributed accordingly to the farmers' supply of fish and it will also be four times the farmers' previous incomes.

Each farmer will earn on average $4,700/year, compared to $1,200 earned previously. The initial CapEx to start our project will be $86,900. The OpEx for the first year is $1,075, 111. The total revenue will generate $286,966 of tax for the state and will create 40 new working positions."

Credits for this project go to the students from Lancaster University Lindsay Akuezumba, Tigran Minasyan, Michele Marchi and Uladzislau Miatselski who designed a ready to launch supply chain for the fisheries sector in early 2019 as part of their module "Innovation in Practice" in collaboration with UC Berkeley under the coordination of Solomon Darwin and Werner Fischer.

INDEX

T

U

V

W

NOTES

Preface and Intro

1. Henry Chesbrough & Marcel Bogers, "Explicating open innovation: Clarifying an emerging paradigm for understanding innovation" In Henry Chesbrough, Wim Vanhaverbeke, & Joel West (Eds.), "New Frontiers in Open Innovation," Oxford University Press (2014), Page 17.
2. See additional data on GDP, current population etc. about India by the World Bank, http://data.worldbank. org/? locations=8S-IN
3. See Geoffrey G. Parker, Marshall W. Van Alstyne, Sangeet Paul Choudary, "Platform Revolution: How Networked Markets Are Transforming the Economy and How to Make Them Work for You," Business & Economics (2016) for understanding the platform economy in fascinating details.

PART I. Why the Smart Village Idea Works

1. What are the Learnings from Previous Rural Development Initiatives

1. See Dambisa Moyo, "Dead Aid. Why Aid is Not Working and How There is a Better Way for Africa" (New York, NY: Farrar, Straus and Giroux (2009), Page 28.
2. Ibid, Page 36
3. Ibid, Page 44. In Africa, Moyo writes, it is not uncommon for a working family member to support as many as fifteen relatives.
4. Ibid, Page 28
5. Ibid, Pages 44 and 45.

2. Why Smart Villages and not Smart Cities

1. "Optimizing Critical City Infrastructures," presentation by Tom Leahy, Executive Manager, Dublin City Council, http://smartcitiescouncil.com/resources/optimizing-critical-city-infrastructures

2. Rio de Janeiro started working with IBM in 2011 to add new capabilities to further improve the city's emergency response system, and give citizens access to information that will help them better manage their daily lives, https://www.wired.com/2011/11/ibm-smart-cities-in-rio-de-janeiro/

3. United Nations Data, http://data.un.org

4. India Census 2011, http://www.census2011.co.in/census/ city/392-hyderabad.html

5. India Census 2011, http://www.census2011.co.in/census/district/122-hyderabad.html, converted from persons per square kilometer.

6. Population Density for U.S. Cities Map, Governing, http://www.governing.com/gov-data/population-density-land-area-cities-map.html

7. Unni Krishnan, "Modi Wants to Replace Crowded Slums in Indian With 20 Million Homes," Bloomberg (2015), http:// www.bloomberg.com/news/articles/2015-02-23/modi-seeks-to-replace-crowded-india-slums-with-20-million-homes

8. "Developing world: Small-scale innovation brings vital help to poor communities," The Financial Times, https://www.ft.com/content/34eb8824-fe25-11e0-bac4-00144feabdc0

9. See also the Keynote from Prof Solomon Darwin presenting to the President of India in 2016, https://www.linkedin.com/pulse/smart-villages-next-emerging-platform-solomon-darwin/?lipi=urn%3Ali%3Apage%3Ad_flagship3_profile_view_base_post_details%3BW6MOfk5jS4W3y4HCF4dwBw%3D%3D

10. ibid.
11. GDP data is compiled from International Monetary Fund (IMF) reports.
12. Based on own research findings when developing frameworks to develop Smart Cities in India.

3. What is the Underlaying Design Philosophy

1. Henry Chesbrough. "Open Innovation: The New Imperative for Creating and Profiting from Technology," Business & Economics (2003).
2. Video: Henry Chesbrough – Open Innovation, https://youtu.be/2UDBaDtwXfI
3. Henry Chesbrough, Christopher Lettl, Thomas Ritter, "Value Creation and Value Capture in Open Innovation," The Journal of Product Innovation Management, 2018.
4. Henry Chesbrough, "Why Companies Should Have Open Business Models", Sloan Management Review, 2007.
5. Video: Insight: Ideas for Change – Open Innovation – Henry Chesbrough, https://youtu.be/02tCs3oKovc
6. Henry Chesbrough, "Open Business Models: How to Thrive in the New Innovation Landscape," Boston, MAP Harvard Business School Press (2006).
7. Buckley Glaister, "Strategic Motives for International Alliance Formation," Journal of Management Studies (1996).
8. See Eric Ries, "The Lean Startup", Crown Publishing Group (2011), for an introduction to this approach in the context of high technology startup companies.
9. The Triple Helix Framework of Innovation was first theorized by Henry Etzkowitz and Loet Leydesdorff in 1995. See Henry Etzkowitz & Loet Leydesdorff, "The Triple Helix – University-Industry Government Relations: A Laboratory for Knowledge Based Economic Development," EASST Review 14, 14-19 (1995).

10. Michael E. Porter and Mark R. Kramer, "Creating Shared Value," Harvard Business Review (2011), Page 50.

11. Ibid, Page 50.

12. Linda Rottenberg and Rhett Morris, "New Research: If You Want To Scale Impact, Put Financial Results First," Harvard Business Review, https://hbr.org/2013/01/new-resarch-if-you-want-to-sc

13. "Reverse Innovation: GE Makes India a Lab for Global Markets," Knowledge@Wharton, http://knowledge.wharton.upenn.edu/article/reverse-innovation-ge-makes-india-a-lab-for-global-markets/

14. "Market-Relevant Design: Making ECGs Available Across India," GE Healthcare Newsroom, http://newsroom.gehealthcare.com/ecgs-india-reverse-innovation/

15. Ronald Burt, "Structural holes versus network closure as social capital," Social capital. Routledge (2017), 31-56.

16. Pierre Bourdieu, "Le capital social: Notes provisories," Acles de la Recherche en Sciences Sociales (1980), 3:2-3.

17. James Coleman, "Social capital in the creation of human capital," American Journal of Sociology (1988), 94: S95-S120.

18. Brian R. Fitzgerald: "Airbnb Host Creates Petition to Change New York Law," The Wall Street Journal (2013), https://blogs.wsj.com/digits/2013/10/14/airbnb-host-creates-petition-to-change-new-york-law/

19. An agreement between Airbnb and the New York state comes after a New York state judge said the original subpoena was too broad, and the attorney general's office refiled with narrower demands. CNBC (2014), https://www.cnbc.com/2014/05/21/airbnb-agrees-to-comply-with-ny-subpoena-to-comply-with-rental-laws-.html

4. What is the Smart Village Idea in Detail

1. The total budget of the town council in Mori Village is roughly
    $8,000 per year, far too little to support any investment in IT
    infrastructure.

PART II. How the Smart Village Idea was Demonstrated

5. Why are Smart Villages Relevant for Villagers

1. The World Bank, http://data.worldbank.org
2. Ibid.
3. Anshul Bhamra et al., "Achieving the Sustainable Development
    Goals in India. A Study of Financial Requirements and Gaps,"
    (2015), http://w w w.devalt.org/images/L3 _ Project Pdfs/
    AchievingSDGsinIndia_DA_21Sept.pdf?mid=6&sid=28
4. Ibid, page 69.
5. Ibid, page 78.
6. Ibid, page 86.
7. Ibid, page 90.
8. Ibid, page 58.
9. The Finance Minister of Andhra Pradesh, Mr. Yanamala
    Ramakrishnudu, presented the Budget for Andhra Pradesh
    for the financial year 2017-18 on March 15, 2017 emphasiz-
    ing the strong financial dependency on agriculture in rural
    areas, PRS India (2017), http://www.prsindia.org/uploads/
    media/State%20Budget%202017-18/Andhra%20Pradesh%20
    Budget%20Analysis%202017-18.pdf
10. See Primary Sector Development: Status, Strategy and Action
    Plan by the Government of Andhra Pradesh (2015), http://niti.
    gov.in/writereaddata/files/AndhraPradesh_Report_2.pdf

11. Soil Quality Information Sheet, Soil Quality Resource Concerns: Salinization, United States Department of Agriculture Natural Resources Conservation Service, https://www.nrcs.usda.gov/Internet/FSE_DOCUMENTS/nrcs142p2_037279.pdf
12. Shocking report about a terrible rape in a village in Andhra Pradesh's Visakhapatnam district where village elders tried to keep this as a secret, Firstpost (2017), https://www.firstpost.com/india/two-tribal-girls-gang-raped-in-andhra-pradesh-village-authorities-try-to-hush-up-crime-3470822.html
13. In January 2017, a county president was murdered over a land grabbing issue as 2019 elections were approaching, The Hans India (2017), http://www.thehansindia.com/posts/index/Andhra-Pradesh/2017-11-18/Peaceful-villages-jolted-by-faction-killings-in-Kadapa-district-/340160
14. Over 8,000 dead in accidents on Andhra Pradesh roads happened in 2017 where hours between 2 am and 5 am were the most dangerous, accounting for 60 per cent of the total accidents, New Indian Express (2017), http://www.newindianexpress.com/states/andhra-pradesh/2017/oct/30/over-8000-dead-in-accidents-on-andhra-pradesh-roads-this-year-1686746.html
15. As per statistics of the National Crime Record Bureau (NCRB) released by the Union Home Minister Rajnath Singh in New Delhi in 2016, The Hindu (2016), http://www.thehindu.com/news/national/andhra-pradesh/crime-against-women-on-the-rise-in-state/article21236540.ece
16. With no electricity, the one-room mud shelter on a farm 240 kilometers (150 miles) east of Mumbai had only the lamp for light – common in India, where power remains unaffordable, inadequate or simply non-existent for 240 million people, Bloomberg (2017), https://www.bloomberg.com/news/features/2017-01-24/ living-in-the-dark-240-million-indians-have-no-electricity;
17. Suparna Dutt D'Cunha: "Modi Announces '100% Village Electrification', But 31 Million Indian Homes Are Still In The

Dark," Forbes (2018), https://www.forbes.com/sites/suparna-dutt/2018/05/07/modi-announces-100-village-electrification-but-31-million-homes-are-still-in-the-dark/#1a3d53fe63ba

18. Energy Outlook 2017, World Energy Outlook Special Report.

19. Julian Sagebiel et al, "Enhancing Energy Efficiency in Irrigation," Springer International Publishing (2016)

20. Anshul Bhamra et al., "Achieving the Sustainable Development Goals in India. A Study of Financial Requirements and Gaps," (2015), http://w w w.devalt.org/images/L3 _ Project Pdfs/ AchievingSDGsinIndia_DA_21Sept.pdf?mid=6&sid=28, pages 108 and the following.

21. https://data.worldbank.org/indicator/SH.H2O.SMDW.RU.ZS

22. See Water Aid's State of the World's Water 2017 report, http://wateraidindia.in/wp-content/uploads/2017/03/English-Release.pdf

23. Anshul Bhamra et al., "Achieving the Sustainable Development Goals in India. A Study of Financial Requirements and Gaps," (2015), http://w w w.devalt.org/images/L3 _ Project Pdfs/ AchievingSDGsinIndia_DA_21Sept.pdf?mid=6&sid=28, page 135.

24. See National Bank of Agriculture and Rural Development (NABARD), All India Financial Inclusion Survey 2016-17, https://www.nabard.org/auth/writereaddata/tender/ 160818 0417NABARD-Repo-16_Web_P.pdf

25. Because Modi's government effectively forced poor citizens into the banking system by linking some welfare benefits to bank accounts, villagers have ended up stuck in long queues and struggling with ATMs that often run out of cash or breakdown, Financial Express (2018), https://www.financialexpress.com/economy/banking-revolution-has-left-rural-india-behind/1247575/

26. Assa Dora and Robin Jeffrey, "Waste of a Nation: Garbage and Growth in India," Harvard University Press (2018).

27. Study by Internet and Mobile Association of India (IAMAI) and market research firm Kantar IMRB (2018),

28. P R Sanjai: "400 deaths a day are forcing India to take car safety seriously," Economic Times of India (2018), https://economictimes.indiatimes.com/news/politics-and-nation/400-deaths-a-day-are-forcing-india-to-take-car-safety-seriously/articleshow/62439700.cms

29. Anshul Bhamra et al., "Achieving the Sustainable Development Goals in India. A Study of Financial Requirements and Gaps," (2015), http://www.devalt.org/images/L3_ProjectPdfs/AchievingSDGsinIndia_DA_21Sept.pdf?mid=6&sid=28

30. "Internal Migrants in India: The Millions Who Cannot Exercise Their Rights," United Nations Educational, Scientific and Cultural Organization (UNESCO), http://www.unesco.org/new/en/newdelhi/about-this-office/single-view/news/internal_migrants_in_india_the_millions_who_cannot_exercise_their_rights/#.V_1Sp2eEAo8

31. "Social Inclusion of Internal Migrants in India: Internal Migration in India Initiative," UNESCO, http://unesdoc.unesco.org/images/0022/002237/223702e.pdf

32. "Internal Migrants in India: The Millions Who Cannot Exercise Their Rights," UNESCO, http://www.unesco.org/new/en/newdelhi/about-this-office/single-view/news/internal_migrants_in_india_the_millions_who_cannot_exercise_their_rights/#.V_1Sp2eEAo8

33. Ibid.

34. "Thousands of Indian Workers Are Stuck in Saudi Arabia as Kingdom's Economy Sags," The New York Times, http://www.nytimes.com/2016/08/02/world/asia/saudi-arabia-indian-workers.html

35. Ibid.

36. Ibid.

37. (Typical wages in Mori are about 180 Rupees to 250 Rupees per day, about $2.65 to about $3.69)
38. Income satisfaction was measured on a 5 point Likert scale with 1 being strongly dissatisfied and 5 being strongly satisfied. Data comes from a conducted survey among over 1,000 small family businesses in Andhra Pradesh, India to research how digital transformation impacts micro-sized entrepreneurship in rural India.

6. Why Governments Participate

1. See "Modi-Obama meet: US to help India develop three smart cities," Times of India (2014), https://timesofindia.indiatimes. com/india/Modi-Obama-meet-US-to-help-India-develop-three-smart-cities/articleshow/43981483.cms

2. Solomon Darwin: "Building Smart Cities In India – Student Projects Add Value," LinkedIn Article (2015), https://www. linkedin.com/pulse/building-smart-cities-india-solomon-darwin/?lipi=urn%3Ali%3Apage%3Ad_flagship3_profile_view_base_post_details%3BW6MOfk5jS4W3y4HCF4dwBw%3 D%3D

3. Solomon Darwin: „Smart City Exchange: From India to the Silicon Valley," LinkedIn Article (2015), https://www.linkedin. com/pulse/smart-city-exchange-from-india-silicon-valley-solomon-darwin/?lipi=urn%3Ali%3Apage%3Ad_flagship3_pro-file_view_base_postdetails%3BW6MOfk5jS4W3y4HCF4dwB w%3D%3D

4. Solomon Darwin: „India Embraces Open Innovation to Propel Growth," LinkedIn Article, https://www.linkedin.com/pulse/india-embraces-open-innovationto-propel-growth-solomon-darwin/?lipi=urn%3Ali%3Apage%3Ad_flagship3_profile_

view_base_post_details%3BW6MOfk5jS4W3y4HCF4dwBw%3D%3D

5. Starting as district collector is a common way to rise up to the state level to become a high official. E.g. the former district collector of East Godavari, Andhra Pradesh is now the principal secretary to the Chief Minister of Andhra Pradesh.

6. See Solomon Darwin, "The Untouchables. Three Generations of Triumph over Torment," Peaceful Evolution Publishing (2018).

7. Corporate Executives from global brands like Google, Cisco, IBM or Ericsson came to the remote village of Mori.

8. Chief minister Chandrababu Naidu has decided to launch the state government's prestigious fibrenet program from Mori on December 29th, 2016, Times of India (2016), https://timesofindia.indiatimes.com/city/vijayawada/mori-a-sleepy-village-in-east-godavari-district-turns-super-smart/article-show/56221937.cms

9. There are certain protocols that mandate local leaders to follow their highest-level government officials of their respective districts, which is the District Collector in the case of Mori.

10. Main contact persons from state government's level were Rajsekhar Budithi (IAS, Principle Secretary, Department of Agriculture), Sri. M. Girija Shankar (Secretary to CM) and Dr. Valli (CEO AP Innovation Society, Government of Andhra Pradesh)

11. See Solomon Darwin & Henry Chesbrough, "Smart Farming in Andhra Pradesh, India: An Open Innovation Approach," white paper handed over to Bill Gates (2017), https://www.slideshare.net/slideshow/embed_code/key/7xVEZz6MILHuRQ

12. See the press article about signing the MoU with the government of Arunachal Pradesh, North East Today (2018), https://www.northeasttoday.in/arunachal-govt-inks-mou-with-sma

13. More information about Arunachal Pradesh is available at: http://www.arunachalpradesh.gov.in/
14. The new team comprises Annu Johny (Regional Associate North), Swapnil Kesarwani (Regional Associate East), Marina Panggeng (Regional Associate Central), Kenny Ete (Regional Associate North), Debabrata Saha (Regional Associate South), Banta Natung (Regional Associate East), Tonya Lollen (Regional Associate West) and Bullo Tagia (Regional Associate Ziro).

7. Why Business Enterprises Engage

1. Linda Rottenberg and Rhett Morris, "New Research: If You Want To Scale Impact, Put Financial Results First," Harvard Business Review (2013), https://hbr.org/2013/01/new-resarch-if-you-want-to-sc
2. Ibid.
3. Ibid.
4. Arnold and Hockerts, "The greening Dutchman: Philips' process of green flagging to drive sustainable innovations," Business Strategy and the Environment (2011), 20 (6), 394–407.
5. Kennedy et al. conducted an in-depth case study of a sustainability-oriented innovation process for a radical new product within a multinational life sciences company. Kennedy, Whiteman and van den Ende, "Radical Innovation for Sustainability: The Power of Strategy and Open Innovation," Long Range Planning (2016), doi: 10.1016/j.lrp.2016.05.004.
6. 21 corporations and startups, which actively worked on tapping into the Indian rural market through the smart village program gave extensive feedback. Although this sample size is not statistically representative, it provides relevant, valuable

insights related to the specific innovation setting faced in rural Andhra Pradesh.

7. Kennedy, Whiteman and van den Ende, "Radical Innovation for Sustainability: The Power of Strategy and Open Innovation," Long Range Planning (2016), Page 2.

8. Ibid. Page 11.

9. Defining CSR by the Mossavar-Rahmani Center for Business and Government, Harvard Kennedy School of Government at Harvard University, https://sites.hks.harvard.edu/m-rcbg/CSRI/init_define.html

10. Following table explains the differences between Corporate Social Responsibility (CSR) and Creating Shared Value (CSV) from Carol Moore, "Corporate Social Responsibility and Creating Shared Value: What's the Difference?," Heifer International (2014), https://www.sharedvalue.org/sites/default/files/resource-files/CFR-047%20Corporate%20Social%20Responsibility%20White%20Paper_FINAL.pdf

Corporate Social Responsibility (CSR)	Creating Shared Value (CSV)
Emphasizes corporate values and corporate citizenship	Focus on designing new products and services that meet social and environmental needs while simultaneously delivering a financial return
Corporate philanthropy: sharing money the company has already made	Access new markets
Contributions-in-kind, pro-bono service and volunteerism: sharing the company's products, expertise, talent and time	Reconfigure and secure the value chain by tapping new or better resources and partners to improve productivity Improve the capabilities (skills, knowledge, productivity) of suppliers

Cause related marketing and Reputation management, Risk management; changing business practices in response to external pressure Compliance with community, national and international standards	Create local clusters to strengthen and capture economic and social benefits at the community level Deploy corporate assets to achieve scale and spur investment
Typically led by CSR, Marketing, Corporate Communications, External/Public/Government Affairs, Community Relations, Sustainability and Foundation departments	Typically led by CEO, senior executive team and individual champions across the company in close collaboration with corporate affairs and sustainability departments

11. Ibid.

PART III. How to Execute the Smart Village Idea

8. How to Establish a Smart Village Organization

1. It involved Lee Omar, Katy Atkinson, BBC Filmmaker, Terry Beaubois, Architect and Professor from Stanford University, David Maracine, Financial Expert, and Manav Subodh, Innovation Accelerator Expert from UC Berkeley.

2. The team involved: Shreya, Srikar, Perumal, Abhiram, Ravi, Maitreyim, Suraj, Uma and Jayaram.

3. Core team consisted of Project Director Shreya Evani, District Directors K. Harshadeep (Srikakulam), Venkat Krishna Kagga (Krishna), YS Michael (East Godavari), Sravani Patnala (West Godavari) and Prashant Nimmagadda (Chittor), Director of Corporate Relations Judah Darwin, Arun Sharma (Data analytics) and Werner Fischer (Director Research).

4. See chapter 3 where dynamic capabilities are explained in detail.

9. How to Develop the Database for Unlocking New Value

1. You can access the village footprints of the 472 villages in Andhra Pradesh here: https://berkeley-apsmartvillage.org/dashboard/

10. How to Execute the Smart Village Idea with an Innovation Framework

1. See David Wijeratne, Gagan Oberoi, and Shashank Tripathi, "The New Ways to Win in Emerging Markets (2017), Strategy + Business, PWC (2017), https://www.strategy-business.com/article/The-New-Ways-to-Win-in-Emerging-Markets?gko=7f566
2. Ibid.
3. Ibid.
4. 2016 report from KMPG and the Organization of Pharmaceutical Producers in India (OPPI), summarized in Business-Standard, http://www.business-standard.com/article/current-affairs/80-of-indian-doctors-located-in-urban-areas-serving-28-of-populace-report-116081900640_1.html
5. See David Teece, Gary Pisano, Amy Shuen, "Dynamic Capabilities and Strategic Management," Strategic Management Journal (1997), 18 (7): 509–533.
6. Zeynep Emden, J. Calantone Roger and Cornelia Droge," Collaborating for New Product Development: Selecting the Partner with Maximum Potential to Create Value," Journal of Product Innovation Management,(2006) 23: 330–341.
7. Henry Chesbrough & Kevin Schwartz, "Innovating Business Model with co-development partnerships", Research Technology Management (2007), Page 55.

8. Lee, Sang M., David L. Olson and Silvana Trimi, "Co-innovation: convergenomics, collaboration, and co-creation for organizational values," Management Decision (2012), 50(5), pp.817-831.

9. Minimal Viable Product (MVP) is a product with just enough features to satisfy early customers, and to provide feedback for future product development, see Eric Ries, "Minimum Viable Product: a guide," Startup Lessons Learned (2009), http://www.startuplessonslearned.com/2009/08/minimum-viable-product-guide.html

10. See Eric Ries, "The Lean Startup," Crown Publishing Group (2011) for an introduction to this approach in the context of high technology startup companies.

11. Henry Chesbrough & Kevin Schwartz, "Innovating Business Model with co-development partnerships", Research Technology Management (2007), Page 55.

12. Ibid.

13. Gene Slowinski and Matthew W. Sagal, "Good practices in open innovation," Research-Technology Management (2010), 53(5), pp.38-45.

14. Henry Chesbrough, Christopher Lettl, Thomas Ritter, "Value Creation and Value Capture in Open Innovation," The Journal of Product Innovation Management, 2018.

15. World Economic Forum, "Collaborative Innovation, Transforming Business, Driving Growth," (2015).

16. The approach to increase NGO performance and overall impact efficacy across every stakeholder comes from the idea of "Impact Investing". Watch hereby the talk from Sir Ronald Cohen at the Stanford Graduate School of Business in 2019. https://www.youtube. com/watch?v=EcXMzkRLB3M

17. Henry Chesbrough & Kevin Schwartz, "Innovating Business Model with co-development partnerships", Research Technology Management (2007), Page 59.

18. Alexander Osterwalder and Yves Pigneur, "Business model generation: A handbook for visionaries, game changers, and challengers," Hoboken, New Jersey: John Wiley & Sons Inc. (2010).

19. See Paul Gertler et al., "Impact Evaluation Practice," The World Bank (2012). See here for detailed methodologies and frameworks for impact evaluation.

20. See Eric Ries, "The Lean Startup," Crown Publishing Group (2011), pp. 77-78.

21. The price of this equipment, were a household to purchase it, would be approximately 5,000 Rupees or $100.

22. Other companies are providing other potential solutions. These two examples are not intended to represent the entire spectrum of proposed solutions, nor are they intended to represent all the companies participating.

23. World Economic Forum, "Collaborative Innovation, Transforming Business, Driving Growth," (2015).

PART IV. What are the Successes and Challenges

11. What are the Success Stories

1. The huge demand on Storeking brought formidable challenges being an early stage startup. Storeking struggled to keep up with the unexpected pace.

12. What are the Roadblocks and their Learnings

1. Solomon Darwin & Henry Chesbrough, "Building Scalable Smart Villages (B)," Harvard Business Review (2018), https:// hbr. org/product/prototyping-a-scalable-smart-village-b/B5924-PDF-ENG. The case builds upon the first HBR Case Study and

reflects mainly the learnings and challenges faced in the extension phase.

2. Dom Galeon: "Tesla Must Overcome Local Production Laws Before Bringing EVs to India," Futurism (2017), https://futurism.com/tesla-must-overcome-local-production-laws-before- bringing-evs-to-india/

3. The US Government elaborates barriers to market entry and local requirements, i.e., things to be aware of when entering the market for India, https://www.export.gov/article?id=India-Market-Challenges

4. Comparing Business Regulation for Domestic Firms in 190 Economies and deriving ease of doing business index for 2017 & 2018, http://www.doingbusiness.org/~/media/ WBG/ DoingBusiness/Documents/Annual-Reports/English/ DB2018-Full-Report.pdf, http://www.worldbank.org/content/ dam/doingBusiness/media/Annual-Reports/English/ DB2019-report_web-version.pdf

5. US based company selling health, beauty, and home care products successfully tapped into the Indian market. See Industry Week (2016), http:// www.industryweek.com/expansion-management/ amway-opens-first-manufacturing-plant-india

6. See Govindarajan and Bagla, "Two Ways to Break into India's Consumer Market," Harvard Business Review (2016), https://hbr.org/2016/10/two-ways-to-break-into-indias-consumer-market

7. V Kamalakara Rao: "'Made in AP' drones from March," Times of India (2018), https://timesofindia.indiatimes.com/city/visakhapatnam/made-in-ap-drones-from-march/articleshow/62595731.cms

8. Tarun Shukla: "Govt issues draft rules for using drones in India," Livemint (2018), https://www.livemint.com/Technology/ vo83e RIbaxljD7LgDBpBbK/Govt-issues-draft-rules-for-using-drones-in-India.html

9. Andhra Pradesh Government's vision and mission to develop a government ecosystem to control also huge parts of the agricultural sector in its state, http://www.ap.gov.in/wp-content/uploads/2015/11/e-Pragati-5Sept-15-Ver3-JS.pdf

10. Reports claim that the Andhra Pradesh government has been imposing the ap fibrenet project and can regulate internet and TV channels in the state, Newsclick (2018), https://newsclick.in/ap-fibrenet-project-mired-controversies

11. Government-owned airline AirIndia has a huge backlog of reforms and is therefore a highly unattractive candidate for private investors to take over, Handelsblatt (2018), http://www.handelsblatt.com/unternehmen/handel-konsumgueter/air-line-in-der-krise-air-india-geht-das-geld-aus/22671170.html

12. Reports claim that the Andhra Pradesh government has been imposing the ap fibrenet project and can regulate internet and TV channels in the state, Newsclick (2018), https://newsclick.in/ap-fibrenet-project-mired-controversies

13. Suprita Anupam: "Startup Watchlist: 13 Indian Blockchain Startups To Watch Out For In 2018," Inc42 (2017), https://inc42.com/features/watchlist-indian-blockchain-startups/

14. CM Naidu convinced Bill Gates to set up Microsoft's development center in Hyderabad 20 years ago, The News Minute (2017), https://www.thenewsminute.com/article/bill-gates-recalls-first-meeting-andhra-cm-naidu-20-years-ago-71793

15. Only 29% of consumers in India have concerns about the amount of personal data that brands have on them compared to 40% globally, Livemint (2017), https://www.livemint.com/Consumer/7CddNl2VWOWjL3gaVP7OAJ/Indian-consumers-comfortable-in-sharing-personal-data-online.html?utm_source=scroll&utm_medium=referral&utm_campaign=scroll

16. Deepika Singhania, "How StoreKing is connecting rural India to the digital world of online shopping," yourstory

(2018), https://yourstory.com/2018/03/ storeking-connecting-rural-india-digital/

17. See Consumer Affairs, Food & Civil Supplies, Government of Andhra Pradesh regarding fair price shops, https://civilsupplies. ap.gov.in/fpshop.jsp

18. CM Naidu speaking at the Open Innovation Forum India 2017 about the importance of embracing technology, The Hindu (2017), http://www.thehindu.com/news/national/ andhra-pradesh/ap-frontrunner-in-embracing-new-tech/article 19596372.ece

19. Anshul Pachouri and Sankul Sharma, "Barriers to Innovation in Indian Small and Medium-Sized Enterprises," ADBI Working Paper 588. Tokyo: Asian Development Bank Institute (2016), available: http://www.adb.org/publications/barriers-innovation-indian-small-and-medium-sized-enterprises/

20. See the 2017 corruption index, https://www.transparency.org/ news/feature/corruption_perceptions_index_2017

21. Larry Downes, The Laws of Disruption: Harnessing the New Forces That Govern Life and Business in the Digital Age," Basic Books (2019)

22. See http://www.worldbank.org/en/news/infographic/2016/ 05/27/india-s-poverty-profile

23. See https://blogs.worldbank.org/developmenttalk/interna-tional-poverty-line-has-just-been-raised-190-day-global-pov-erty-basically-unchanged-how-even

24. After launching the AP fibernet in Mori, the expansion to 1 million households is planned, Televisionpost (2016), http:// www.televisionpost.com/ap-fibernet-project-launch-and-cable-tv-biz/

25. CM Naidu reviews the progress of implementing the AP fibernet boxes across Andhra Pradesh, Knn India 2018), http://knnindia.co.in/news/newsdetails/state/

ap-cm-reviews-progress-and-achievements-of-department-of-energy-infrastructure-investment

26. Problems of local cable operators emerged when being responsible for implementing AP fibernet in Andhra Pradesh, Times Of India (2016), https://timesofindia.indiatimes.com/city/visakhapatnam/Recognize-local-cable-operators-SCOWA-tells-APSFL/articleshow/51593402.cms

27. Report on Buying Behavior of Rural Consumers in India (2016). Department of Consumer Affairs, Ministry of Consumer Affairs, Food & Public Distribution. Government of India, New Delhi. http://consumereducation.in/ResearchStudyReports/RuralIndia2016.pdf

28. Ibid. page 2.

29. Ibid. page 15.

30. Abheek Singhi, Nimisha Jain and Kanika Sanghi, "The New Indian: Many Facets of a Changing Consumer," BCG (2017), https://www.bcg.com/en-in/publications/2017/marketing-sales-globalization-new-indian-changing-consumer.aspx

31. Report on Buying Behavior of Rural Consumers in India (2016). Department of Consumer Affairs, Ministry of Consumer Affairs, Food & Public Distribution. Government of India, New Delhi. http://consumereducation.in/ResearchStudyReports/RuralIndia2016.pdf

32. Ibid. page 15.

33. eCommerce players like Lenskart adapt the rural consumer behavior when setting up physical stores to build brand awareness and trust, Economic Times India (2014), https://economictimes.indiatimes.com/industry/services/retail/niche-E-Commerce-players-like-lenskart-setting-up-physical-stores-to-build-brand-awareness-trust/articleshow/43844605.cms

34. Report on Buying Behavior of Rural Consumers in India (2016). Department of Consumer Affairs, Ministry of Consumer

Affairs, Food & Public Distribution. Government of India, New Delhi, page 16, http://consumereducation.in/ Research StudyReports/RuralIndia2016.pdf

35. The Thums Up story – Coca Cola adapting to rural consumer behavior, http://guruprasad.net/posts/part-13-thums-up-story-ramesh-chauhan-sells-parle-brands-coca-cola/

36. Report on Buying Behavior of Rural Consumers in India (2016). Department of Consumer Affairs, Ministry of Consumer Affairs, Food & Public Distribution. Government of India, New Delhi, page 16, http://consumereducation.in/ Research StudyReports/RuralIndia2016.pdf

37. See https://www.statista.com/statistics/240647/approval-of-arranged-maariage-in-todays-india/

38. Report on Buying Behavior of Rural Consumers in India (2016). Department of Consumer Affairs, Ministry of Consumer Affairs, Food & Public Distribution. Government of India, New Delhi, page 17, http://consumereducation.in/ Research StudyReports/RuralIndia2016.pdf

39. See https://economictimes.indiatimes.com/tech/internet/acute-urban-rural-divide-in-internet-penetration-in-india-report/articleshow/62997468.cms

40. See http://povertydata.worldbank.org/poverty/home/

41. Portrait about Napanta, Ozy (2017), https://www.ozy.com/fast-forward/why-farmers-in-india-are-taking-their-own-lives-and-how-to-stop-it/81840

42. Abheek Singhi, Nimisha Jain and Kanika Sanghi, "The New Indian: Many Facets of a Changing Consumer," BCG (2017), https://www.bcg.com/en-in/publications/2017/marketing-sales-globalization-new-indian-changing-consumer.aspx

43. A Indian fast-moving consumer goods company has overtaken several older and more experienced rivals when focusing on Indian specific goods, VC Circle (2017), https://www.vccircle.

com/how-patanjali-outsmarted-older-rivals-to-become-indias-no-2-fmcg-firm/

44. Abheek Singhi, Nimisha Jain and Kanika Sanghi, "The New Indian: Many Facets of a Changing Consumer," BCG (2017), https://www.bcg.com/en-in/publications/2017/marketing-sales-globalization-new-indian-changing-consumer.aspx

45. Calestous Juma, "Innovation and Its Enemies: Why People Resist New Technologies," Oxford University Press (2016)

13. What are the responses from the stakeholders

46. "More than philanthropy: SDGs present an estimated US 12 trillion in market opportunities for private sector through inclusive business," UNDP (2017), https://www.undp.org/content/undp/en/home/blog/2017/8/25/More-than-philanthropy-SDGs-present-an-estimated-US-12-trillion-in-market-opportunities-for-private-sector-through-inclusive-business.html

47. "Sustainable Signals: Growth and Opportunity in Asset Management," Morgan Stanley's Institute for Sustainable Investing and Bloomberg L.P (2019).

48. GEM report on social entrepreneurship (2015), https://www.gemconsortium.org/report/gem-2015-report-on-social-entrepreneurship

49. Edelman Trust Barometer (2018), https://www.edelman.com/sites/g/files/aatuss191/files/2018　-10/2018_Edelman_Trust_Barometer_State_of_Business.pdf

Made in the USA
Coppell, TX
10 September 2020